DEALI CES

Soci e

DATE DUE

DEALING WITH DIFFERENCES
An Introduction to the
Social Psychology of Prejudice

Edward E. Sampson
California State University at Northridge

Harcourt Brace College Publishers

Fort Worth   Philadelphia   San Diego   New York   Orlando   Austin
San Antonio   Toronto   Montreal   London   Sydney   Tokyo

Publisher	*Earl McPeek*
Acquisitions Editor	*Carol Wada*
Market Strategist	*Kathleen Sharp*
Developmental Editor	*Christine Abshire*
Project Editor	*Andrea A. Johnson*
Art Director	*David A. Day*
Production Manager	*Angela Williams Urquhart*

ISBN: 0-15-505312-4

Library of Congress Catalog Card Number: 98-87391

Address for Orders
Harcourt Brace College Publishers, 6277 Sea Harbor Drive, Orlando, FL 32887-6777
1-800-782-4479

Address for Editorial Correspondence
Harcourt Brace College Publishers, 301 Commerce Street, Suite 3700, Fort Worth, TX 76102

Web Site Address
http://www.hbcollege.com

Printed in the United States of America

8 9 0 1 2 3 4 5 6 7   0 6 6   10 9 8 7 6 5 4 3 2 1

Harcourt Brace College Publishers

Dedication

To my wife, Marya, whose humanity under adversity keeps my own optimism alive.

To my friend and colleague, Archie Smith, whose experiences with racism remind me that people can be good in a world that too often is not.

To my lesbian and gay friends who have flourished in spite of the fears that surround them.

To my son Mark, and my daughter Marta, who continue to teach me in ways they perhaps will never fully appreciate.

Finally, to the people of my heritage who have helped me never to forget what must never happen again, even while sadly, it continues to happen.

TABLE OF CONTENTS

Section 1

Section 2

Section 3

Section 6

PREFACE

I have been in the business of higher education for some 38 years, teaching primarily in psychology departments first at Berkeley, then at Clark University, and now at California State University at Northridge. At no time during those nearly four decades has prejudice in some form *not* been a constant presence infecting most people's lives. It is because of this presence that I feel this book is necessary. Its historical, sociological, and psychological perspectives help students see a more complete picture of prejudice.

Although I am considered to be a privileged white male, when I began my professional career, consciousness had not yet been raised sufficiently for me even to be aware of those features of my identity, nor for that matter, that I had any special privilege because of them. How much I have learned! How many lessons remain for all of us to learn! Some would argue that the sensitivities to our differences (to which most of us are now aware), have proved to be anything but helpful. Yet most would agree that knowledge of our social identities as shaped by "race," ethnicity, gender, sexual orientation, and religion, and the privilege or penalties we receive from those social identities are essential steps on the way to challenging the prejudices that these differences have brought.

At the beginning of each term, I stand in front of my class to take attendance. In this simple act, the entire story of social change appears, and with it, much of the rationale for this book. I confront a veritable rainbow of students. My students want to learn about the reasons why troubles between various people have existed for such a long time in human history, and especially, what they can do about it.

In other words, a book using the broad perspectives of history, social science, and psychology to study prejudice is a pressing necessity today in the study of prejudice. Paradoxically, this is a topic of study we all fervently hope will someday no longer be needed. Unfortunately, that day has not yet arrived. And while a book of this sort cannot remedy all the problems it addresses, it is my hope that this book can help us better appreciate the roots of prejudice and some avenues we might call upon to reduce its grip on all of us.

EES
Berkeley, California

DEALING WITH DIFFERENCES
An Introduction to the
Social Psychology of Prejudice

S E C T I O N

Introduction: Definitions and Overview

There are few topics as disturbing to write about and to read about—and yet as important to understand—as the topic of prejudice. Prejudice is something that many of us know close-up and firsthand, something that—in spite of all the advances in technology and human knowledge—seems never to have disappeared completely from our world. When thousands of people each year become the victims of hate crimes directed towards them only because of their race, religion, or sexual orientation; when the opportunity to achieve the American dream can be thwarted because of a person's race, ethnicity, gender, or appearance; then we know that no matter how much progress in human relations we have already made, the journey has many miles yet to go.

Chapter 1 begins our own journey by examining the definition of prejudice and some of the important issues that the definition entails. We continue by providing an overview of the text, calling on Allport's (1954) early but still useful idea of looking at prejudice through various lenses. Each lens gives us a slightly different viewpoint—not only for examining prejudice but also for understanding and eventually challenging its grip.

Whenever we find prejudice, we find differences. Thus, Chapter 2 examines the link between diversity (i.e., differences among the variety of human kinds that exist in the world) on the one hand and prejudice on the other. The world in which we live has always been filled with peoples and cultures that cover a wide range of differences. Yet, before modern means of travel and rapid communication systems made contact with these cultures readily available to almost anyone, the richness and depth of human diversity was little known to most people who spent their lives in familiar, often homogeneous surroundings.

But today, even if many people still live in a homogeneous community and have never had personal contact with the many varieties of people in the world, they have been made aware of different cultures and lifestyles through the media. This has meant that most people now encounter differences between themselves and others on a near daily basis.

Some find those differences enriching to their own lives. Others are unsettled by the differences they encounter, even if indirectly through television. Few of us, however, meet differences with quiet indifference. Dealing with differences, as we will see in Chapter 2, is a central theme in the study of prejudice. It is in these efforts to deal with differences that we will find the seeds of prejudice.

Chapter 1

Defining Prejudice

Each of you is invited to come along with me to the first day of classes. We arrive together in a familiar place filled with unfamiliar faces. After nearly four decades of teaching, I continue to be shocked and deeply disturbed as I listen to the many stories of encounters with prejudice and discrimination that students have already experienced in their young lives. Aisha tells of being followed by security personnel when she enters a store, as though she were a shoplifter, apparently just because she is black. Jorge talks about being harassed by the police because in their view a Latino should not be driving such a fine car, especially in this classy neighborhood. But, of all the stories, Shonnique's is among the most poignant:

> Shonnique was the very first member of her family to enter college. She graduated from high school in June and all summer long her father, mother, brothers, and sisters looked forward to helping Shonnique move into her dorm. She was about as excited as she had ever been, and her family shared this great sense of joy and anticipation. In September, they packed up the family car and drove the 2 hours from home to campus.
>
> After wandering around a little lost, they finally located the dormitory and took turns hauling Shonnique's gear up the elevator to her room. She can still recall the feeling she had on entering her new home. It was wonderful! Large, airy, and bright: two beds, two dressers, and two closets—one for her and one for her soon-to-be roommate. She wondered who would come through that door to move in with her.
>
> Shonnique and her family were getting the finishing touches completed when they looked up and saw another young woman standing in the doorway with her father and mother each holding suitcases. This was Shonnique's new roommate. Shonnique stood up and moved forward, smiling eagerly, extending her hand to greet her roommate. She was met first by a cold stare, followed by a puzzled look. "Sorry," said the young woman standing in the doorway, "there must be some mistake here. I must have the wrong room." "No," said Shonnique, "if your name is Karen, then this is your room."
>
> Karen, however, thought differently. Her parents seemed to agree. They all turned and walked out.

Shonnique knew what was taking place, what had ruined her excitement. Her parents also knew this too-familiar experience.

A half hour passed before the resident director came into the room to explain: Shonnique would be getting a different roommate sometime later.

Definition of Prejudice

There are few topics of interest to social psychologists that have proven to be as controversial and yet as vital to understand as the study of prejudice (e.g., Puckitt, 1994; Harding et al., 1969). This makes it all the more important to be as clear as possible at the outset about what we mean when we refer to prejudice. Most of us know that the term itself is comprised of the affix *pre-*, meaning "before," and the word *judgment*, usually involving a positive or negative evaluation. A prejudice then would be an evaluation we make before all the facts are known—a *bias*, in other words. But we need more than this general view to guide our own study. Here is a definition of prejudice derived from Allport's (1954) pioneering work, among others (e.g., Jones, 1997), that I have found useful:

Prejudice involves an unjustified, usually negative attitude directed towards others because of their social category or group membership.

This deceptively simple definition contains three elements that we will consider in somewhat more detail. First, although the definition uses the phrase *usually negative*, keep in mind that prejudice can involve either positively or negatively biased evaluations. Second, although we are interested in prejudiced *attitudes* as well as prejudiced *behavior*, it is important to maintain a distinction between what we believe and feel (attitudes) and what we actually do (behavior). Finally, the definition tells us that prejudices are *unjustified* evaluations. This final point raises some additional complications as well as introducing us to the idea that prejudice involves treating people in terms of their social category or group memberships rather than in terms of their uniquely individual qualities.

Prejudiced Evaluations Can Be Positive or Negative

Obviously we have positive prejudices about certain things in our world as well as negative prejudices about other things. My *favoring* someone simply because he is white, for example, is every bit as much a prejudice as my *disliking* someone because of his race or ethnicity. I recently went to a flea market and found a silver bracelet I was eager to purchase. The woman selling it assured me that it was genuine sterling silver. Learning that she was not only its maker but also an Israeli convinced me that I had good reason not to doubt her, even though the bracelet did not have the usual jeweler's markings that signify real silver. In this case, my evaluation revealed my favorable prejudice toward people from Israel.

In a similar manner, the stereotypes we hold about others—those so-called "pictures in our heads"—may be positive as well as negative. When Bob considers women to be soft, gentle, and nurturant, a generally positive evaluation, he is prejudicing his evaluations of any specific woman he meets based on the stereotyped picture he holds for all women. It has been shown that even these positive evaluations can have demonstrably negative consequences—for example, when a particular woman is passed over for a promotion because her "soft" qualities dominate her evaluators' ratings, leading them to consider her not "good leadership material" (e.g., see Benokraitis & Gilbert, 1989). In short, even Bob's positive evaluations can reflect prejudice, insofar as they are based on a biased view of any specific woman he meets.

Nevertheless, when we think of prejudices, we usually think of negative biasing—that is, viewing a specific person negatively because of his or her social category or group membership. Shonnique's prospective roommate Karen had no knowledge whatsoever about Shonnique; her responses were guided solely by her negative view of African Americans as a group. Although it would also be an example of prejudice if Karen eagerly embraced Shonnique, rather than rejecting her—once again the evaluation, though positive, would not be based on information about Shonnique herself.

In general, however, we typically think of prejudice as taking the negative rather than the positive form. After all, it is likely to be harmful to others when we reject rather than accept them because of their group memberships. Yet, as we also noted, even positive evaluations can have harmful effects, such as when a person is not promoted because her otherwise positive stereotypical female attributes are held against her when it comes to decisions about her leadership potential.

Prejudiced Attitudes vs. Prejudiced Actions

Social psychologists usually distinguish between the attitudes people hold and their actual behavior (e.g., Ajzen & Fishbein, 1980; McGuire, 1969; Wicker, 1969). For the most part, our attitudes involve the beliefs we hold about people and things in our world as well as our feelings towards those people and things. For example, Janet believes that black men are aggressive and dangerous, and so she feels fearful when in their presence. This would describe Janet's attitude and fits the definition of prejudice as a negative attitude directed toward others because of their group memberships, in this case because they are black and male.

Although we commonly would expect people to act in ways that are consistent with their attitudes, the distinction between attitudes and actions calls attention to the many instances in which there is more discrepancy than consistency between what we believe and feel (our attitudes) and how we behave (our actions). Let us consider two contrasting cases that highlight the importance of this distinction: first, when attitudes are prejudiced, but actions are not discriminatory; and second, when attitudes are unprejudiced, but actions are discriminatory.

Prejudiced attitudes without prejudiced actions   This situation is likely to occur when people who hold negative attitudes toward others (e.g., their beliefs are racist) find themselves in circumstances where it would be inappropriate to act on these racist beliefs and feelings. For example, Jim comes from a community in which the public expression of racial prejudices is commonplace. He has been brought up thinking it quite proper to use racial epithets in referring to African Americans, Asian Americans, Native Americans, and Latino and Latina Americans. When he leaves his community to attend the state university, however, Jim quickly realizes that one does not publicly express these clearly prejudiced attitudes. In this case, then, we have an illustration of prejudiced attitudes that do not result in prejudiced or discriminatory behavior.

Prejudiced behavior without prejudiced attitudes   While it might appear that whenever behavior is discriminatory toward others simply because of their group memberships there must also be prejudiced beliefs in operation, there are many instances in which this is clearly not the case. For example, Robert works in the Human Resources Department of a large corporation. Although he personally harbors no prejudiced attitudes toward women or African Americans, his hiring and promotion recommendations follow company policy, which denies opportunities to specific groups of people. Thereby, his decisions contribute to discriminatory actions even though he personally has no prejudiced attitudes.

Let us consider a somewhat different example. The South Forks Fire Department has established criteria for its firefighters, requiring that they not only achieve a certain score on a multiple-choice test given to all prospective candidates, but must also attain a particular score on a demanding test of physical prowess (see Norris & Reardon, 1989). Although 98% of the males and 95% of the females who take the multiple-choice test qualify to be firefighters, 43% of the males and 0% of the females qualify based on their scores on the test of physical abilities. Those establishing the tests as well as those administering the tests reasonably claim not to be prejudiced against women; they are simply reporting the factual scores that men and women achieve. This would then appear to be a case in which attitudes are unprejudiced, but the outcome discriminates against women.

A legal challenge was raised by a woman on behalf of both herself and the class of women who had passed the written test but had failed the physical test. The challenge claimed bias and discrimination in the selection of items for the physical abilities test, arguing that the items were not relevant to the actual job of firefighter and rather served primarily to keep women out of firefighter positions. The courts agreed, concluding that "the test was not content valid because the abilities measured were not the most observable abilities of significance to the job" (Norris & Reardon, 1989, pp. 57–58); in other words, this was a case of discriminatory behavior without any necessary prejudiced attitudes.

Rereading our definition reveals that prejudice emphasizes attitudes—that is, what people think, believe, and feel—rather than their actions. Although, as these examples illustrate, knowing that someone's attitudes are prejudiced may or may not invariably inform us about their likely behavior, it is nevertheless important to deal with prejudiced attitudes because of the many occasions in which such attitudes do underlie actions, even if subtly. I think it fair to conclude that we must be interested in both prejudiced attitudes and prejudiced actions. We cannot afford to ignore either.

Are Prejudiced Attitudes Ever Justified, or Are They Always Unjustified?

For better or worse, most of us know people we personally dislike: They are obnoxious people, intrusive, hostile, and generally to be avoided. Is it prejudice, however, when we dislike such people? According to our definition of prejudice, we would have to answer "no." It would not be a case of prejudice, therefore, if you happen to find a particular woman with whom you work on a daily basis to be obnoxious. It would be an instance of prejudice, however, if your view of her was shaped primarily by the fact that she was a woman (a member of a specific social category), in this case basing your opinion solely on gender. In other words, some negative attitudes we have toward others are not examples of prejudice because they are clearly personal and specific to a given individual. In this sense, such attitudes can be said to be justified. As Allport (1954) noted years ago, attitudes are unjustified when we judge a particular person entirely on the basis of their social category or group membership. This is clearly the case with Shonnique's prospective roommate Karen, who disliked and rejected Shonnique, not because she knew her—after all, this was their very first meeting—but rather because Shonnique was African American and Karen held negative views of African Americans.

In this view, all prejudices are incorrect because they involve making a judgment about specific individuals based on ideas about the characteristics of the social category or group in which those individuals have membership. Even if we could assess a group's "real" characteristics, we would invariably be in error in insisting that every single member of that group had exactly the same characteristics to exactly the same degree. Thus, even if there were a kernel of truth to our perceptions (see Chapter 8), it could not hold true for every case.

In their consideration of the accuracy of stereotypes, for example, Judd & Park (1993) raise this same point. Suppose, for example, we think that Germans are a highly efficient people. Suppose further that we could measure the trait of efficiency for the entire population of Germans. Is it not still preposterous to presume that all Germans have this trait or have it to the same degree? In this sense, therefore, all prejudices are invariably inaccurate and thereby unjustified as they seek to paint the individual with the broad colors of the group, an endeavor fraught with errors of judgment.

Furthermore, prejudice produces harmful effects for everyone, including its targets, its agents, and the larger society itself. The harmful effects of Karen's prejudiced attitudes on Shonnique are clear for all to see: Her great day was ruined. But Karen was also harmed by acting in terms of her prejudiced attitudes about African Americans: She missed an opportunity to have her beliefs challenged and proved incorrect. And all of us suffer when instances of this sort are multiplied every day across the entire nation. And so, unless we are prepared to approve of such extensively harmful effects, we must agree that its harm-doing makes prejudice necessarily unjustified.

Finally, failure to consider prejudice to be unjustified, using the argument that to do so is to take sides and make a value judgment, is in itself taking sides and making a value judgment! When people are harmed and we wish to avoid the dirty business of calling this evil, we have taken a position. In fact, there is no way *not* to be on some side in the great debates and controversies of our time and place. There is no way to stand nowhere. Trying to remain neutral and avoid adopting any point of view is, as some have argued (e.g., MacKinnon, 1989; Sampson, 1991), in itself adopting a point of view.

My students challenge me   Perhaps you can imagine my surprise when, having presented the foregoing arguments, several of my students protested. I think it will prove helpful to consider their protest. Their main problem was with the third part of our definition of prejudice: the idea that all prejudices are unjustified. Here is an example they literally threw in my face:

> "Since you are Jewish, do you still insist that if you were to dislike Nazis, your prejudice would be unjustified, especially given the horrible things the Nazis did to the Jews? And, if a group of gun-toting, Jack-booted Nazis were to pound on your door, coming to drag you away, would you continue to insist that your negative view of Nazis was unjustified?"

I was momentarily taken aback, for they had indeed found an example that appeared to press me up against the classroom wall. If I claimed that all prejudices were unjustified, then wouldn't I have to agree that harboring negative views toward all Nazis simply because of their membership in the Nazi Party was also unjustified, even if the Nazis were responsible for the slaughter of millions of Jews?

In the heated discussion that followed, I stuck to my guns. I insisted that to harbor negative feelings toward all members of the Nazi Party without knowledge of any specific case would be to hold a prejudice. On the other hand, disliking those guys pounding at my door was justified (and so not prejudice) because my reaction to them was not based on their membership in a particular group, but rather on the immediate threat they posed to me.

I quickly countered with my own examples, hoping to restore confidence in my ability to clarify the meaning of prejudice. "It is prejudice," I argued, "If a women has a negative reaction when a black man gets on the elevator with her." After all, her reaction is to the social category and not to the specific person riding in the elevator. "To be upset under specific conditions of real threat is not prejudice," I continued, "but to be upset simply because the person is black is prejudice." Under specific conditions of threat our responses are not based on group membership but on evaluating the specific situation that confronts us. The store clerk who follows a black customer around merely because that customer is black is revealing prejudice; it would not be prejudice, however, if the customer is observed stealing items from the shelf and is then followed about to document the case.

Several of my students remained dissatisfied, raising yet another point that bears thoughtful consideration. Let me paraphrase:

> "Surely, membership in all groups is not the same. Nazis join a political party voluntarily, or at least in a way that members of many other groups (e.g., racial, gender-based, ethnic) do not. And so, I may be justified in disliking an individual who I learn is a Nazi, knowing that person voluntarily agreed to join this political group with its well known murderous designs on many people. I would not be justified in the same way, however, in my dislike of another individual simply because he or she is black, female, or Latino."

This challenge raised a very interesting point that, in all honesty, I had overlooked in my attempt to establish a definition for prejudice. I had to admit that there were those kinds of groups—including the Nazi Party and many others as well—that people more or less voluntarily joined and that clearly marked them as a certain kind of person who might indeed warrant a justified dislike on my part. Groups that were defined by their steadfast opposition to commonly shared humane values—for example, groups dedicated to violence and harm-doing—might be the very kind of exception that renders prejudiced attitudes justifiable.

And so, on meeting Bill for the first time, if I am informed that he is a member of a group that eagerly consumes child pornography and favors the sexual molestation of young children, my antagonism to him, while indeed based on his group membership and not on any personal knowledge of him beyond that, is justified in a way that responding negatively to someone simply because of his or her racial group membership is not.

At this point, I had to confess to my class (and now to my readers) that a close scrutiny of most definitions opens the door to a virtual Pandora's box of potential complications. It is a safe bet in general, however, to stick to the notion that most prejudices are unjustified attitudes based on a negative evaluation of persons merely because of their group memberships. Yes, there may be some noteworthy exceptions, but for the most part the instances of prejudice we will consider in this book and that dominate newspaper headlines in our society and around the world today are unjustified evaluations, not conclusions reached after a thoughtful examination of either the specific individuals involved or knowledge of the meaning of their group affiliations.

Some Further Questions About Prejudice

Several additional questions about prejudice remain to be addressed before we proceed.

First, is there any single, all-encompassing theory that can explain the wide variety of forms that prejudice has taken, or must we learn to live with a loose collection of different theories addressed to different aspects of prejudice?

Second, has the face of prejudice changed, as some have suggested, from its more traditional, bigoted version to a politically correct, modern form, or should we consider only the traditional form to be the true expression of prejudice?

Third, because our focus in this text is primarily on those groups that have typically been the targets of prejudice because of their race, ethnicity, gender, ability status, religion, or sexual orientation, does this mean that only white male heterosexual Protestants are the carriers of prejudice and that everyone else is free of its grip? And almost as a corollary to this third point, we usually think of prejudice as something the majority directs toward a minority. But, what do the terms *majority* and *minority* mean when, for example, women may be the targets of prejudice but are clearly not in a numerical minority?

One Theory or Many?

Most social psychologists hope to discover a unified theory of whatever it is they are studying, including prejudice, that will somehow explain all the various forms it takes. Some compelling evidence exists suggesting that there are commonalities running through all prejudices—in other words, that "prejudice is not target specific, but rather is a generalized hostility towards a number of outgroups" (Weigel & Howes, 1985, p. 126; also Altemeyer, 1994). Furthermore, those who insist that prejudice is often based on normal categorization processes that describe how all people function (see Chapter 8) similarly argue that a single, all-encompassing theory of prejudice will someday be found if it is not already in our possession (i.e., prejudice results from the way we think and organize our world). According to this view, then, perhaps there is a single theory that explains all forms of prejudice.

On the other hand, we have the position advocated by Young-Bruehl (1995), who selects the four well known targets of prejudice—based on race, religion, gender, and sexual orientation—and argues that a different underlying psychological process operates in each case. She argues that what is required to understand one form of prejudice does not serve us well in trying to understand the other forms; for example, what drives racism is different from what drives anti-Semitism, and so on.

Allport's recommendation   Allport's (1950, 1954) advice would seem appropriate here. He first suggested that prejudice, like most other complex topics, "should be viewed through a series of lenses" (1950, p. 23), including historical, cultural, and psychological. He next warned us not to be narrowly seduced by whatever particular lens guides our own work into believing that our lens is the only lens or even the best lens. To paraphrase Allport, we must remain respectful of all the lenses that might be used to explain prejudice. Allport's advice suggests that our hope of discovering a unified theory of prejudice is a vain one insofar as no theory can possibly integrate such diverse perspectives as those provided by historical, cultural, and psychological studies.

Although we will not resolve the issue in this text, we will cover a variety of theoretical bases, some of which are pretenders to the kind of unification that is surely unwarranted, others of which do give us a useful sense of the roots of some but clearly not all forms by which prejudice gains a foothold in a population. These will become apparent in the lenses we use throughout this text.

Has Prejudice Declined or Simply Changed Its Face?

Most observers of the contemporary situation in the United States note that many of our former prejudices either have declined or have changed the form in which they appear. There is some controversy, however, over which it is: decline or changed face. For example, it is commonly observed that whereas once it may have been routine to make racist and sexist jokes and to subscribe to ideas that focused on the fundamental "inferiority" of blacks, women, and other groups, for the most part few today subscribe to such views, at least publicly (but see Chapter 6 for some noteworthy exceptions). And yet, there appears to be strong evidence of the continuing marks of both prejudice and discrimination.

Therefore, some social psychologists have found it useful to distinguish between old-fashioned and modern forms of prejudice.

The old-fashioned forms of prejudice have been described as traditional or rednecked and emphasize both their rough and blunt quality (e.g., the use of racial epithets such as "nigger") as well as their tendency to consider certain groups to be fundamentally inferior when compared with white males, who presumably dwell at the top of the evolutionary ladder.

By contrast, modern forms of prejudice are said to have taken on a more subtle and socially polite form, and have been termed symbolic or aversive (e.g., Dovidio, Mann, & Gaertner, 1989; Kinder & Sears, 1981; McConahay, 1986; McConahy & Hough, 1976; Spotlight on Research, 1996). Not only are those epithets unlikely to appear in polite, politically correct conversation, but also absent is the hint that one can arrange humankind according to a ladder ranging from superior to inferior. If some people do not do as well as others and so end up on the ladder's bottom rungs, this is not because of any basic inferiority they have, but rather because they are simply less motivated to succeed.

Consider some of the research findings that have led some investigators to claim that the face of prejudice has changed. In 1946, only 45% of a white sample agreed that blacks should have as good a chance as whites to get a job, whereas by 1972, fully 97% of the whites agreed with this statement (Dovidio et al., 1989). In a similar manner, the majority of whites today would not say that discrimination in schooling or in housing is a good thing or that black stereotypes of being lazy, dumb, shiftless, and superstitious still hold true (see Chapter 8). And yet it is also clear that many of the same whites who would not openly endorse negative views of blacks, for example, continue to subscribe to racist views when they feel they can rationalize them in terms other than race: "I did not stop to help the injured black man, not because he was black, but rather because many others were around to help." Evidence also suggests that whites are very reluctant to endorse negative descriptions of blacks; what they are willing to do, however, is to endorse even more positive descriptions of whites: "blacks are not lazy; it is simply that whites work harder" (Dovidio, et al., 1989).

Not all social psychologists who have noted the possible shift in the expression of prejudice from harsh to softer forms, however, have agreed with this distinction between traditional and modern forms of prejudice (e.g., Sniderman & Tetlock, 1986; Weigel & Howes, 1985). One argument these critics raise is based on an evaluation of the tests used to measure both traditional and modern forms of prejudice. Because the correlations between scores on such tests are high, it can be argued that rather than there being two distinct forms of prejudice, perhaps only one form exists. In other words, if you give people two tests, one of which is said to measure traditional prejudice and the other its modern form, and the scores on both tests are highly similar—that is, those who score high on one test also score high on the other; those who score low on one likewise score low on the other—perhaps there is really only one kind of prejudice that is being measured, not the two forms as claimed.

These same critics also suggest that the ways designed to measure the modern forms of racism confound political values with prejudice. For example, if you were to argue that affirmative action as a social policy is something you oppose, would this be properly scored as racial prejudice or as a value position based on accepting the traditional American ideal of individual achievement? And, although it seems clear that some who oppose affirmative action do so as a modern disguise for racist or sexist prejudices (e.g., see Dovidio & Gaertner, 1996; Tougas, Crosby, Joly, & Pelchat, 1995), not all opposition is similarly motivated.

Furthermore, Sniderman and Tetlock (1986) take issue with those who claim that modern racism is different from its traditional, rednecked version. They go so far as to suggest that where racism once referred to genuine prejudice in the form of "a deep-seated, irrational insistence on the inferiority of blacks, and contempt and hostility to them" (p. 186), efforts to define its modern form in terms of support for conservative political beliefs and social policies (e.g., anti–affirmative action policies) destroy all of its meaning and current relevance. In other words, when conservative political values are called racist, does this reveal a new form that prejudice has taken or a political bias on the part of the investigators as these critics suggest?

It is clear that most people today are hesitant to state publicly any prejudicial views they may have. It is also true that the debate over certain current social policies mixes political values with prejudice in a way that is offensive to some but accurate to others. I suppose there is really no way around confounding prejudice and politics when indeed prejudice and politics have always been somewhat strange bedfellows (see Sidanius, Pratto, & Bobo, 1996). More on all of this later.

So Who Is Prejudiced?

Most of us have learned to think that prejudice is something that whites may have toward blacks, that straights may have toward gays, that the able-bodied may have toward persons with disabilities, that Christians may have toward Jews, and that men may have toward women—the familiar litany of racism, homophobism, sexism, and so forth. We have also learned that prejudice is something that the majority has toward minorities. On first sight, therefore, this emphasis might make it appear that minorities and the various targeted groups are themselves without prejudice.

It is important to state at the outset that while we do in fact emphasize those prejudiced attitudes and actions directed toward typical target groups, this is not done because the targets are themselves pure and without prejudice. Although we explore this issue more fully in Chapter 16, one of the major reasons for this emphasis is based on a question of *power,* its effects, and therefore whose prejudiced views matter most. Let us take the case of sexism—men's prejudice toward women—to illustrate how power is involved and to set our own agenda for studying prejudice in this text.

In the first place, in the United States at least, women are not in the numerical minority relative to men: They comprise more than half of the U.S. population. In the second place, women may engage in as harsh a verbal bashing of men as the reverse is true, suggesting that as a group women are hardly without prejudice. Yet, in spite of these facts, women are deeply underrepresented in the corridors of social power, whether those corridors are in business, education, industry, or the government (e.g., women's wages continue to be significantly lower than those of men doing comparable work).

Given these circumstances, whose prejudiced views are more likely to have significant effects that range throughout the society: the prejudiced attitudes of those with little power or the prejudiced attitudes of those with much power? We are all quite capable of harboring prejudice. The prejudices of some groups, however, are farther reaching in their consequences than others, and it is the former more than the latter, therefore, on whom we focus in this text.

But, there is another, related reason for our particular emphasis. Prejudice has a history. The attitudes we find today did not spring suddenly from nowhere; they reflect the history of social relations among the various peoples within a society. This history has usually not been neutral or without passion but reflects some very powerful interests. As we will see in Section 2, for example, one cannot hope to understand black-white relations today without understanding the history of slavery that divided black and white in the first place. Whose prejudices are we most interested in understanding: the masters or the slaves? Our emphasis is on the former more than the latter.

None of this is to excuse anyone's prejudice. Rather, I have suggested a basis for the direction that our own study of prejudice takes and why most of our focus is on the historically dominant groups' prejudiced views of others more than on those others' prejudiced views of those who have historically and, in many cases, currently remain dominant.

Overview of the Text

Although it was not a direct part of the definition of prejudice, there is one property that all forms of prejudice seem to share: Prejudiced attitudes are directed toward *differences*. In other words, when we find prejudiced attitudes, we find human differences often drawn very large and exaggerated. Section 1 therefore includes in our study of prejudice a consideration of the meaning of differences and how prejudice is structured around dealing with differences.

The next three sections of the text are organized around three of the lenses proposed by Allport for understanding prejudice (see Figure 1.1): the target, the prejudiced person, and intergroup relations.

Section 2 examines those efforts to understand prejudice that argue that perhaps there is something about the targeted groups that would explain why they are thought ill of and perhaps even treated differently from the rest of "us."

Section 3 refocuses our study from the targeted groups to the prejudiced person, arguing that perhaps there is something about people who are prejudiced that we must examine in order to understand this troubling topic.

Our final lens appears in Section 4, where we argue that because prejudice is an intergroup phenomenon, involving how people from one group deal with those from other groups, perhaps it is best to examine prejudice in terms of intergroup relations.

Our story, however, is not finished. No study of prejudice could possibly be complete without addressing two additional issues: the consequences of prejudice (Section 5) and what to do to reduce prejudice (Section 6).

By the conclusion, the reader will have been taken on a fairly ugly tour of the darker side of human life, less designed to depress, however, than to mobilize into actions that challenge prejudice wherever it may appear and in whatever guise it may wear. The task is not easy, but the rewards are surely substantial for generations yet to come.

Figure 1.1
Three lenses for viewing prejudice

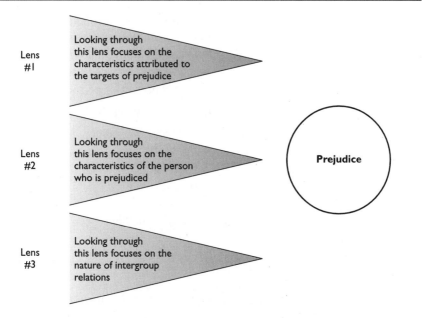

Chapter Summary: Key Learning Points

1. Prejudice is defined as an unjustified, usually negative attitude directed toward others because of their social category or group memberships.

2. This definition can be broken into its three central elements:

   a. Although our primary interest in this book will be with prejudices that involve negative evaluations of others, prejudice can also be positive, at times with equally harmful effects.

   b. We distinguish between prejudiced *attitudes,* beliefs about and feelings toward various people and groups in the world, and prejudiced *behavior,* the actions we direct toward those persons or groups. We can have prejudiced attitudes that do not lead to prejudiced behavior; we can have prejudiced behavior that does not derive from holding prejudiced attitudes.

   c. We consider prejudices to be unjustified primarily because they involve an incorrect generalization, treating individuals in terms of their group memberships rather than relating to them as the unique individuals they are.

3. The chapter considered whether one theory is adequate for addressing the complexities of prejudice, concluding that Allport's wise counsel

to view prejudice through various lenses is a far more reasonable approach. We introduced three central lenses that would guide our own study:

a. Examining prejudice in the form it has taken throughout much of human history: dominant groups seeking characteristics of others to warrant their attitudes toward and treatment of these others.

b. Examining prejudice by seeking characteristics not of the groups targeted, but rather of the persons who harbor prejudice.

c. Examining prejudice as an issue of intergroup relations.

4. We considered two additional issues about prejudice:

a. Is prejudice as prevalent today as in the past, with the only difference being that its form has become softened? Or should we insist on treating as prejudice only those more extremely bigoted old-fashioned forms?

b. Does the focus on the typical groups who have been the targets of prejudice because of their race, gender, religion, sexual orientation, or other differences mean that the targets are themselves without prejudice? We saw that this is not true—but that issues of power plus a lengthy history of prejudiced social relations recommend that we focus more on the prejudices held by the dominant social groups than on those held by persons in less dominant positions.

Chapter 2

Differences and Prejudice

Consider the following exercise. Take out a piece of paper and describe several occasions in which you have experienced yourself to be the target either of someone's prejudiced attitudes or prejudiced actions—that is, when you were either treated poorly or thought ill of by others simply because of your membership in some social group or category. Students in my own classes offered the observations that follow.

First, without exception, all students, regardless of their background, reported a time in their lives when they felt targeted for prejudice. The experience, unfortunately, is something all have encountered—some, of course, more than others.

Second, none of the students had any difficulty in knowing what prejudice involves. For them, any poor treatment, any hostile, rejecting, or negative attitude they received merely because they were seen as a member of a specific social group or category was sufficient for them to feel targeted for prejudice.

Both Aisha and Jamil, for example, described times in which they went shopping, only to be carefully monitored by wary salespersons simply because they were black.

Jorge described an embarrassing and all too frequent occurrence when he is stopped by the police, he says, not because he had done anything wrong, but simply because he was a Mexican American driving a flashy new car. In fact, in the African American community, there is even a name given to what Jorge experienced: DWB or "driving while black," a humorous but all too real take-off on the DWI charge of "driving while intoxicated."

Janet wore a leg brace for the first 18 years of her life; others' stares and whispered comments never let her forget her differences.

James tells of the time in high school when his bookpack was forcibly taken from him by another student, who beat him up and then kicked him off the school bus, and all because he was gay. He also remembers talking with the school counselor the next day about what had happened and being told that this could not be what really happened to him because there is no prejudice at Madison High!

A third observation is that all of my students generally shared much the same sense of what it means to be treated poorly: It is to be the target of a negative, hostile, derogatory, or personally diminishing attitude or to be discriminated against in housing, in jobs, in friendships. As we saw with James, some students also report being physically attacked or harmed by others simply because of the racial, ethnic, gender, or sexual orientation group in which they have membership.

Fourth, it may seem obvious yet is still significant that my students offered no examples in which the prejudice they encountered was based on their *similarity* with another person or group. Prejudice, it seems, is connected with *differences.* Janet does not describe a time when she was the target of prejudice because of some quality she had in common with others, but only when she stood out as different in some way from others. There is a correlation, therefore, between differences and prejudice.

Fifth, the kinds of differences that the students say produced prejudiced responses are well known to all of us, or at least to those of us reared in the modern Western world. The relevant differences include the familiar categories of race, ethnicity, nationality, culture, religion, ability, appearance, age, gender, sexual orientation, and so forth. In each case, it was the student's difference from others in one or more of these categories that resulted in his or her being targeted for prejudice. For example:

> Roger told of a time in which people judged him to be aggressive and dangerous simply because he was much taller than others, when, in fact, he was a gentle (not a dangerous) "giant."

> Shaunte described the experience of being black in a white school and how this difference made her the target of others' racist comments.

> Abdan, a visitor from a developing nation, told of being the target of prejudice based on his cultural differences from the predominantly American students in his classes.

> Karen described the rejection she experienced when others learned she was lesbian; and James's coming out as a gay student, as we previously saw, led to a physically abusive encounter with a fellow student.

A sixth observation, however—and to my way of thinking, one of the most interesting points of all—is that when it comes to being targeted for prejudice, not every difference between people makes a difference; in other words, not all differences evoke a prejudiced response. Obviously, people are similar in many ways and differ in many ways as well. If the ways in which people are similar tend not to produce a prejudiced response, it is also true that not all of our differences lead to prejudice. For example:

> Allen has brown eyes while Betty's eyes are blue. It was Betty's gender, however, not her eye color that was central to her being the target of prejudice.

Roberto and Paul differ in their weight by some 40 pounds. But, when Roberto describes a time in which he was the target of prejudice, it was his Latino heritage that was central, not this difference in weight.

In brief, not all differences make a difference when it comes to prejudice. And it turns out that this sixth point is one of the keys to understanding prejudice. It suggests that in order to know which differences make a difference in prejudice, we must examine the society within which people live and the kinds of distinction that over time have been *marked* as important ways to differentiate people within that society. In other words, in order to discern which differences lead to liking and which evoke hatred or fear, we need to know more than psychology; we also need to know about the history of social relations within a given society, a point stressed by the pioneer of psychological work on prejudice, Gordon Allport (1954) and seconded recently by others (e.g., Gaines & Reid, 1995; Hirschfeld, 1996). In short, we must have a *social psychology* of prejudice, not simply an individual psychology.

This then brings me to the seventh lesson to be learned from this classroom exercise. The differences that lie at the heart of prejudice exist more in the eyes of the beholder than out there in the world as such (e.g., Hirschfeld, 1996). These are the differences that one society or major group determines to be an important way of categorizing people and distinguishing them from their own kind. In short, the kinds of differences that enter into understanding prejudice are those that exist only because some societies and groups have made them important.

Most of us in the United States, for example, have grown up learning that the pigment of a person's skin is an important factor to be used in categorizing people. Yet, if we were reared in Brazil, we would have learned to minimize skin color as being such an important way to divide people (e.g., Fish, 1995; Hirschfeld, 1996; Westie, 1964). Fish notes, for example, that if a hypothetical Brazilian couple comprising what to us is one black and one white parent were to have 10 children, "the children might well receive 10 different 'racial' classifications" (p. 45).

Hirschfeld (1996) agrees, adding the apparently well known Brazilian saying that "money whitens": Money and economic standing play a key role in the Brazilian system of categorizing human variety. For example, "members of the same family may be designated as belonging to different races, depending on their socioeconomic status" (Hirschfeld, 1996, p. 163). This situation would be inconceivable in the United States, where race is thought to be an essentially fixed and immutable quality of the person, not something that can change from birth onward as the person's economic standing changes.

Hirschfeld also tells us that while we in the United States and many other Western nations continue to emphasize race as a key marker for dividing human kinds, in parts of Asia *occupation* plays the same kind of organizing role that race does for us. As noted above, we tend to consider a person's race to be something that is intrinsic, a matter of birth and generally immutable. For us, people may change occupations, they may change clothing and their general appearance, and in some rare cases, may even change their sex, but never their race. You are born into a given race, live your entire life as a member of that racial grouping, and end your life in the same racial category as you began. In South Asia, by contrast, it is occupation that functions in this same manner. Occupation is said to be part of a person's intrinsic nature, not something that is incidental to his or her essential character and so modifiable. It would be as though we were to insist that "You were born to be a carpenter; that is who you really are and will always really be." As we reflect on these examples, we must come to the realization that how people are sorted into different types is less a function of some natural qualities of difference that mark human variety and much more a matter of cultural and historical conditions that define what are and are not the salient ways for sorting human kinds.

Let us consider one further example. If you were brought up in the African nation of Zimbabwe, skin pigment but not race as such would be an important marker of difference. In this case, however, being albino—that is being black by birth yet white in skin pigment—would produce many of the same kinds of prejudice and discrimination that blacks with black pigment encounter in the United States (e.g., McNeil, 1997). Albinism is a somewhat rare genetic disorder in which the genes needed to code melanin are defective, rendering the person's skin white, even if born of two black parents. Albinism is estimated to affect about one or two persons in every 5,000 in Zimbabwe and about one person in every 20,000 in the United States. Prejudice against albinos is much more severe in Zimbabwe, however, than in the United States: Some people spit on seeing an albino in the hope that this will ward off the curse they suppose had produced this condition and that might infect them as well; many refuse to shake hands with an albino or share food lest they too become infected; albinos find it difficult to get employment, to date, to marry, or to engage in a normal social life, being shunned by many in their society. In this case, skin pigment is employed socially to categorize people, but in reverse of the pattern employed in the United States and many other Western nations. Nevertheless, we find much the same effects on the persons so categorized: Their differences mark them as the targets of prejudice and discrimination.

Why Differences Become Socially Marked

As we probe further, we must wonder why skin pigment was selected as a marker at all. Why is it that some societies and groups are so concerned with the pigment of a person's skin in the first place, while others (e.g., Brazil) care so little? This same question can be asked about any of the differences that have been selected by some social groups throughout their history to be important markers of difference. Why religion? Why sexual orientation? Why ethnicity?

So that we will not be confused, the question I am asking us to consider is *not* why people seem to insist on making categories to sort human kinds, but rather why the particular kinds of categories that predominate in a given society at a particular time in its history are formed: why this way of dividing the world rather than another? Considering that people may be sorted by age, height, weight, eye color, hair color, and so on almost endlessly, why have certain ways of sorting become dominant? Why is race, why is gender, why is sexual orientation currently so critical to the way that we in the United States (among other nations) organize our understandings of the world's people? The point of all of this is to teach us that the ways we sort are not based on natural features of the world as much as they are based on socially selected and marked features that, for some reason, we have deemed to be important.

Although part of the story involved in answering this question seems to be based on humanity's apparently natural tendency to sort, group, categorize, and organize (matters we consider in more detail in Chapters 8 and 9), we must keep in mind that societies use that natural tendency to sort in their own peculiar ways. Extensive research as reported by Hirschfeld (1996), for example, suggests that all people engage in what he refers to as *essentialist thinking*—that is, to assume that the major categories by which their society has taught them to organize the world are somehow natural and essential defining properties of the persons and objects that have been sorted, a part of the world rather than of the societal perceivers. As we already observed, for example, in the United States and many other Western nations race is assumed to be an essential property of people by which they may be sorted, whereas in parts of Asia, occupation functions in much this same manner.

Our question at this point, then, is not why people sort and categorize— this is what the human mind seems geared to do—but rather, why they comprise the particular kinds of categories they do. To help us answer this question, let us consider five points.

First, differences that make a difference in prejudice have been selected, emphasized, and marked by some social groups in order to distinguish themselves from other social groups. For example, it is not religious beliefs (or skin pigment, etc.) *per se* that matter as much how some groups use religious beliefs (or skin pigment, etc.) to divide people into various categories so as to distinguish their own people from these others.

Second, this selection is usually not done overnight, but reflects a history of social relations among the various groups in a society. Indeed, the social relations between groups in a given society effectively create the important categories by which people in that society sort one another. For example, as Hirschfeld (1996) notes, it was slavery that created a single race out of the diverse populations of Africa. In other words, the diversity that marks indigenous African groups was overwhelmed by the role that slavery played: Slavery helped to make these diverse groups appear to be all the same. Because they did not undergo a comparable history of slavery, Latino and Latina Americans currently tend not to be considered a race, but rather are thought to be an ethnic group defined more by culture and class than by the biological category of race. As we shall shortly see, however, other immigrant groups have been racialized in much the same way as African Americans. All of this suggests that if we wonder why particular categories have predominated in any given society, we must first examine the history of social relations among the various groups that comprise that society. Not surprisingly, we will often find that power and domination (as with slavery) are central features of many of the ways that people categorize one another.

A third point is that although any one individual may have her or his own peculiar way of sorting other people (or even oneself), for the most part the differences that really matter are marked by social groups within a society. The individuals brought up in that society learn these distinctions and incorporate them into their own way of viewing the world. In other words, skin color has become important in the United States not because each of us individually has made it so, but rather because the color of a person's skin has been selected by our society as a key marker distinguishing members of groups within our society. To grow up in a society that has made skin color so important, then, is to learn its ways of organizing people by dividing them into coloration categories. Indeed, it would be almost impossible to grow up within a society that has marked skin color without learning to do so oneself.

For the same reason, it is almost impossible to grow up in a society that harbors prejudices against various groups without having those prejudices seep into our own fabric of being, however well intentioned we hope to be. Ezekiel (1995) captures this idea through a metaphor. He asks us to imagine that we live next to a cement factory churning out fine particles of cement dust that covers everything for miles around. This daily dust becomes the very air we breathe. Eventually, we never even know what clean air is like. In a similar manner, we ingest our society's prejudices; like the cement dust, they too become an unwelcome yet important part of us.

Fourth, which types of differences are emphasized and which are ignored is usually a choice made by the social groups that occupy positions of dominance within a society. These are the groups that have the power to make their definitions of who is one of them and who is different stick. Dominant groups not only select the qualities of difference that will be emphasized but also develop the rationale to explain why those differences mean one group should be treated differently from another.

For example, when the dominant groups brought slaves to the United States, skin color became a key mark of free (white) and slave (black). In addition, these dominant groups offered a reason that explained why it was only "natural" for dark-skinned people to be enslaved. We learn, for example, that the Founding Fathers did not truly intend that the freedoms promised to "all" really meant *all people*. After all, argued Chief Justice Taney of the U.S. Supreme Court in 1857, because slaves and former slaves were inferior beings, they were not fit to associate with the white race. And, as Tetlock, Armor, and Peterson (1994) remind us, because black slaves brought over from Africa were considered *subhuman,* it was not an inconsistency in logic for a white slaveowner to support *human* equality while simultaneously owning slaves. Because slaves are not humans, they do not deserve to be treated equally!

Our fifth and final point here is this: Those human differences that become central to a dominant social group are important to that group's sense of its own identity—that is, to its sense of itself as a people. For example, the whites' sense of themselves as a free people is built upon the sense of blacks as an enslaved people. I will shortly have more to say about this important matter, but for now let me simply note that one of the central purposes served by a dominant group's choice of qualities to define itself and others involves the dominant group's desire to form and sustain a positive view of itself. The Puritans who landed in New England encountered a native culture they considered to have issued from Satan (e.g., Segal & Stineback, 1977). If the native culture was satanic, then the Puritans must be God's own chosen people sent to convert, conquer, or destroy these savages!

There is nothing intrinsically better or worse about the pigment of people's skin, their gender, their appearance, or their sexual orientation that requires either their marking or their ranking. Nor is the particular selection of qualities that are marked today in the United States necessarily the same as those that have been marked in the past or in other current societies. Some social groups have marked these dimensions as important features by which the world of humanity is to be organized and have assumed that one side is better than the other. This means that when a student says she is the target of prejudice because she is black, she is not reporting something objective about herself as much as she is telling us about a complex story of the society in which she lives in which her skin color, which may in fact be more cream than black, has been said to be an important determinant of her character and destiny.

Differences, Purposes, and Identity

As we further probe this study of the relationship between differences and prejudice, note that there are two interconnected reasons why one group distinguishes itself from others and even ranks its difference as superior. One reason has to do with group identity, the other with collective interests and purposes. We will revisit aspects of this same idea later in Section 4. Figure 2.1 illustrates this argument.

Identity

One way for *my* people to appear especially civilized is to consider *your* people to be uncivilized. The ancient Greeks had a good word for this, so good in fact that it has come down to us as representing the essence of people without civilization and culture: *barbarians.* For the Greeks, all foreigners were

Figure 2.1

Why differences can lead to prejudice

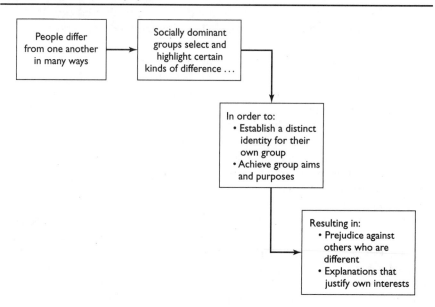

considered to be barbarians, a term based both on the strange sounds of their language and the alien quality of their customs.

Of course, the very terms *strange* and *alien* tell us less about the foreigners than about the Greeks, for whom any sounds but those of their own familiar language and any customs but their own were considered to be not only different, but lesser, barbaric. This point is generally true about all the cases of difference we consider. Differences, then, are less about the characteristics of nondominant groups (e.g., the barbarians) than about those characteristics marked by the dominant groups in their search for their own identity. Thus, we could reasonably argue that the barbarians were less barbaric than the Greeks' image of them, which was devised so that the Greeks themselves could appear to be civilized by comparison.

Carol Tavris (1992) applies this same analysis to the story of male-female relations throughout much of Western history. She effectively argues that the dominance of males as a group has both provided the male point of view as the implicit standard by which everything else is evaluated and made the female the group that lacks what this standard possesses. As Tavris puts it, "Men are normal; women, being 'opposite,' are deficient" (p.20). Obviously, she is not arguing that women are *in fact* deficient, but that they have been constructed as such in order to serve as the needed comparison for males' search for their own identity.

We are quite used to this way of thinking even if we are unaware that we employ it in our daily conversations. For example, we readily talk of "the opposite sex," which assumes that men and women have opposite characteristics. And so, if men are strong and rational beings, women, being opposite, must be weak and irrational, governed more by their emotions than by their intellect. Indeed, as Tavris suggests, men's identity as strong and rational beings requires considering women as opposite. How do men know their own rationality but through this kind of comparison with another (woman) made opposite?

During the time of Western explorations and imperialistic expansion, the "civilized" Europeans encountered many contrasting cultures. The civilized quality of the European culture was affirmed only by considering these natives to be heathen savages, uncivilized primitives (e.g., McGrane, 1989). Indeed, the very concept of "primitive" requires a contrast with a civilized comparison group. Of course, this rendering ignores the qualities of the others' culture. They become "primitives" so that the dominant groups can identity themselves as "civilized."

Cornell West (1993) tells us that "without the presence of black people in America, European-Americans would not be 'white'—they would be only Irish, Italians, Poles, Welsh and others engaged in class, ethnic, and gender struggles over resources and identity" (p. 156). To be white, in other words, demands that another group be designated as black.

Author Toni Morrison (1992) adds to this, commenting that for whites to consider themselves free and desirable as a people, they had to distinguish themselves from a people they had made enslaved and undesirable. In short, white identity was carved out of the comparison with others, without whom the whites could not be who they claimed to be. If this is correct, then as one author states it (Anderson, 1995), all we know about African Americans relates to the kind of *blackness that whiteness has created*. And much the same can be said about our knowledge of *whiteness* itself (e.g., see Dyer, 1997; Frankenberg, 1993).

Let me now briefly summarize this collective identity-making process that these several examples have illustrated. I have assumed that both individuals and social groups hope to answer the key identity question, "Who am I?" One of the major ways of answering that question is through a comparative process by which the characteristics of one's own group are given only by being contrasted with characteristics of other groups. Thus, my whiteness is given only by my having made you black; my masculinity exists only by virtue of having construed you as an opposite, feminine; my civilization exists only by virtue of considering yours to be uncivilized and barbaric. Obviously under such conditions, the actual qualities of your group (or mine) are concealed. But, if my group has the power to make its definitions stick, then we proceed in this manner until events interrupt and change the distribution of power.

Interests and Purposes

While all of this might seem to be quite unfair, and in most respects clearly is, it describes an important reason why certain differences have been selected by dominant social groups to be marked, and how the dominant groups maintain their dominance and sense of self-worth as long as they can effectively keep others "in their place." Thus a second reason for marking certain differences is based on a group's collective interests and purposes. Dominant groups who seek to use others in their own service—for example as slaves or as a conquered people whose land and resources are available for exploitation—typically develop a theory of group differences that not only *sorts* people and *explains* why others are different from themselves but that also *justifies* why the dominant group must take the actions toward them that it does (e.g., see Hirschfeld, 1996).

In the early history of the United States, for example, and even before they fled England, the Puritans had a well developed theory about the satanic land they were about to inhabit and the savages who already populated that land (see Segal & Stineback, 1977). Their theory, namely that these savages were the offspring of Satan, effectively sorted the world into savage and civilized and justified the necessary attempts of the Puritans, being civilized, to appropriate the savages' land for their own purposes. What the theory ignored, of course, was that these so-called savages simply had a different culture and worldview than did the Puritans.

For example, the Indians believed that the land had been given in sacred trust to the entire community and so could not be sold or bartered away by any individual member of the tribe. By contrast, the Puritans believed that all land was a private possession; they also believed that when it was vacant, as it typically was among these native peoples, it was available to be appropriated and made useful. Citing biblical chapter and verse, the Puritans justified taking over the land from these savages for whom it seemed (in the Puritans' view) to hold no purpose whatsoever. In a similar manner, the Puritans' ideas about the satanic qualities of the Indians saw them as a challenge to their own virtue, a group to be subdued in the name of Christian civilization. These ideas justified the continuing expansion of the early colonies as well as the destruction of the native culture.

In Germany preceding the Nazi era, attempts had been made to define Jews as a separate race with distinctive and dangerous racial qualities (e.g., Efron, 1994). When the Nazis came to power in the early 1930s, these theories provided a comfortable basis for rounding up members of this separate race and seeking their destruction in the name of purifying the Aryan type (Burleigh & Wipperman, 1991). In other words, dominant groups develop theories about others that not only serve to firm up the identity of their own kind, but additionally present these others as ripe for conquest and, if necessary, elimination. In the German case, typical of many such examples, these others (e.g., Jews) were used to help unify the nation by providing a shared *scapegoat* to blame for societal ills.

The following example from U.S. history demonstrates how dominant groups sort other people in a manner that justifies their own position and their treatment of others, and how these dominant groups develop a theory of sorting that creates racial divisions in much the same way that diverse African cultures were sorted into a single racial category and that Jews in pre-Nazi and Nazi Germany were sorted into one race that stood apart from all others. In the mid-19th century and early 20th century, when the Irish fled starvation in their own nation and came to the United States (among other countries) seeking what all immigrant groups have historically sought in a new land, they found themselves quickly involved in a racial confrontation (e.g., Alba, 1985; Gordon, 1990, 1994; Roediger, 1991, 1994; Shanklin, 1994). Although the Irish Catholic's skin color was clearly white, the Northern European and Protestant majority claimed that these Irish immigrants were a distinctly different race. They were treated as though they were not white, or as one author termed it (Roediger, 1991), as "not yet white." Indeed, worry about race mixing at that time tended to be focused less on the union of black with white than on the even more feared union of Protestant with Irish Catholic (e.g., Gordon, 1990). But it was not only Irish Catholics who were racially sorted into the nonwhite category. As others have observed (e.g., Alba, 1985), the dominant majority in the early part of the 20th century also argued that Italian immigrants were similarly not really white. It seems fairly apparent that dominant groups use a racial sorting to distinguish themselves from others they consider inferior, to justify why those others never quite accomplish the same lofty achievements as their own kind, and why racially distinct others receive the treatment they do. And all of this uses a theory of race that, as our examples illustrate, has very little to do with natural differences such as skin pigment.

Wallerstein (1991) offers another type of example that clearly reveals the "economics" and "politics" of dividing the world into various types of groups. During the era of apartheid, the South African government carefully sorted the country's local human world into distinct "racial" categories with distinct legal rights: Europeans (the privileged group), Bantus (the native African groups), Coloureds (those born from the union of Africans and Europeans), and Indians (those primarily from India). Each person was not only sorted into one of these presumably racially defined groups, but having been so categorized had certain legal rights that defined his or her conditions of living, working, and playing. Europeans, of course, were at the top of the social ladder, with Bantus and Coloureds being at the bottom, highly restricted as to where they could live, work, and play.

A problem emerged, however, when Japan became a major economic force in the world and Japanese businessmen traveled worldwide to conduct their commercial affairs. In this case, the business of Japan was economically important to the business of South Africa. But, into which category should these Japanese businessmen be placed? They did not fit neatly into any of the governmentally devised categories and yet were of major economic importance to the South African government and its economic well-being.

The problem was solved, Wallerstein tells us, simply by referring to these Japanese businessmen as "honorary whites"! Cynically, but accurately, Wallerstein comments: "In a country whose laws are supposed to be based on the permanence of genetic categories, apparently genetics follows the election returns of the world-economy" (p. 80). In other words, because it was economically convenient for the South African government (the dominant group in this case), persons were categorized as "honorary whites" and given the legal rights and privileges available only to those who are "white." If ever anyone doubted the economic and political side of "racial" groupings, this example should serve to wipe away that skepticism.

Chapter Summary: Key Learning Points

1. To understand prejudice requires that we examine the various kinds of difference on which it is based.

2. These differences, however, turn out to be less a quality that people naturally possess than the result of a complex historical and social process by which dominant groups have marked out or highlighted certain qualities as important ways to distinguish between groups.

3. We considered two main reasons why socially dominant groups tend to be concerned with distinguishing between themselves and others:

   a. Socially dominant groups achieve a sense of their own identity by highlighting differences between their group and others.

   b. Socially dominant groups highlight differences in order to justify their attitudes toward and treatment of others, thereby securing their own group interests.

Explaining Prejudice: Characteristics of the Targeted Groups

As we have seen, an important lesson to be learned about understanding prejudice is that its complexity demands that we remain open to approaches from a variety of disciplines. With this in mind, Section 2 draws on history, political science, and anthropology—as well as psychology—so that we can examine prejudice in the form it assumed for several thousand years of human history. Although the term *prejudice* was never associated with this form, I believe that we cannot successfully understand prejudice today without probing its past as well as some current survivals of that past.

The predominant form that prejudice took for thousands of years explained the negative attitudes and actions of one group toward another primarily in terms of the characteristics of the target group. Needless to say, what to us is prejudice, because it involves one group's negative view of another group, was not understood as prejudice by "our" ancestors, who explained their negative feelings by focusing on characteristics that the targeted group presumably possessed. In no way did they consider themselves to be acting with prejudice. They were simply responding to what they argued was the true nature of those they had to deal with. In order to make this idea easier to grasp, let me simplify matters a bit.

Let us suppose that one group of people, the Apollonians, encounters another group of people, the Wollonians, whom they experience as different from themselves: Wollonians seem to be primitive and uncivilized. Let us further suppose that this difference evokes a negative evaluation among the Apollonians and thus, *by our definition,* is an instance of prejudice. There are two ways that Apollonians might try to understand their negative views.

First, they might try to explain their negative attitudes toward the Wollonians by referring to the characteristics that Wollonians possess. Whenever several Apollonians meet and discuss the great issues of their day, they explain the problems they have with these unruly Wollonians by noting the peculiar characteristics of the Wollonian people: Wollonians are backwards and primitive, they lack the finer sensitivities, they are ruled by their passions, and so are always a problem to the civilized world. I would describe this process as seeking explanations for prejudiced reactions by focusing attention on characteristics that the objects of prejudice are presumed to have. And indeed, this process is the focus of the three chapters in Section 2.

But there is a second possibility. Rather than explaining their negative view of the Wollonians in terms of qualities Wollonians possess, Apollonian social scientists might search for characteristics evident among those members of their own group, the Apollonians, who harbor negative attitudes. If anyone were to wonder why some Apollonians think so negatively of the Wollonians, the answer would be sought by looking for specific characteristics of those Apollonians who felt and acted in this prejudiced manner. The focus, in other words, would shift toward asking about the qualities that describe the prejudiced person (e.g., Samelson, 1976, examines this shift in the United States). This second option, focusing on the prejudiced person, will be examined in Section 3.

Now for a brief look at the chapters in Section 2:

Chapter 3 examines some historically early efforts to explain differences. In the days before science provided a more rigorous method for probing the secrets of human life, those secrets were conveyed through a combination of religious beliefs, cultural myths, and common folklore. The early seeds of prejudice appear in this prescientific trio of religion, myth, and folklore. These seeds are carried by beliefs about the characteristics said to describe those groups who emerged as the targets of special attention.

Chapter 4 offers a preliminary view of how science has addressed the question of difference. The chapter first looks at the relation between science and society, and then introduces three different paradigms (or models) involving scientific efforts to explain group differences: a biological model, a sociocultural model, and the more recent bidirectional model. We illustrate aspects of these models with several early scientific attempts to explain group differences by focusing on qualities within the groups that have been the targets of prejudice (e.g., women, Jews, African Americans, homosexuals) that may account for the kinds of responses these groups evoke. Is there something inherent about women, for example, that might explain men's responses to them and also help us better understand why, as a group, women have not achieved as highly as men? As we will see, although religious doctrine and folklore may have yielded to science, many of the answers we consider in Chapter 4 remain steadfastly focused on characteristics of the target groups.

Chapter 5 continues to examine the role of science in understanding group differences, moving beyond the earlier efforts discussed in Chatper 4 to some of the more recent debates, many of which center on race and intelligence—and which, I contend, continue to carry the seeds of prejudice in the guise of scientifically re-spectable data about differences in IQ (intelligence quotient, a measure of intelli-gence) between various racial groups. This chapter also considers another group dif-ference that seems to have come into its own as we move toward the close of the 20th century: homosexuality.

Now, here are some things to look for while you read the three chapters in Section 2:

First, notice that the specific groups whose differences from the majority pose a problem to the majority tend to shift through time as historical circumstances change. Although women and Jews have had a rather lengthy history as the targets of preju-dice, other groups are more recent entries. Homosexuals, for example, were not the targets of prejudice in classical Greek times to the extent that they are in many soci-eties today. This means that we will see different kinds of difference emerging at dif-ferent times in history to pose a problem that the majority feels it must address. In-deed, one can learn a great deal about the majority by examining the kinds of difference they find most troublesome at a particular point in history.

Second, be aware that much of the material in Section 2, both prescientific as well as scientific, often appears to be more of a way to justify a group's prejudice than to understand it. For example, it takes little imagination to see how men, by viewing females as innately inferior to males, manage to justify their own positions at the top of the social ladder and women's standing well below. This is not to claim that those who seek explanations by probing characteristics of the targeted groups have invari-ably done so in a self-conscious attempt to justify their own attitudes. It is to say, however, that regardless of their intent, the result often serves to justify inferior and superior social ranking in which, not surprisingly, the chief explainers are themselves members of the socially superior group.

Finally, let me repeat the warning we first encountered in Section 1. Because this section emphasizes prejudice on the part of those who are in dominant social posi-tions, the reader might *incorrectly* conclude that those who are its targets are them-selves without prejudice. Nothing could be further from the truth or from the intent of the three chapters in this section. Admittedly, this section focuses primarily on those whose prejudice includes searching for qualities among the targeted groups that justify the prejudiced attitudes and behaviors taken toward them. However, the mere fact that this is our current focus does not imply that the targeted peoples are with-out their own forms of prejudice.

Thus, although at this point we are primarily examining how dominant groups have expressed their prejudices by seeking qualities among certain targeted peoples that explain and justify their attitudes toward them, we must remember that the tar-geted groups themselves can and typically do also harbor prejudices. For example, homosexuals may be the targets of some strong prejudices that seek to explain cer-tain qualities they possess that might warrant nonhomosexuals' attitudes toward them. At the same time, however, homosexuals may also harbor prejudices toward hetero-sexuals. The same is true of other groups who have been the targets of prejudice.

Although this warning needs to be carefully considered as you read the three chapters in this section, it is also important to keep in mind that the prejudices harbored by the socially dominant groups in any society tend to be more consequential for the shape of human relations in that society than are the prejudiced views of the typical targets. Remember, it was when the Nazis came to power that their views of Jews (among others) produced the horrors of the death camps. Although many Jews may have harbored prejudices toward the Nazis, their prejudiced attitudes did not produce consequences as horrible or significant as did the prejudices of the then-powerful Nazis.

Chapter 3

Religion and Folklore Explain Group Differences

Few groups in the Western world have had as lengthy a history of being the targets of prejudice as have women and Jews. Before going further, two preliminary observations are in order. First, keep in mind that as historical conditions change, different groups emerge as problems of concern either to the dominant groups within a society or to groups aspiring to such dominance. Second, remember that this concern waxes and wanes. For example, neither women nor Jews have *always* been a problem to the dominant groups within society—but, when a group (such as women or Jews) becomes a serious concern to the majority, the prejudicial process we are examining in this section—that of justifying negative attitudes and actions by attributing certain characteristics to the target group—seems to take hold.

For instance, I cannot accurately pinpoint the exact moment in history when women as a group emerged as a problem to be explained. But we know from reading early Greek philosophy that even in those ancient times, women posed enough of a challenge that men felt the need to explain why women were not only different, but also inferior to their male counterparts.

We also know that when Christianity emerged from its early Jewish roots and began to stake out a territory of its own, seeking to expand and solidify its hold on the populace of what was then the civilized Western world (about 200-300 C.E.), the Jews stood out as a serious problem to be dealt with by the emerging new Christian religion. The difference in this case involved the Jews' refusal to accept Jesus as the Christ (Messiah), and their insistence on retaining their own beliefs and ritual practices. This refusal to become Christian led some key Christian figures of that era to explain the Jewish difference by looking for something unique, even satanic, about Jews as a group.

Later in the chapter we will also examine how this early form of prejudice operated within the contexts of colonialism and slavery. But to begin, let us look more closely at the relationships between women and men and between Christians and Jews.

Women and Men

Greek Philosophers Confront Women's Difference

Plato and Aristotle were two of the greatest Greek philosophers of the classic age. Many of their ideas continue to influence Western thinking even today. Each offered what many would now find to be shocking appraisals of the nature of women. Even more clearly than Plato, Aristotle established an explanation of women's essential difference that survived for centuries.

Everything seemed fairly obvious to Aristotle, who lived in the 3rd century B.C.E. He tells us that women had not been created to be as complete as men. At best, women were *partial or incomplete* men (e.g., Whitbeck, 1976). According to Aristotle, women lacked the heat that men possessed. This made them unable to cook their own vital fluids (menstrual blood) into the final refined stage which, Aristotle argued, was found only in the male element, semen. Aristotle also called upon an ancient distinction that is as modern as today's stereotypes: Men were mind or spirit; women were body. As spirit was considered to be superior to body—after all, bodies decay and die and are thereby impermanent as compared with the eternal quality of spirit—so too were men superior to women.

What marks humans as distinct from animals, continued Aristotle, is their ability to think and reason, their possession of what he termed "the deliberative faculty." Although all humans (even women!) are distinct from beasts and so possess this faculty, in women, it is *defective.* And so, lacking an ability to think and reason clearly, women are necessarily lesser than men, giving men the legitimate right to rule in all human affairs.

Thomas Laqueur's (1990) analysis of the early understanding of male and female anatomy adds further to this picture. For example, Galen, the great 2nd-century Greek physician and anatomist, argued, as had Aristotle, that because women lacked the heat that men did, they were unable to move their genitalia from their imperfect location inside their bodies to the more perfect location outside. Location, however, was the only difference in male and female genital anatomy! In Galen's view, women's ovaries, which by the 19th century had become a biological marker of their distinct difference from men, were not even given a name of their own but were referred to by the same term used to designate male testes. In this case, then, sameness erases women's unique difference while retaining their inferiority: After all, they did not ever have the ability to move their sexual organs to their proper and perfect location outside the body.

The theory of women's difference and inferiority to men also found root in the dualistic notions that took hold in early Greek philosophy, especially among the followers of Pythagoras (Synnott, 1993). We already encountered one example of this dualism: spirit (male) versus body (female). According to this dualistic notion, the world is composed of opposites: odd-even, one-many, right-left, light-dark, good-bad, straight-curved, and so forth. A central dualism is the opposition *male-female*. And, not surprisingly, "female" was associated with darkness and those items on the negative side of the list, whereas "male" was associated with lightness and everything positive. In early philosophy, therefore, women were said to be the opposite of men, or as we now say, women are the "opposite sex." Therefore, if men have reason, rationality, order, and mind, women—as opposites—represent nonreason, irrationality, chaos, and body.

While there is nothing factually opposite about men and women, the dualistic descriptions that have come down to us from ancient times have persisted in framing our understanding in these oppositional terms. We continue to consider men and women not only to be different but to be opposites.

I hasten to note that not every early Greek philosopher was as negative about women's difference as the Aristotelians and Pythagoreans. Plato, for example, offered a somewhat more ambiguous assessment, at times portraying women and their world in harshly negative terms, at times presenting an equality between men and women. The overall thrust of this early philosophy, even Plato's, however, was its portrayal of women's difference as lesser and inferior as compared with men.

Women as a group were clearly a problem and a challenge for men as a group. And men rose to this challenge by developing theories about women's characteristics that established very early in Western tradition some of the notions that live with us today and that carry on the message of prejudice: a negative and unjustified view of women as a group.

Rabbis and Church Fathers Confront Women's Difference

Before opening this next topic, it is important to introduce a brief preface to provide a context for what follows. For many people, the Bible, both Old and New Testaments, represents the literal words of God, recorded by men and handed down in the forms we know today. Yet, as numerous biblical scholars have demonstrated (e.g., Coote & Coote, 1990; Pagels, 1981), the Bible involves the words of men written in order to solidify their particular groups' interests and advantages. In other words, rather than the Bible recording God's words, it records men's words designed to justify powerful group interests. Take the Genesis story of Adam and Eve, for example.

Although debates over its meaning continue (e.g., Pagels, 1988; Pardes, 1992), the Genesis story of Adam and Eve remains a central piece of early religious faith that has come down to us today as "common knowledge and wisdom." After all, was not Adam made in God's image and Eve made from Adam? And, did this ordering of creation not give men priority over women and place women in a secondary standing with respect to men?

This was an idea to be told later by Paul in his letter to the Corinthians (I Corinthians 11:7-9). Paul reminds the Corinthians that just as Christ is supreme over every man, the husband is supreme over his wife; that because it is man who reflects the image and the glory of God, he has no need to cover his head, but woman must because she does not reflect God but rather reflects the glory of man; that man was not created from woman, but woman from man; that man was not created for woman's sake, but woman was created for man's.

In both the Jewish and the emerging Christian traditions, women, of course, had their place, but that place was not as a full equal to men. In the Jewish tradition, for example, women were excluded from reading the most holy of books, the Torah; nor were they permitted to participate in the many rituals of the religion other than those relegated to women in their reproductive and homemaker roles. One rabbi is reputed to have exclaimed to a woman who was "obviously" claiming a better place for herself, that "it was better to burn Torah than to allow a woman to handle it" (Brown, 1988, p. 145). Women's monthly uncleanliness, it was felt, made them unfit for these sacred roles.

Early Christianity somewhat improved the lot of women in religion, at least until the institutionalized church took firm hold, when women's voice was stilled (e.g., see Fiorenza, 1989). Early Christianity, however, not only sought to silence women (e.g., Paul's reputed letter in I Corinthians 14:34-35), but in addition subscribed to the then well known split between spirit or mind and body that we encountered in classic Greek thought. All matters of the body were dangerous and threatening, as they deflected man from his spiritual path to God. Since women were "body," they were especially dangerous to men: "Women were the cause . . . of 'double-hearted behavior' . . . thought to stir up the lust and jealousy that pitted males against each other" (Brown, 1988, p. 39).

For one early church father, Tertullian, women were the devil's gateway: "With their alluring hairstyles and disturbingly unveiled faces, the women of the church of Carthage were regarded by Tertullian as a breech in the defenses of the church" (Brown, 1988, p. 153). So concerned were men about women that they sought to avoid appearing womanish and to remain virile in all that they thought and did (Brown, 1988). Can we recognize, in this early religious view of gender, the current concern of many men not to appear effeminate?

Evaluating the Early Philosophical and Religious Explanations

Let us pause for a moment and take stock of where we have been and what lessons we should learn from these early efforts of philosophy and religion to explain both women's difference and their inferiority to men. In the first place, we see that the writers and theoreticians, all male at the time, were attempting to grapple with the differences between themselves and women. In case after case, and extending from ancient Greek philosophy through early religious doctrine, both Jewish and Christian, this difference was interpreted as revealing something fundamentally—that is, *naturally*—inferior about women. Men were the model for the proper human; women were lesser. Women's sexuality and association with the body made them dangerous to men. Men were beings of the spirit who could be seduced by women and distracted from their own loftier, godly mission. Is this ancient history or contemporary folklore?

In the second place, however, if anyone in that era even worried about holding accurate rather than biased views—and Greek philosophers were clearly concerned with truth and correct knowledge—these views about women were not seen to be a sign of male prejudice towards women, and hence were not considered incorrect judgments; they were simply truisms about the nature of male-female differences. Men were not prejudiced, irrational, or foolish. Their attitudes towards women were based on "fact" as it was then known. Men felt the way they did about women because of the deficiencies that women themselves possessed.

Thirdly, the treatment of women that today some might consider discriminatory—such as not permitting women a voice in the church or rule in the governing centers of society—were seen as the natural result of natural processes. God did not make woman in man's image. Women were not endowed with abilities to think and reason in the same manner as men. It was only *natural* to give women lesser positions in all the institutions of society.

In sum, what we today might refer to as *sexism,* involving clear-cut prejudice and discrimination toward women, was explained by turning to qualities of the target, women in this case, that made it only right and proper to think poorly of them and to treat them differently. It was not women's fault that they were the way they were, nor were men particularly biased for thinking of them as lesser beings: They simply, plainly, and naturally *were* lesser beings. And that was that.

Keep these ideas in mind as we move from the past in this chapter into more modern times in Chapters 4 and 5—from religion and folklore, to scientific efforts to explain differences; from differences between women and men, to those of the various other groups whose differences seem to provide concerns for the dominant groups in society. Although both historical conditions and the focus have shifted over the last several millennia, the story line turns out to be all too much the same: It is not prejudice but rationality that leads one group to think poorly of another group and to treat that other group differently.

Christians and Jews

According to the ancient Greeks, all non-Greek foreigners, referred to as *barbarians,* were a problem because they lacked the niceties of civilization and self-control that were thought to be essential to maintain Greek society in an orderly and unitary form (e.g., Vernant, 1995). For the newly emerging

Christian religion, barbarians were less the source of difficulty than were fellow Jews whose refusal to accept the Christian view of the world, especially the story of Jesus as the Christ, threatened the unity of all mankind they sought to achieve.

One biblical scholar, Daniel Boyarin (1994), uses Paul's letter to the Galatians (Galatians 3:28) to hammer home this point. On the one hand, Paul's letter seemed very inclusive in arguing that all distinctions between people should be eliminated: Persons were neither slave nor free, male nor female, Christian nor Jew, but were essentially all one under Christ Jesus. In short, argued Paul, under the rule of the Christ, differences would melt and all persons would be equal because they would be one.

On the other hand, this act of inclusiveness could readily be inverted and become exclusionary if one group declined to accept Paul's terms. Jews, who refused to accept Jesus as the Christ, became a problem at that time, and in many cases have remained a problem for certain groups throughout history. Their refusal marked them as special, but not in the positive sense of that term. Their refusal to accept the emerging doctrines of Christianity, especially when coupled with the view that they were responsible for the death of Jesus, laid the foundations for their exclusion and eventual denigration as a group.

The dilemma these early Christians faced was how to account for this Jewish refusal to accept the doctrines of the emerging Christian church. It was only a small step to believe that perhaps Jews were not the children of God, but of Satan—agents not of good, but of evil. The biblical scholar, Elaine Pagels (1995) tells us how in the book of Mark, Jesus' ministry is described as "involving continual struggle between God's spirit and the demons, who belong . . . to Satan's 'kingdom' " (Pagels, 1995, p. xvii). She observes how Mark's vision has "been incorporated into Christian tradition [serving] to confirm for Christians their own identification with God and to demonize their opponents—first other Jews, then pagans, and later dissident Christians called heretics" (p. xvii). "Obviously," this Jewish refusal to accept what everyone else knew to be true was a sign of their being Satan's offspring. Here we see once again how a difference is construed as a failing in the character of one group, thereby justifying their being the targets of negative feelings and actions.

The demonization of Jews survived early biblical times to enter later discussions of the Christian-Jewish difference, including both official church doctrine as well as widely shared cultural myths and folklore. Medieval myths prevalent throughout western Europe, for example, carried the idea that Jews were the devil's children and even had characteristics of the devil himself. Jews had horns, for example:

> In 1267 the Vienna Council decreed that Jews must wear a 'horned hat' . . . a provision which later councils sought to strenuously enforce; and Philip III required Jews of France to attach a horn-shaped figure to the customary Jew badge (Trachtenburg, 1943, pp. 45-46).

If you visit Rome today and view Michelangelo's wonderful statue of Moses, you are immediately struck by the clearly depicted horns coming out of Moses' head. While there is some ambiguity over what this meant for Michelangelo (see Trachtenberg, 1943), there is little doubt that the mythology of the Middle Ages held that because they were offspring of the devil, all Jews had horns.

The myths and folklore of the Middle Ages also viewed Jews as sorcerers who could cast spells and summon forth demons. In addition, because they were kin of the devil, Jews were said to have a peculiar odor reflecting both their bestial origins as well as the animal familiarly known to associate with the devil, the goat. Jewish men were said to be especially prone to peculiar diseases that compelled them to require Christian blood as therapy. And, surprising to us but less so in the Middle Ages, folklore suggested that both Jewish men and women menstruated, another blood loss that required replacement by capturing young Christians and bleeding them!

What lessons, then, do we learn from this rapid journey through early history? We can now add Jews to women as another group whose difference had to be explained. And here as before, the explanation turned to characteristics of the target group, Jews. People maintained that their reactions to Jews were not signs of prejudice, not irrational, but rather quite reasonable and rational judgments given the special and, in this case, decidedly evil and satanic qualities of the Jews. For the most part, today, one will not usually find these same accounts given by Christians about Jews except among the most extreme groups whose ideology of Christian Identity we will encounter later (in Chapter 6).

Colonialism and the "Discovery" of the Primitive

One of the significant periods of Western history was the age of exploration, with its well known voyages of discovery. During this time, many of the major European nations encountered exotic new lands, peoples, and cultures. In most cases, these voyages of discovery were driven not so much by curiosity as by other familiar motivations: new lands to claim for the crown heads of Europe, more resources for the coffers of the country's rulers. This was the era of imperial expansion and colonization.

The colonizers faced several challenges, not the least of which involved explaining both why these exotic people were different from the Europeans and why their very difference *invited* European colonization. This challenge was solved, one might say rather neatly, by assuming that the difference was one of *degree of civilization,* and that it was only right and proper for those with the greatest civilization to govern those with the least. And so now savages and primitives took their places alongside women and children to be guided by those who were the most civilized and capable of leading.

Theories developed rather quickly to fit this picture. There was a Great Chain of Being (Efron, 1994), an ordering of the world in terms of evolutionary progress, with the most evolved being the European (this would soon become the Aryan or Nordic European) and the least evolved being the savage primitives encountered worldwide, hardly distinct from the surrounding beasts. This theory was convenient for those at the top of the Great Chain (who, of course, had developed this theory in the first place!). After all, they were not being exploiters when they conquered these primitive peoples and took their resources. It was a burden that these white Europeans had to bear, a "white man's burden": taking care of those less fortunate than themselves.

Consider the Puritans we met earlier in this text. On landing in what is now New England, they encountered Indians (primitive savages to them) who not only were not Christian (and so in need of saving if this were at all possible), but also sufficiently backward that they did not even know how to deal with their vacant lands. This made it necessary for the Puritans to take action to tame the land, which they, of course, would thereafter own. It was only right and proper given the characteristics of these savages.

As a highly critical analyst of this process of colonization, Memmi (1967) observed a common theme. On meeting the primitive native and observing his way of life, the European saw a *lazy* person:

> It is easy to see to what extent this description is useful. . . . Nothing could better justify the colonizer's privileged position than his industry, and nothing could better justify the colonized's destitution than his indolence. The mythical portrait of the colonized therefore includes an unbelievable laziness, and that of the colonizer, a virtuous taste for action. At the same time, the colonizer suggests that employing the colonized is not very profitable, thereby authorizing his unreasonable wages. (p. 79)

Laziness explains the colonizer's attitudes towards the primitives while simultaneously obliges him to act forcefully to manage these lazy and potentially unruly people. This entire story is told without even a hint of prejudice. The colonizer's account tells of his virtue and the primitives' lack of civilization. The colonizer must use repressive tactics to keep order among a people who are childlike, impulsive, irresponsible, and thus unable to govern themselves.

Black Africans and Slavery

The story told in the United States when black Africans were brought over and enslaved is much the same as the story we have just considered for colonizers worldwide. To justify slavery, the white masters had to depict black Africans as somehow lesser than normal humans, as subhumans who lacked the qualities that marked the true human being as distinct from beasts. And so, for their own good, the slaveowner had to use harsh tactics.

Some of the great figures in American history, Thomas Jefferson for example, were not only slaveowners, but advocates of a theory of the black slave that explained even as it justified their treatment. Jefferson attributed to blacks a lesser need for sleep and a courage that was based on their inability to anticipate dangers because of their lesser mental abilities (see Jordon, 1968; Sampson, 1976). Somewhat childlike in their inability to hold much of anything in mind for longer than a brief moment, blacks were also unable to think creatively. Their powers of reason were dull. In short, their inferior social position was more than amply warranted by their generally lesser abilities than the whites who, of necessity, ruled them.

Chapter Summary: Key Learning Points

1. When a group becomes a problem to the dominant groups within a society or those groups aspiring to dominance, the dominant groups emphasize the ways in which their people differ from those problem people.

2. Dominant groups use these now marked and highlighted differences both to explain and to justify their views of these other peoples and their treatment of them. They build their case around certain qualities, traits, and characteristics that these others possess (e.g., they are satanic, imperfect copies of the ideal, lazy, etc.).

3. Rather than considering their own attitudes to be signs of prejudice, it is more typical for the dominant groups to believe that their attitudes and actions are reasonable responses to the characteristics that these other people possess (e.g., men must rule because of women's inferior character).

4. This chapter has emphasized how philosophy, folklore, and religion have often served to legitimate the rule of the dominant groups over others. Although the specific groups that emerge as problems for the dominant groups have varied historically, the process has remained very much the same: Once a group is identified as a problem, the dominant group begins to attribute certain negative characteristics to the targeted group in an effort to explaining why it is a problem.

Chapter 4

Science Explains Group Differences, I: Preliminary Considerations

During that time in human history when religious belief, cultural folklore, and mythology dominated human understanding, as we have seen, attitudes that today we would consider prejudicial were prevalent. But during the latter part of the 16th century and onwards—when science as we now know it began to take root in the Western world, when raw superstition and intuition were replaced by reason and empirical methods of investigation designed to get at the truth—then surely human understanding would dramatically change. Science would put an end to those *false* beliefs about women, Jews, people of color, and primitives, and replace them with cold, hard, objective facts. Of course, differences between people would remain. But rather than using differences to justify advantage for some groups and disadvantage for others, science would eliminate the politics of difference and provide us at long last with knowledge of the real truths about humankind. Or would it?

This chapter and the next must walk a delicate line. My intent is neither to condemn science nor to deny the great advances in understanding that it has brought. I do not wish to suggest that scientific methods of inquiry and verification and the search for objective facts are more flawed than the myth and folklore that preceded them. Rather, I hope to let us see how in its relatively brief history, science has not always fared better than the prejudiced mythologies it replaced.

A Quick Course on Science and Society

Some people have so mythologized science that they assume it to be a perfect way to achieve truth, where "perfect" means without error or bias. But, science is a human endeavor, conducted by human beings who live in the same world that you and I inhabit. Scientists are subject to many of the same biases and cultural beliefs as the rest of us. For most people doing the everyday work of science, it is a job, not a magic act. Its laborers have most of the same pressures facing everyone who must work to earn a living. And, even as the rest of us respond in various ways to those pressures, bending this way and that to ensure that in bad times we will keep our jobs, scientists too may find themselves responding in less than saintly ways.

Yet one quality that the *system* of science itself has as a disciplined way to achieve knowledge, even if no single one of its workers may be so described, is that the scientific system is *self-correcting*. Unlike most matters involving religious belief or folklore, science is in a continual process of movement, change, and correction. Old truths are fair game to be challenged and replaced by new truths, which in their turn will be challenged and either survive or more often than not be transformed. The very science that first told us not to worry about the health hazards of smoking, for example, was corrected by scientists who documented a connection between smoking and disease such that few today do not believe that excessive smoking has harmful health effects.

As we examine the role of science in explaining group differences, we will see that in certain respects it has been employed in much the same prejudicial manner that we encountered with religious belief and cultural mythology. Let us keep in mind, however, that for every scientific finding I present that confirms society's prejudicial attitudes about this group or that, there is either a scientific challenge already in place or one waiting in the wings. The problem, then, is not science itself, but a society that is often all too eager to accept the worse news about certain groups, and some scientists who seem only too eager to help feed these public prejudices.

Some of the same groups that were considered a problem for the dominant social groups of the earlier historical period in the Western world have remained problems during the scientific era. We should not be surprised, therefore, but perhaps disappointed, to see science now affirming some of the same biases about women's characteristics that we have already met.

For example, Anne Fausto-Sterling (1997), a Brown University professor in the Department of Molecular and Cell Biology and Biochemistry and a critic of these abuses of science's treatment of "the woman question," cites several scientific works that have fueled the popular media frenzy that appeared in front-page stories during the mid-1990s in such major national magazines as *Time, Newsweek,* and *The New Republic.* These popular renditions of scientific research review biological findings that appear to demonstrate some clear-cut "facts" about women's fundamental differences from men. While appearing to document several hardwired biological differences between men's and women's brains, the subtext of these stories is to set the terms within which any social changes and social policies must of necessity operate. For instance, if women are fundamentally wired differently from men, then some social programs designed to get more women into certain scientific careers may be misguided, as women simply do not have "the right stuff" for such work.

Although by the end of the 19th century, Jews had exited from serious scientific concern in most parts of the Western world, they continued to remain a problem in certain nations, including the United States during the period of great immigration from eastern Europe and especially in Germany both prior to and throughout the Nazi era. In the United States, we find scientists using intelligence testing to confirm the fundamental inferiority of eastern Europeans, including many Jewish immigrants (see Samelson, 1976). Meanwhile, German race science sought to demonstrate that Jews were not only a separate race, but also had traits so despicable and dangerous to the rest of the world that only their elimination, much as one would eliminate a deadly virus or cancerous growth, could solve the Jewish question (e.g., Efron, 1994; Rose, 1990).

When slavery was ended in the United States and black Americans were free to take their places in society as equals, they became a group once again to be explained by the white majority. Classifying people who suddenly became equals as subhuman primitives, as had previously been the case, would no longer suffice. New justifications for the failure of blacks to be integrated fully and equally into white society were sought. And, in an often overly accommodating manner, certain scientists obliged—discovering traits within blacks that destined them to remain in the lower echelons of society or that explained why they were a danger to respectable white citizenry (e.g., Hirsch, 1981; Samelson, 1976).

Many other groups, too, have emerged as challenges—because of their *appearance* (too fat, too slim, too whatever), their *age* (too young, too old), or their *ability status* (hearing, visually, or mobility impaired). But for some in the final years of the 20th century, the one group that has come to the fore as a serious problem is characterized by its sexual orientation. In many respects, the homosexual difference marks an important new direction of serious societal concern in the United States. This difference seems to challenge the very core values held by the heterosexual majority and its view about what is and is not proper sexual conduct and lifestyle. And once again science has entered the fray with its efforts to discover the "real" basis for this homosexual difference within the characteristics—especially genetics and brain structures—of the gay and lesbian person (e.g., Gladue, 1994; LeVay, 1991).

Three Models of Scientific Inquiry

Before we can advance our examination of science and prejudice, we must enter what has been and remains a thorny and often misunderstood debate.

Figure 4.1

Scientific explanations of group differences: The swinging pendulum

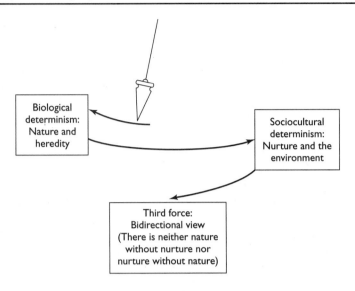

Unfortunately, in the public's eye and at times even in the eyes of scientists who should know better, the battle lines are formed around two apparently opposed positions: nature versus nurture, heredity versus environment. Plomin and Petrill (1997) provide a useful portrait of the swings in the pendulum between these two views as well as the kind of resolution toward which science is now moving—a direction I might add, that when understood will no longer feed the public's nor the media's desire for "facts" that affirm ancient prejudices. Figure 4.1 illustrates the swings between these three models of scientific inquiry.

It was Charles Darwin's cousin, Francis Galton, who in the 19th century coined the two terms *nature* and *nurture,* then set them in opposition to one another and declared that nature wins hands-down over nurture in all matters of importance for understanding human life. This declaration captured the public and well as the scientific imagination of its era and moved the pendulum steadily toward a firm position on the side of nature.

With significant changes in world events—for example, the abuses that the Nazi regime imposed in its attempt to create a genetically pure race of supermen, and the emergence in the 1920s and 1930s of *behaviorism* in the United States—the pendulum began to move from nature back toward nurture. The founder of American behaviorism, J. B. Watson, for example, insisted that simply by managing the social environments in which infants were reared, he could develop any kind of human adult he wished. In other words, it was the environment and nurture, not nature, that set the course for human life. With the growth of cultural anthropology and sociology during the 1940s and

1950s, and with the lingering memory of Nazi attempts at racial engineering still fresh in mind, the pendulum remained rather steadily fixed at the nurture end of the scale.

The scale, however, was to make yet another shift as the still young science of genetics began to make some exciting new discoveries about the human gene and its relation to diseases and perhaps even complex forms of human behavior. With increasingly sophisticated techniques producing new discoveries nearly every day, the pendulum began its march back toward nature and away from nurture. In other words, human genetics—not the environment, as had previously been believed—seemed to be the source of human destiny.

Once again, however, certain interpretative excesses of scientific data raised serious doubts about nature's role and threatened to move the pendulum back again into the nurture camp. At the same time, however, what might be best considered a third force that took sides with neither nature nor nurture seemed to be catching hold, at least among some major scientists if not yet the media or public. This third force held out the hope of extricating science from the unprofitable debates between the two extremes of nature and nurture and providing what might perhaps turn out to be a view that contributes less to public prejudices than enlightenment.

Let us first enter this original debate as though we are unaware of these current developments of the third force, so that we can better appreciate how science not only can but unfortunately too often has participated in cultural wars involving prejudiced beliefs about certain group differences. We will then consider this third force so that we can better see both the scientific critique of these earlier views and the less prejudicial directions that scientific discoveries can offer. As I said earlier and will repeat again, although prejudice and science have all too often been a bit too cozy with one another, this tells us less about the system of science than it does about certain scientists and their pursuit of simplistic understandings that feed social prejudices.

Model 1: Biological Determinism

On the one side, we find proponents of a biological or natural determinism. In one form or another, their arguments suggest that human differences are determined by some basic, fundamental properties of the human biological organism. Some phrase this as "anatomy (or genetics) is destiny"—implying that human destiny is shaped by our genetic makeup. A recent newspaper article, for example, noted that because it is too expensive and of dubious value to freeze a person's entire body after death, perhaps what should be frozen and preserved for eternity is the person's genetic material. After all, says the article, this is the *true essence* of the individual.

In a similar manner, others insist that the evolutionary demands made on the human species cause the large group differences we find. For example, men and women are said to differ in their preferred mating strategy: Men prefer to mate with many different females, while women prefer one good resource-rich male to help them and their offspring survive pregnancy and lactation. These preferences play out today in much the same manner as they did in the ancient past. In other words, ancient evolutionary demands that are different for men than for women continue to shape dating and mating behavior of men and women today (for a good statement of this evolutionary form of biological determinism, see Buss, 1994, 1995, and Buss & Schmitt, 1993; for critiques of this approach, see Caporael & Brewer, 1991, and Fausto-Sterling, 1997).

There are two points we need to consider about the relation between this sort of biological determinism and the story of prejudice. First, we are presented with a kind of inevitability about human life. We are what we are by virtue of something built in or hard wired into our very structures: our brain, our body, our hormones, our genes, our evolutionary history as a species. And so, men and women have built-in characteristics that determine their feelings, abilities, and approach to life and that thereby destine them for certain roles in society: Each group's destiny is said to be biologically determined.

Second, the particular groups whose differences are said to be important to examine have not so much been chosen by science as they have been deemed important by the particular society in which the scientific work is undertaken. In other words, if the larger society believes certain groups require some explanation for their difference—for instance, why men rule and women do not, why blacks are in lesser social positions than whites, why same-sex desire is unnatural—then biological arguments are applied to uncover these differences.

It is relatively easy to see how prejudices can be carried by this approach and yet not be seen as prejudices. After all, if women are destined by their very nature to be homemakers and men to work in the fields (figuratively), and if it is *unnatural* to do otherwise, wherein lie any harmful prejudices? And, if blacks are genetically of lesser intelligence than whites, there are neither prejudiced attitudes nor discriminatory behaviors involved if we find that blacks earn significantly less than whites. These are simply the results of scientifically verified truths about inborn group differences that, however much we may find them distasteful, are facts nevertheless.

It is also relatively easy to see how even if scientists do not themselves press home such extreme conclusions, popular opinion that may harbor certain prejudices (about women and blacks, for example) can all too readily be encouraged by these findings. And, needless to say, there is something very seductive for the scientist who suddenly becomes a well known figure appearing on the cover of major newsmagazines and being courted for interviews on radio and television talk shows. How tempting it must be to exaggerate one's findings and their interpretations, just a little, to make oneself more marketable.

Model 2: Sociocultural Determinism

On the other extreme we find those who insist that the story of human life, including group differences, is told in terms of culture, society, and the environment. For them, the major player in this human drama is nurture, not nature. The nurture side searches within the fabric of society for its explanatory story line. If the biological determinist finds genes the culprit, the sociocultural determinist blames poverty and discrimination. If the former says that because of something inborn, in their very nature, women's place is rightfully as the family caretaker, the latter suggests that women have been placed in this role less because of their nature than because of the desire of men to maintain their own positions of power. If the former tells us that the reason why blacks tend to be lower on the social ladder is because of some innate lack of intellectual ability, the latter tells us that the reason must be sought in conditions of poverty and institutional discrimination.

In other words, in the sociocultural view, social conditions rather than a group's innate characteristics shape their destiny. Although this explanation clearly challenges a significant basis of prejudice, it may inadvertently absolve the target groups from taking any steps to act on their own behalf, and so indirectly may contribute to maintaining the very qualities that generate some of the prejudiced attitudes that members of the group experience. We return to some of these ideas in Chapters 15 and 16.

Most of us have encountered this all too familiar debate between nature versus nurture, or biological versus social determinism. During this section of my course, many students enter the debate with the common preconception that you must choose sides between these two unalterably opposed options. The problem with all of this lies in the very term *versus* and its implication of two opposed sides.

Model 3: The Third Force, or the Bidirectional Thesis

Although this is not a textbook whose purpose is to teach about the contributions of nature or nurture to human life, in our efforts to understand how prejudiced attitudes and behaviors are all too often carried by scientific inquiry and interpretation, we must of necessity touch on the current state of the arguments we have been considering—and so introduce, if only briefly, the third force to which I alluded earlier. There are two central arguments involved in what I have referred to as the third force in the debates about nature and nurture. The first asks us to distinguish between levels of analysis and directs us to ask level-appropriate questions and seek level-appropriate answers. Borrowing a term favored by Fausto-Sterling (1992)—*bidirectionality*—the second argument helps us see the meaninglessness of attempting to oppose nature and nurture.

Argument 1: Levels of analysis   Because it seems so obvious, we might wonder why this first point has not been a more significant part of either the scientific or popular debates about nature and nurture. This obvious feature involves the level of analysis to which our questions are directed. The following example—a variation of the analyses provided both by Fausto-Sterling (1997) and Peters (1958)—will illustrate what I mean.

Suppose we observe Jim crossing the street and wonder why he did so. At one level, our question might direct us to inquire about his physiology and anatomy. That is, we would have to know something about his physical condition that permitted him to walk, and perhaps even something about the emergence of bipedal locomotion as the outcome of a complex and lengthy evolutionary process. However, if we focused only at this level, we would fail to observe that he crossed the street in order to make a purchase in a convenience store; nor, obviously, would physiological, anatomical, or evolutionary data be adequate for understanding the cultural and historical meanings required in order to know what a convenience store is or what one can do there. This would require a very different level of analysis and understanding.

As another investigator states the issue of levels (e.g., Bruner, 1990), we would do better to see biological explanations of behavior as describing both the *constraints* and the *conditions* for human action, but not the immediate causes of such action. In other words, argues Bruner, Jim's motor abilities biologically constrain and condition his locomotion abilities—for instance, he is not likely to curl up into a ball and roll across the street—but this knowledge does not inform us very much about what has caused Jim's behavior of seeking out a convenience store in the first place.

The idea that biology constrains and conditions is also seen in another very familiar form of locomotion. Human beings are not able to fly as birds do: Our past history as a species and current bodily configurations constrain us from such activity. Yet, we all can and many do "fly" rather extensively and for long distances because of a cultural invention: the airplane. If we stuck only to the biological level in our analysis, we would never find a satisfactory answer to questions about human mobility. These questions involve much more than biology and take us into the world of culture—with planes, buses, trains, and automobiles, all of which make people highly mobile creatures well beyond the anatomical limits set for our species.

Fausto-Sterling (1997) uses this idea of levels to remind us that when our questions concern group differences (e.g., differences between men and women), answers at the physiological or anatomical level may prove to be only minimally useful. While it is true that we cannot act without some biological involvement, *why* we act in the particular manner we do usually must be answered at the level of our culture and the kinds of options it makes available to us. Physiologically, women and men are both quite able to read; culturally and historically, women have often been discouraged from reading certain holy texts. To understand why this occurs, we must know about the culture and its prejudicial beliefs about women more than we need to know about matters of pure biology.

Argument 2: Bidirectionality   The nature-nurture debate's emphasis on the idea of opposition (or *versus*) misses the central relationship that binds nature with nurture. In a world in which biological and social factors are intimately intertwined, the very idea of "versus" is a problem. Obviously, we are biological creatures, and that feature of our existence does make a difference. Just as obviously, we are also social beings; and that too makes a difference. But, as several scientists tell us, even more significantly, the line between the biological and the social, between nature and nurture, cannot be sustained (e.g., Fausto-Sterling, 1992; Lewontin, 1991; Neisser et al., 1996).

For example, even prior to conception, the conditions of both sperm and egg cells are not simply determined biologically but also by the social conditions of their bearers. And with conception, the interweaving of both biology and social experience becomes even more complex. The environment within which the fertilized egg develops is not simply biologically programmed but is also influenced by the intrauterine environment, which in turn is affected by such extrauterine factors as the social world in which the woman lives—her nutritional status, her habits and addictions, her stress levels, and so forth. Where does biology end and society begin in this scenario? The two are inextricably intertwined, making the "versus" more a story of prejudicial ideology than real science.

In a nutshell, the issue is not whether any group difference is to be explained by nature *or* nurture, but rather how the intricate and intertwined operation of both occur at every single step of the process. Nature *and* nurture not only contribute a share in the beginning, but continually and throughout the entire process of human growth and living. Fausto-Sterling offers a helpful illustration using the brain's structure as the basis for the view she refers to as *bidirectional* in order to capture this interplay between the biological and the social:

> The physical structure of the brain of the adult, including its size, number of cells and its neuronal pathways, establishes itself in intimate interaction with the environment of the developing individual. (p. 74)

In other words, the brain is not an instrument that determines our life, independent of the very life that determines the qualities of that brain itself.

Hence, for example, nutrition, exercise, physical contact with other people, exposure to varying sorts of visual and cognitive stimuli all influence the emerging structures of the brain. How difficult it is then to accept the idea of nature *versus* nurture, but especially to accept those misguided efforts to adopt an extreme form of biological determinism. It is in this form that science helps sustain social prejudices about so-called problem groups by locating the causes of their difference and hence the root of their problem within the very inborn characteristics of the members of the group.

An eminent group of psychologists (e.g., Neisser et al., 1996) have arrived at much the same conclusion regarding the need to eliminate the "versus" from our thinking:

> It must be emphasized at the outset that gene action always involves an environment. . . . Thus all genetic effects . . . are potentially modifiable by environ-

> mental input. . . . Conversely, all environmental effects . . . involve the genes
> or structures to which the genes have contributed. Thus there is always a ge-
> netic aspect to the effects of the environment. (p. 84)

Both Lewontin (1991) as well as Bronfenbrenner and Ceci (1994) join with
their colleagues in affirming the bidirectionality of nature and nurture:

> Environmental variation and genetic variation are not independent causal
> pathways. Genes affect how sensitive one is to environment, and environment
> affects how relevant one's genetic differences may be. The interaction be-
> tween them is indissoluble. (Lewontin, 1991, p. 30)

Given this widespread recognition within scientific circles of the essential
bidirectionality of the nature-nurture relationship, one can only wonder about
the agenda of those scientists who fail to heed this view. Why do they continue to seek inborn qualities of the groups who have historically been the targets of prejudice in order to explain some of the reasons why these groups are
treated differently?

Some Vivid Examples: Science Confronts Differences

I believe that we are now armed with an understanding about what science is
and how it may inadvertently affirm societal prejudices. Keep in mind, however, that for every published scientific study that demonstrates the innately biologically inferiority of this group or that, there will be another spate of scientific studies that challenge this very finding and suggest that what we are
seeing is prejudice not scientific fact. The problem therefore is not with science as a disciplined way of obtaining and verifying knowledge, but rather
with the manner by which science is often employed to confirm the very prejudices toward selected group differences that were once confirmed by religious belief, myth, and folklore.

Men and Women: Then

Suppose you were a male scientist living in Europe in the late 1800s. As you
went about your everyday business, you might make the observation that few
women, very few indeed, were in positions of either power or fame. You go to
a concert, for example, and see a male orchestra, conducted by a male, playing
music written by a male. You visit a museum and see paintings by male artists.
You examine articles in your scientific journals and read major scientific
books—all written by men. And in your leisure hours when you curl up with a
good book to read, once again, it is likely that the author is a man. Wouldn't it
be reasonable for you to assume that this failure of women to be represented
in the higher reaches of your society must be due to something about women?

Hardly different in this respect than the ideas we encountered in Chapters 2 and 3.

And so, captured by the images of your own time and place, you decide to undertake a scientific investigation of this phenomenon, hoping to determine just what there is about women that accounts for their obvious absence from the important positions in society. Perhaps it has something to do with the female brain: After all, "because physical differences were so obvious in every other organ of the body, it was unthinkable that the brain could have escaped the stamp of sex" (Shields, 1975, p. 740).

It was only a small next step to evaluate this possibility by conducting a scientific investigation in which the brains of men and women were weighed in order to determine which were heavier. The assumption, of course, was that with a heavier brain comes higher intelligence, and with higher intelligence, higher placement in society. And not surprisingly, men's brains did weigh more than women's, apparently settling the question of who really is more intelligent!

A similar argument developed in scientific circles around the late 1800s concerning the so-called maternal instinct:

> The female's energies were directed toward preparation for pregnancy and lactation, reducing the energy available for the development of other qualities. This resulted in a "rather earlier cessation of individual evolution" in the female. Woman was, in essence, a stunted man. Her lower stage of development was evident not only in her inferior mental and emotional powers but also in the resulting expression of the parental instinct. . . . She was primarily responsive to "infantile helplessness." (based on Herbert Spencer's writings as reported by Shields, 1975, p. 749)

It was easy to assume that women were naturally designed to nurture the young. If this were the case, then there was little question about her incapacity to engage in other kinds of activities for which men were clearly designed and better suited.

Men and Women: Now

Reading this, you might properly proclaim, "But that was the late 1800s and early 1900s. Surely, no one believes that nonsense today!" Some do! Several contemporary scientists report a correlation between brain size, variously measured, and intelligence involving both women compared with men and blacks compared with whites (e.g., Jensen, 1995; Jensen, & Johnson, 1994; Rushton, 1991, 1995, 1996). Others (e.g., Peters, 1995) cite contradictory research findings. The point, however, is that measuring brain size and seeking to correlate it with intelligence and various social outcomes was not simply a pastime among European scientists some 100 years ago; it continues to be an area of current interest to some scientific investigators, who have added racial differences to sex differences while retaining their biologically deterministic worldview. We take this up in Chapter 5.

The point is that *now,* as in our past, groups that pose a problem for the dominant groups within society have become the targets for careful scrutiny designed to figure out why they are the way they are, and perhaps to justify why we feel toward them the way we do. It may no longer be fashionable to speak of women as incomplete or failed men, yet their brains are weighed in order to provide a scientific explanation for what some continue to believe is their innate inferiority.

While examining brain size has not entirely waned in interest among certain scientific investigators, the search for a biological basis of male-female difference has also focused on other features of the brain. Those regions of the brain assumed to deal with higher mental functioning were first examined well over 100 years ago to determine if men's brains were more developed in these areas than women's (see Shields, 1975; Fausto-Sterling, 1992). By the end of the 19th century, for instance, the frontal lobes had emerged as significant in human reasoning and advanced intellectual functioning, qualities in which men were assumed to be more proficient than women. And so the neuroanatomists of the day discovered that the female frontal lobe was smaller and less developed than that of the male, thus providing what then seemed to be a solidly scientific explanation for observed male-female differences and of women's natural inferiority to men.

And today, research has shifted to still other areas of the brain. Scientific probing today has focused on such brain structures as the *corpus callosum,* the region that facilitates communication between the brain's left and right hemispheres (see Fausto-Sterling, 1992; Neisser et al., 1996). Some research demonstrates that the female brain is less lateralized than that of the male— meaning that the often discovered inferiority of women in visual and spatial performance and in mathematical ability (but see next paragraph) is to be explained by this lack of specialization that describes males. Other brain structures have also emerged to take their place in efforts to scientifically document male-female differences and so offer a biological explanation for the differences found in the social world.

A current debate concerning male-female differences with its own biological twist pertains to the dual areas of math ability, in which men seem to outperform women, and spatial ability, in which once again men outperform women (e.g., Hyde, Fennema, & Lamon, 1990; Kimball, 1989; Voyer, Voyer, & Bryden, 1995). These are not trivial abilities, as they provide the foundation for several important career options in the sciences, options that may be denied to women because they do not score as well as men on tests designed to measure these abilities. Their failure to match male performance has led some to argue that there must be an inborn, biological reason for this difference (i.e., biological determinism strikes again).

Such an analysis, however, fails to note certain "puzzles" for any purely biological argument. One puzzle, for example, is the finding that differences between males and females in spatial abilities do not seem to arise until after age 13 (Voyer et al., 1995). A genetic analysis might have a problem with this finding as we assume that the genetics do not suddenly change after age 13. Given the hormonal changes that occur at puberty, however, perhaps a hormonal interpretation would fare better. But even this argument has difficulty in addressing the fact that only *some* spatial tests reveal a sex difference, and that sex differences emerge at a wide variety of ages, not just at puberty. In other words, in their eagerness to provide a simple biological explanation for some observed sex differences in spatial ability, several scientists have rushed too quickly to judgment and ignored contradictory evidence.

Many of these same problems have appeared in the work of scientists who seek a biological explanation for male-female differences in math achievement. Some have used these differences in math achievement to support the differential placement of men and women in particular scientific careers. Doing this, of course, fails to take cognizance of the extent to which young girls, who appear to excel in math in the early school years and then do worse as they enter high school and beyond, are actively discouraged from taking higher math courses and are less involved than boys in the very kinds of activities that would increase their math ability. In other words, it is not simple biology, but biology and environment intertwined indissolubly that we need to consider (see Halpern, 1997; Hyde et al., 1990; Kimball, 1989).

These small examples will be multiplied as we move through this chapter and the next. They suggest that prejudices about men and women are carried through scientific research that adopts a strictly biologically deterministic position, the nature side of what cannot truly be a debate between opposites. Once again, we see an effort to locate social distinctions between men and women somewhere in the realm of innate biology—to explain women's lesser standing in society, for example, not in terms of something like prejudice (e.g., discouraging women from taking advanced math) but rather in terms of natural differences that have destined women for the places they occupy. I am not claiming that the scientists conducting this research are themselves prejudiced against women, but rather that in their search for some biological basis for the observed differences between men and women, they have often ignored other causes and so give a kind of natural inevitability to their explanations.

German Race Science and the Jewish Question

To some it will seem obscene to think that science played any role whatsoever in the Holocaust. However, in those European nations that already had a lengthy history of anti-Semitism and where *nationalism* had become a central driving force—Germany fits the bill on both counts—Jews were considered to be a problem group. German scientists were called on to explain the Jewish difference and to suggest what might be done to deal with this nagging Jewish question.

While nationalism can take many forms, in Germany prior to the beginning of World War II it took the form of a search for German national identity: What did it mean to be a German? This search took on near religious tones. Many leading Germans felt that Germany had an important role to play in the coming world revolution on behalf of humanity (see Ros?, 1990).

The historical urgency of this moral mission, which drove German thinkers from the 18th century onward, need not concern us here. What is of concern, however, is the degree to which the historical tradition inherited from early Christianity—the belief that Jews were the devil's children—joined the fervor with which Germany sought to redeem the world and restore humane values, to coalesce around a virulent form of anti-Semitism. The Jew became a symbol for all that was wrong with the world. Jews were said to be a distinct race apart not only from Germans but from all persons of goodwill everywhere. Only their destruction could restore harmony to the human race.

When Hitler and the Nazis finally came to power in the early 1930s, their ideas fit this long developing climate of opinion in which the Jew was the dangerous enemy whose elimination was essential for Germany and the world. Some argued that Germany would be doing a service to the entire world by taking bold steps to get rid of the Jew once and for all—a step that others could not countenance.

Science was called on and seemed willingly to agree to document the case against the Jews. First, it was critical to establish that the Jews were not simply another group of people but a *distinctive race* with distinctive and readily discernible racial characteristics. Certain prominent 19th-century scientists proved helpful here:

> We all recognize the Jewish type. We immediately distinguish him by his face, his habits, the way he holds his head, his gesticulations or when he opens his mouth and begins to speak. And it is always possible . . . to recognize even the most assimilated, because he always bears some characteristic of his race (quoted in Efron, 1994, p. 22, from the 1881 original by the scientist, geographer, and ethnologist Richard Andree).

Second, it was critical to demonstrate that this race was bent on the destruction of the world, and that the only cure was its elimination. German race science cooperated only too eagerly in both endeavors.

Anthropologists joined in the effort to position the races of the world on a scale ranging from superior to inferior. At the top, closest to God, were the Nordic and Aryan peoples; at the bottom, farthest from God, were the bestial races. Not only were the various racial groups so arrayed, but in addition, it was up to scientific anthropologists to inform the world about which specific characteristics would reveal a person's racial category. Needless to say, as the previous quote tells us, as a race, Jews were easily identifiable.

Being white was essential to being at the top, closest to God. Having a proper facial angle—that is, a face that when seen in profile had a relatively small angle and thus was far removed from the angles of apes' and dogs' faces—was also critical (Efron, 1994). In addition, the chosen races were active and manly, thriving in cold climates. The weak races, those at the bottom of the racial ladder and farthest from God, by contrast, were from warmer climates and were passive and effeminate. Indeed, so intent was this attempt to link climate with race that some scientists sought to show that Jews were an *exception* to the rule that climate could influence a person's characteristics. A Jew was always a Jew *wherever* he or she lived. In other words, climate had no impact on this genetically discernible racial group!

It was also said that because the Jewish difference was racial and thus genetic in nature, it could never be erased through Christian baptism. Even converts were permanently marked by their Jewish racial characteristics; conversion could not change their Jewishness. Thereby a Jew was an identified Jew regardless of what he or she professed as a religious belief and regardless of where she or he lived. All of this sounds exactly like the "one drop of Negro blood" theory (i.e., it only takes one drop of African blood to categorize a person as black) that was applied to African Americans (e.g., Hirschfeld, 1996, discusses this "rule" and its current use among children).

Having established their distinctive racial features, their dangerous character readily followed. This was the easy part, given the background of Jewish hatred found in earlier Christian mythology and belief. Jews, this race apart, could never be German. The mark of their crimes against humanity would forever be upon them. Jews were a selfish people, an evil people, a loveless people:

> The Jews had formerly resisted Christ; now they resisted love and humanity. . . . The redemption that Jews had earlier spurned from Christ they were now seen as continuing to rebuff in a modern enlightened age by refusing to become truly human through embracing authentic love; they preferred to cling to money and self-love. (Rose, 1990, p. 28)

So poisonous were Jews thought to be that some felt the only way to save the world from this menace was their final elimination from the world's body.

When the Nazis came to power and avowed as part of their official policy to engage in the final solution to the Jewish question, they were not met by a shocked public, but rather a public who had been long prepared for just these ways of thinking (see Goldhagen, 1996). It was the duty of Germany to take on this task, as onerous as it might be, and save the world so that the pure races, the Nordic and Aryan peoples, could finally take their place at the top where they naturally belong.

Not only were medical doctors involved in this final solution, providing scientific methods to help destroy the Jews, but science in general had signed on the Nazi train and found a hospitable place in which to conduct experiments, write scientific papers, and prove beyond all doubt that Jews were a race apart and a threat to the well-being of all good peoples everywhere. Rarely in the course of human history have so many people—scientists and others, including academicians, religious leaders, lawyers, and judges—joined in such a destructive, genocidal effort.

There are many lessons to be learned from this horrific tour through Nazi race science. But the point I wish to make involves the role of certain scientists in seeking and then finding characteristics in those groups targeted by their society as problems and in eventually agreeing to eliminationist social policies. Here was science walking arm and arm with prejudice.

Chapter Summary: Key Learning Points

1. Although science as a system is more self-correcting and open to continuous modification than any of the prescientific systems that have attempted to explain the differences among humankind, science and scientists remain sufficiently part of their societies to have often participated in confirming common social prejudices about various groups (e.g., men are superior to women; Jews are a dangerous race of people).

2. We considered three different paradigms or models of scientific inquiry addressing group differences:

    a. The *biological determinist* model treats nature as the prime mover of all human destiny. This model has historically been associated with sustaining commonly shared prejudices by emphasizing certain innate qualities that groups possess that might serve to justify the kinds of attitudes held toward them and the kinds of treatment they receive.

    b. The *sociocultural model* emphasizes nurture over nature—that is, society, culture, and the environment are the prime determinants of human destiny. This model has historically been set up in opposition to the biological view in the hope of undermining its potentially prejudiced formulations of human difference.

    c. The third force or *bidirectional model* states that nature and nurture are understood less to be in opposition than to function as necessary coproducers of all human destiny. The bidirectional model undermines the justifications for prejudice that have often been associated with the biological view, while encouraging people to take active control over the environmental forces that also participate in their destinies.

Chapter 5

Science Explains Group Differences, II: The IQ Debates and Other Recent Issues

While the virulence of the Nazi scientists and their dedication to the destruction of a specific group of people disappeared from the world's scientific scene with the defeat of the Nazis, elements of the same race science did not disappear with their departure. The use of science, in this case ostensibly to discover those unique biological features of African Americans that make this group a problem to white America, has taken off with a vengeance. Fortunately, there are many critics for whom this race science is as obscene today in the United States as German race science was in the Nazi era.

Race: An Idea in the Eye of the Beholder

According to some (e.g., Fairchild, 1991; Hirschfeld, 1996; Lewontin, 1991; Yee, Fairchild, Weizmann, & Wyatt, 1993; Zuckerman, 1990), part of the problem lies with the very concept of race. As we saw in the case of Jews in Germany, the effort to define the Jews as a distinct race was part and parcel of the initial effort to isolate this group of people from other Germans and to characterize them in such a way that they could then be systematically eliminated from society. But, you might wonder, how can something so simple and apparently straightforward as the very idea of race be a piece of the puzzle of prejudice? Let us start with a genetic fact:

> About 85 percent of all identified human genetic variation is between any two individuals from the same ethnic group. Another 8 percent of all the variation is between ethnic groups within a race—say between Spaniards, Irish,

Italians, and Britons—and only 7 percent of all human genetic variation lies on the average between major human races like those of Africa, Asia, Europe, and Oceania.

So we have no reason *a priori* to think that there would be any genetic differentiation between racial groups in characteristics such as behavior, temperament, and intelligence. . . . The nonsense propagated by ideologues of biological determinism that the lower classes are biologically inferior to the upper classes, that all the good things in European culture come from the Nordic groups, is precisely nonsense. It is meant to legitimate the structures of inequality in our society by putting a biological gloss on them and by propagating the continual confusion between what may be influenced by genes and what may be changed by social and environmental alterations. (Lewontin, 1991, pp. 36–37)

I might add that the author of this quoted passage, R. C. Lewontin, holds the Agassiz chair in zoology at Harvard University and is an internationally known geneticist. This reminds us that science in itself is not the source of the prejudices that often come from the mouths and actions of some of its practitioners.

The story gets even more suspect when we learn from Fairchild (1991), for example, that the very concept of race that we now almost automatically assume is a necessary way to divide the peoples of the world into three classifications—white, black, or Asian—is not only an invention of the European world designed to affirm the advanced standing of one group and the inferior standing of others, but as we have also seen, flies in the face of the known genetic facts that we have just reviewed: *Homo sapiens* is more common than different in its genetic history. Evidence thereby "points to one race, not three or thousands" (Fairchild, 1991, p. 103).

In other words, the very idea of race, that people can be divided into distinctive racial categories, is highly suspect. Indeed, as the lead editorial in the *Los Angeles Times* observed (February 22, 1995), the very concept of race is scientifically vacuous, lacking a serious basis in scientific fact. Of course, as the editorial also noted, most of us have grown up believing that race is a natural feature of the world rather than a creation of society designed to serve particular social purposes. Once we can understand that race is more in the eyes of the beholder than a fact of nature, the very idea that the world's people can be divided according to race, let alone ranked racially from superior to inferior, becomes a clear matter of prejudice.

The IQ Debates

Although you and I may now know the "truth" about race, efforts still continue hoping to document a genetically based, biologically determined case about the so-called black races of the world. For instance, during the 1960s, in his published work and in public addresses at scientific meetings, the Stanford professor William Shockley (a 1956 Nobel laureate in Physics) gave respectability to a view that has had a long history, even predating the German efforts to purify the Germanic racial stock by means of eugenics. Shockley believed that selective breeding, much as one breeds dogs, cows, and horses to improve the stock, was essential in order to increase the numbers of those with good biological makeup and eventually to eliminate those with less valued biological stock (see Hirsch, 1981, for a good summary of Shockley's works). And because blacks as a race were genetically inferior, argued Shockley, it was important to minimize their polluting impact on the rest of the world.

Shockley's widely reported contribution to the eugenics debate was followed in 1969 by the publication in the prestigious *Harvard Educational Review* of an article by Arthur Jensen, an educational psychologist associated with the University of California at Berkeley. Jensen presented empirical data demonstrating that intelligence, as measured by intelligence tests and indexed by the single IQ score (intelligence quotient) was not only significantly inherited (i.e., carried genetically) but in addition showed a gap between whites and blacks of some 15 or so points. In other words, Jensen's data supported the notion of black intellectual inferiority and the parallel notion that this inferiority was genetically determined in a significant way and thus presumably very difficult if not impossible to change through educational or social opportunities.

Since 1969, Jensen has continued with this same program of work, concluding in a recent commentary, for example (Jensen, 1995) that black-white differences in intelligence appear most clearly on those tests of cognitive ability that contribute most to general intelligence; those tests that are least important to general intellectual ability, by contrast, do not show significant black-white differences. This is another way of confirming his original and oft-repeated findings concerning a firm and significant genetic basis to the black-white differences in IQ.

In 1974, a Princeton psychologist, Leon Kamin, published a work challenging the accuracy of data originally reported by a British researcher, Sir Cyril Burt, whose findings were central to Jensen's own conclusions. Kamin suggested that Burt's data were in fact fraudulent, more ideological than scientific. In 1977, a well respected British psychologist, H. J. Eysenck, rebutted Kamin's challenge, accusing Kamin of being the ideological player and not a true scientist as were Burt, Jensen, and of course Eysenck himself. The debate continues to this day, with two recent books refuting the allegation of fraud directed at Burt, but leaving open some questions about the quality of Burt's data that Jensen had used (see Green, 1992).

Beginning in the late 1980s a Canadian scientist, J. Phillipe Rushton, published his own data and addressed highly prestigious scientific meetings (e.g., the 1989 meeting of the American Association for the Advancement of Science) affirming Jensen's earlier findings of innate superiority of whites over blacks, to which he added a slight superiority for Asians even over whites. But whatever else emerged clearly from Rushton's report was the finding of a major gap between whites and blacks, a gap that was, he argued, clearly biological in its basis:

> I have concluded that on more than 60 variables, including brain size, intelligence, speed of maturation, personality, reproductive behavior, and social organization, measured in Africa, Asia, and Europe, as well as in North America, a distinct pattern emerges with Mongoloids and Negroids at opposite ends of the spectrum and Caucasoids occupying an intermediate position, with a great deal of interracial variability within each broad grouping. (Rushton, 1991, p. 983)

And, here is what Rushton has to say about the sources of these racial differences: "No known environmental variable is capable of . . . causing so many diverse variables to correlate in so comprehensive a fashion. There is, however, a genetic one" (p. 983). And so, he continues, "A truth must be faced . . . readers may fervently wish that genetically based race differences in behavior did not exist, but the data show otherwise" (p. 984).

The story, however, is not over. In 1994, with a prepublication blast of publicity, two scientists, Richard Herrnstein and Charles Murray, published a work they entitled *The Bell Curve*. While treading a careful line between declaring and denying any genetic or biological determinism, their work nevertheless concluded that the clear-cut black-white differences of some 15 IQ points must have a significant genetic contribution. Sounding very much like Rushton, Herrnstein and Murray tell us that "however discomfiting it may be to consider it, there are reasons to suspect genetic considerations are involved" (Murray & Herrnstein, 1994, p. 32). And so, therefore, "preschool programs may be good for children in others ways, but they do not have important effects on intelligence" (p. 34).

The preceding examples illustrate the shape of race science in the United States today. Many white people in the United States have grown worried about people of color. The climate of public opinion thereby seems ripe for seeking and even believing scientifically generated reports implying that the disturbing group differences we find—including the lesser educational, occupational, and income attainments of blacks compared with whites and their apparently higher presence in prison populations—may be significantly caused by innate biological factors. If these group differences are caused by biological factors, then surely there is neither prejudice nor discrimination involved among the white population. After all, whites are simply responding to the facts of nature. Where have we heard this before? How much more comforting it is for whites to consider black inferiority to have nothing to do with white prejudice and how much more comforting to have several respectable scientists reporting from highly prestigious universities (Stanford, Berkeley, Harvard) confirm what many suspected or hoped for all along.

Critiques of the IQ Debates

One of the main reasons it is important for us to consider the several critiques that have emerged in these IQ debates is so that we can better understand how badly practiced science can all too readily encourage social prejudices and how a more sophisticated science using the bidirectional model can undermine those very prejudices (see Figure 5.1).

As I have repeatedly observed and must say yet again, science itself is not the cause of prejudice, but its often unintended effect may be to contribute to the hold of prejudice in a society. In response to the publication of *The Bell Curve* and related works, and in an effort to dilute its hold on the all too receptive public imagination, several groups of scientists published their own critique demonstrating the errors in methodology and interpretation perpetrated by those who adopt a simplistic, biologically determinist view of group differences (e.g., Fraser, 1995).

Although some of the major critics have come from the social and behavioral sciences (e.g., Sternberg, 1995), we have already encountered critics from within the home of biological and genetic science itself—including, for example, Lewontin (1991), Fausto-Sterling (1992, 1997), and Plomin and Petrill (1997), to name a few. While the former focus primarily on the key social factors that may account for the group differences in intelligence between whites and blacks, the latter call on all sides to tone down their rhetoric and focus instead on the newer view of the relationship between genetics and environment. All agree that a change in scientific understanding is necessary so that science will not contribute to increasing prejudices by building a case for differential social treatment (e.g., of blacks and whites) on genetic information alone. Read what Plomin and Petrill (1997) write on this point:

> Evidence for genetic influence . . . does not imply that differences among individuals are immutable or irremediable—novel environmental factors could make a difference. . . . Conversely, expert training that can produce impressive skills does not contradict evidence for genetic influence. . . . No research tells us *what should be* because this is a matter of goals and values. (p. 56)

Figure 5.1
What causes what?

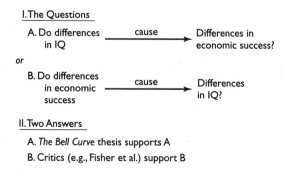

I. The Questions

A. Do differences in IQ ——cause——▶ Differences in economic success?

or

B. Do differences in economic success ——cause——▶ Differences in IQ?

II. Two Answers

A. *The Bell Curve* thesis supports A

B. Critics (e.g., Fisher et al.) support B

In other words, and echoing others on this same point (e.g., Carroll, 1997; Ceci & Williams, 1997; Fausto-Sterling, 1997), to leap from citing genetic influences on intelligence to abandoning efforts to improve environmental conditions for all persons not only misses the meaning of the genetic findings, and so is bad biological science, but, I would add, smacks more of the use of science to encourage social prejudices than to inform social policy.

Further Critiques

The American Psychological Association   In response to public misconceptions of the scientific reports on the biological bases of complex human behaviors, especially including racial differences in intelligence, the American Psychological Association convened a panel of experts to address one specific issue: what is known about intelligence and what remains to be learned (e.g., Neisser et al., 1996).

The report raises many different questions about intelligence: What is it? Is intelligence one general ability or many diverse ones? How well and in what ways is it measured? To what social outcomes is intelligence related? For our own purposes, the central question concerns the nature of group differences in intelligence: Are such differences found, and if so, are they attributable to genetics or environment or both, and in what proportion?

The answer provided by Neisser and his colleagues is both clear and an open-ended invitation to continue searching. Yes, there are measurable group differences between blacks and whites on the usual tests of intelligence. There is also an indication that these differences have decreased over time. Significantly, as the reports notes, there is "no support for a genetic interpretation" (p. 97) of these group differences. In fact, the authors conclude that currently there is "no adequate explanation of the differentiation between the IQ means of Blacks and Whites" (p. 97).

Because genetics and thus any simplistic, biologically determinist argument has been found to lack empirical support, the authors probe other contenders, two of which are interesting to consider although without much solid support. The first involves arguments about the discrepancy between the culture of the school and the culture of the African American community. Children are not simply taught subject matter in school (math, history, language); they are also taught cultural values (tell what you know, not how you feel; take individual responsibility for your successes and failures; work steadily on boring tasks that may eventually have a payoff) (e.g., see Heath, 1989). These ideals may be in conflict with what some have identified as African American ideals about "verve, affect, expressive individualism, communalism, orality" (Neisser et al., 1996, p. 95). This discrepancy may alienate many black children and so not provide them with a meaningful school experience. This would account for their poorer performance on IQ tests.

The second argument, also potentially valuable though still in need of confirmation, involves the notion of a people's being a "caste-like minority" (e.g,

Ogbu, 1978). Caste-like minorities differ from other minorities—for example, most immigrant groups. The latter can anticipate improving their situation; people in a caste-like minority are convinced that their life is already set for them and will forever be restricted. Research shows that the children of caste-like minorities tend to do less well in school and to quit earlier. This, of course, would contribute to lower intellectual test scores on measures such as IQ that are closely linked with formal schooling.

Bowles and Gintis   Writing originally in 1972 and 1973, Samuel Bowles and Herbert Gintis, adopted a critical view of the very meaning of IQ in the United States. They argued that rather than IQ measuring intelligence, it served another purpose: to "legitimize an authoritarian, hierarchical, stratified, and unequal economic system of production, and to reconcile the individual to his or her objective position within this system" (p. 2).

That is quite an allegation. Read again what Bowles and Gintis are saying. Intelligence, as measured by standardized tests, for example, is employed in order to legitimate the system of inequality in United States society and to help people accept their positions within this system. Intelligence, then, is not the real issue; rather, what is at issue is the *use* of intelligence testing to legitimate various types of inequality.

Bowles and Gintis did not make this assertion casually, but arrived at it after carefully reviewing a variety of data. For example, they examined the correlation between IQ and economic success under various conditions. Let us examine some of their figures, remembering that a high number indicates a strong relationship between the two variables involved.

First, they report the correlation between IQ and economic success. They tell us that this correlation is .52, a rather substantial figure. By itself, this strong correlation suggests that people who have a higher IQ tend to be more economically successful than people with a lower IQ. Thus, if IQ were found to be significantly determined by genetics, then we have completed the chain of evidence: Groups that are genetically inferior intellectually cannot rise as far up the ladder of economic success as groups that are genetically superior in intelligence. In other words, inequalities in economic standing are nature's way of placing people, not a result of prejudice or discrimination.

If we stopped at this first correlation, however, we would have made a very serious error in our understanding. It is to unfold the nature of that error that Bowles and Gintis present several other correlations. For example, the correlation between economic success and years of schooling is .63. That is, the more schooling a person has, the more economically successful he or she is likely to be. Next, they find that the correlation between economic success and social class background is .55; the higher one's class background, the more one is likely to be economically successful.

At this point you might argue that perhaps IQ is the key to both years of schooling and social class standing, and thus IQ remains a central determinant of economic success. To check out this possibility, Bowles and Gintis present the correlation between IQ and economic success for persons of the *same* social class and with the *same* number of years of schooling. This correlation turns out to be .13, hardly better than no relationship at all. In other words, when you look at how IQ influences economic success, after having eliminated the effect that years of schooling and social class have on economic success, you find no relationship! IQ matters little in determining economic success; schooling and social class background matter much more.

Recognizing that some people look at a collection of numbers such as these and shudder moments before they blank out, let me simply call attention to the major conclusion that one can draw from these figures: IQ is only minimally related to economic success; years of schooling and social class matter more. Translating this back to our original inquiry, it would be fair to say, then, that inequality in economic success is more a function of one's social class and schooling opportunities than so-called native intelligence. And so, even if IQ were totally determined by genetics, its role in determining people's placement along the social ladder would be minimal.

It is precisely because IQ is unrelated to social inequalities that Bowles and Gintis formulated their own ideas about the functions it must serve in society. Since IQ does not determine whether one succeeds, then all the hoopla about intelligence must be designed to legitimate inequality rather than to explain it. And obviously, those who benefit most from the existing systems of inequality must find this use of IQ as a godsend, helping them explain why they made it and others did not and doing so in a manner that absolves society (and them) from any causal role in this process.

Update: Fischer and colleagues   Writing more recently, Fischer, Hout, Jankowski, Lucas, Swidler, & Voss (1996) raised many of the same points as Bowles and Gintis. The very title of their book, *Inequality by Design,* captures the direction of their work as well as the conclusions they reach.

In their view, social inequalities are not the result of differences in intelligence or any other natural properties of individuals; rather social inequalities are the consciously designed, though at times unintended, consequences of social policies that benefit some social groups at the expense of others. Inequality, in other words, is part of a social design. To claim that inequality reflects basic group differences in ability or native intelligence is a useful cover story employed by those on top to explain their position and to provide solace to those who are not permitted to make it because they are said to lack the requisite abilities.

One of the most striking demonstrations Fischer and his coauthors provide for this conclusion comes from their examination of the proportion of U.S. households in 1993 that would appear at each income level if everyone had the *same* IQ. The proportions are almost exactly the same! That is, if everyone had the same IQ, the proportion of households falling at the high and the low ends of the income distribution would change only minimally. This supports Bowles and Gintis's conclusions. IQ plays a very minor role in determining social inequalities: "if we could magically give everyone identical IQs, we would still see 90 to 95% of the inequality we see today" (Fischer et al., 1996, p. 14), a conclusion also recently confirmed by Ceci and Williams (1997).

So what does it all mean? The answer is contained in their frequently repeated conclusion: *"It is not that low intelligence leads to inferior status; it is that inferior status leads to low intelligence test scores"* (Fischer et al., 1996, p. 18). Mull that one over. What it tells us is that IQ does not cause inequality but rather that inequality produces differences in IQ. This is a conclusion that is based not only on work conducted on populations within the United States, but on populations around the world. Fischer and his associates observed, for example, that regardless of the racial and ethnic identities that are involved, on a worldwide basis, groups that occupy inferior status in their society score lower on measures of intelligence and related psychological characteristics than groups with superior status.

They cite Koreans as a good case in point. Within the United States, where Asian Americans tend to score relatively high in measures of intelligence, we would consider Koreans to be highly intelligent. In Japan, however, where Koreans occupy much lesser social standing, we find Koreans considered "dull." But you do not have to compare racially identical groups today (e.g., Koreans) to confirm this. In the history of the United States, an immigrant group who on entry around 1900 or so were considered to be intellectually inferior are today considered among the intellectual elite: These are the Jews who were once thought to be of borderline intellectual capability.

In case after case, Fischer and his colleagues find that status determines IQ rather than IQ determining status. Groups that occupy lesser, inferior, or caste-like status positions within their society score lower in intelligence than groups that occupy higher status positions within their society. All of this suggests the extreme costs of being located in a lower caste within society— costs, however, that are not the result of the way nature divides the world, but rather of the way people exercising social policies design inequality into their world.

The designs for economic inequality about which Fischer and his colleagues write cover an extensive range. Income policies such as tax deductions of mortgage interest, for example, benefit those social classes that can afford to own homes at the disadvantage of those who cannot. Even taxes levied for highway construction benefit those who can afford cars and who live far from the central city and must use cars to commute to and from work. It is difficult to see how a new freeway from the center of town to a fancy suburb built with taxpayer dollars helps taxpayers living in the inner city who have neither cars to drive nor the time to drive anywhere even if they had cars.

Not every social policy, however, contributes to maintaining inequalities. Affirmative action, for example, was designed to reduce inequalities by giving people once denied employment opportunities a better chance to enter the job market and try to make a success of themselves. Indeed, the entire affirmative action movement is a document to the extent to which social inequalities are not built into nature but are built into society: In affirmative action, we have an intentional policy designed to make the playing field more even for everyone by eliminating the advantages that once automatically went to certain people simply by virtue of their group memberships.

Unfortunately, as noted by Fischer and his colleagues, among today's Western industrialized nations, the United States is one of the leaders in designed-in inequality. This means that more policies within the United States are designed to maintain or even increase inequalities between groups than are designed to flatten out these inequalities.

There is little doubt that behind many of these designs for inequality lurks the stealthy hand of prejudice. How else can we understand some of these figures (from Fendel, Hurtado, Long, & Giraldo, 1996)? Although they comprise only 33% of the U.S. population, white men have 85% of the tenured professorships at U.S. universities and colleges, 85% of the partnerships in major law firms, and hold between 90% and 95% of the seats in Congress (in the early 1990s). Men are five times more likely to be high earners than women, and three times more likely than black and Hispanic men. Furthermore, they hold 95% to 97% of the senior managerial positions in the top U.S. companies, are less likely than blacks to be denied mortgages and so find it easier to own homes, and (because home ownership provides one of the major contributors to a person's net worth) are better able than blacks to pass on their accumulated wealth to their children—and so on without end.

It is simply too easy to assume that the basis for the preceding inequalities lies in the better qualifications that white men possess when compared with every other group in society. Doesn't this strain one's credulity? Figures of this sort lend credence to the arguments of Bowles and Gintis and of Fischer and his colleagues regarding what is really going on when claims of superior qualifications are employed to justify prejudices rather than to explain resulting inequalities.

Let me summarize the current debate involving the use of science to document important differences, intellectual and otherwise, between whites and other groups, especially blacks. To put it simply: The debate is ongoing. For instance, earlier in the 20th century we saw how the prejudicial use of biologically determinist arguments was used by Nazi Germany to eliminate those groups seen to be troublesome to the dominant majority. But the process survives—as elsewhere in today's world, purity movements and ethnic cleansing have taken on their own genocidal meanings. This ongoing debate is a reminder of how science can be used to perpetuate prejudice and even contribute to the destruction of human well-being.

While those proposing the biological position in no way see themselves as being prejudiced or as playing into the hands of cultural prejudices—as the critics of the biologically determinist position argue and as we have seen too often—biology has become ideology in the service of facilitating one group's domination over another, justified now by reference to innate characteristics possessed by those target groups.

Homosexuality: The Story Continues

In the latter part of the 20th century and especially in the United States, yet another group emerged to challenge the dominant majority's understanding. Its difference from the majority lies in the area of sexual orientation, a type of difference that seems to cut to the core of many people's anxieties. This chapter has been concerned with the forms that prejudice takes when science focuses on special qualities of a targeted group and when the public uses that science to justify its attitudes and treatment of the members of that group. Biological determinism has entered the homosexuality debate as well, attempting to document a strong case that a person's homosexual orientation is biologically determined (e.g., Gladue, 1994; LeVay, 1991).

Will this biological turn increase or decrease prejudice toward homosexuals? This remains an open question. But if society's treatment of other groups whose biology has been claimed to be relevant (e.g., women, Jews, and blacks) offers any clue, then it is likely that biology will provide a scientific justification for sustaining prejudice against still another group who, in biology's terms, cannot help but be what they are. After all, neither can women or blacks, and this "fact" has not shielded them from prejudice.

Background

Before we can enter the biological debates about homosexuality, we need a little more background about homosexuality itself. Most observers have noted that the idea that a person is or is not homosexual is relatively recent, with the very conception of a homosexual identity being dated from only about 1870 (see Connell, 1987) and *preceding* the definition of someone as having a heterosexual identity. That is, the identification of a person in terms of sexual orientation (specifically same-sex as opposed to other-sex) was a rather late-appearing idea in Western culture.

This does not mean that in the 19th century same-sex acts were suddenly recognized, but rather that someone who sought sexual relations with persons of the same sex became a special category of human being. Anyone familiar with ancient Greece is well aware of the extent to which it was normal for older men of certain elite classes to have sexual relations with younger men. These were relations undertaken in the normal course of growing up in ancient Greece; they were not indicative of a special type of human being (the homosexual) or of someone who would later fail to engage in sexual relations with a woman and produce children (see Dover, 1978; Foucault, 1978, 1985, 1986; Halperin, 1990; Winkler, 1990).

Furthermore, those familiar with cross-cultural materials from Melanesia will be aware of the extent to which same-sex relations are not only normal but also an essential part of the developmental process by which young boys eventually become men (Herdt, 1984). The issue, then, is not whether persons have sex with members of their own sexual category, but rather, whether that fact becomes a predominant feature defining who they are, and in turn, makes them a problem for the rest of society.

As a group, homosexuals were once defined as a problem by the mental health establishment. Psychiatry and psychology wrestled with the definition of same-sex desire. Was it pathology, or simply a healthy but different form of human sexuality? The implications of this choice are substantial. If homosexuality is a pathology, then people will require interventions to change them back to normalcy. But, if homosexuality is a healthy alternative, then only if someone experiences a problem would there be a need to intervene, and not to change the person into a heterosexual, but to help that person feel more comfortable with his or her sexuality. While the issue seems to have been resolved in favor of viewing same-sex desire as a nonpathological form of human sexuality, the pathological view has never really disappeared; it is now caught up in larger societal debates (e.g., permitting same-sex marriages).

Some Current Scientific Attempts to Uncover the Roots of Homosexuality

After reviewing how science sought to find the secrets of women, Jews, and blacks within their biology, it should come as no surprise to find science once again working diligently to discover the unique biology of the homosexual, primarily the male homosexual (women receiving short shrift once again!). A variety of evidence from several sources seems to coalesce around the idea that homosexuality is a condition to be understood in terms of human physiology and neuroanatomy (e.g., Fausto-Sterling, 1992; Gladue, 1994; LeVay, 1991). Male homosexuals have areas in their brains that are said to be different in size or shape from those areas found in the brains of "normally" sexed males. Indeed, some researchers report a similarity between the brains of homosexual males and normal females, suggesting that the stereotype about gay men being effeminate is as well and good in scientific circles as it is among the larger public. Twin studies likewise seem to confirm that between 30% and 70% of a person's sexual orientation is genetically determined (Gladue, 1994). These and similar findings appear to provide a clear biological basis for sexual identity, thus demonstrating the degree to which homosexual brains, neuroanatomy, and hormones *cause* same-sex orientation.

Critics Critics (e.g., Fausto-Sterling, 1992) have pointed out the many problems with the founding assumptions of much of these biologically rooted efforts to locate sexual orientation. Some of the same concerns expressed earlier about the either-or quality of most biologically determinist arguments can be raised in this case. Let us look at a few of the problems associated with these efforts.

First, how do we identify the very population to be studied? This is not unlike the problem with the definition of race, which, as we have seen, is a concept without much scientific backing. Who is and who is not to be counted as a homosexual male? Do you accept what people say in identifying themselves? Do those who freely admit their sexual orientation differ in any manner from those who do not? And, how would we ever know this? At what point in a person's life do you conclude that he or she has decided on a sexual identity? How do you deal with men who spend part of their lives engaging in heterosexual conduct and who then focus primarily on same-sex relations, and perhaps later turn back and forth a few more times? How do you deal with both historical and cultural examples of persons who socially pass through a period of same-sex activity on their way to other-sex activities? If your analysis emphasizes the genes or some other biological factors that come hard wired within the person, then how do you deal with people who move freely between different orientations as a function of cultural dictates? Also, how does one deal with the understanding of human sexuality, not as an either-or matter but more as a continuum with no simple dichotomy into male or female?

Second, as Fausto-Sterling among others has pointed out, the analysis of cause and effect is faulty. Biology is presumed to be the cause when in many cases it may be the consequence or effect of different behavioral patterns. In other words, rather than biology causing homosexuality, homosexual activity may produce differences in human biology that are then detected by the researchers and misattributed to a biological cause.

Without expanding further, let me simply observe that I believe we have another example here of a prejudice toward a particular group, in this case persons with same-sex desires, masquerading as a scientific search for a truth about this group's distinctive characteristics. Given the rather lengthy and tragic history associated with the scientific search for unique qualities that make one group differ from another, some elements of which we have considered in this chapter, one can only approach this current scientific attempt with a great deal of skepticism.

When all is said and done, the particular groups that come to the attention of science for further study and closer examination are not chosen by scientific curiosity but by social demands to offer explanations that will transmute prejudiced judgments into rational judgments, and that will permit people to justify their attitudes and explain the existing social ordering of group differences. It comes as no surprise to find that the groups selected for this special scientific treatment are those whose difference disturbs the majority, either because the majority requires a comforting explanation for its own superiority or because the different minority openly challenges the majority's way.

Homosexuals could be tolerated as long as they remained firmly closeted. Because the marks of homosexuality were often not as readily obvious as the marks of color and gender, remaining quietly closeted provided a comfortable denial for the majority. Mental health and criminal justice professionals could deal with those few who made their presence known.

But when the movement for homosexual rights took firm hold with what is usually attributed as the key 1969 Stonewall Inn riots in New York (Deitcher, 1995), the public's awareness of "these people and their difference" demanded responsive action. And a great part of that action involved enlisting one group of scientists to seek homosexuals' unique biology in order to explain their difference, and another group to challenge the first group's attempts to reduce homosexuality to a biological fact and thereby dismiss its underlying challenge to the larger society.

The presumptively nonhomosexual population is now coming out of its own closet and having to take a further look, not just at homosexuality but also at so-called normal sexuality and the institutions that have supported it. What does the very concept of family and child rearing mean when it does not demand a man and a woman, but when two men or two women can be a family? What does it mean to the idea of marriage when two men or two women can marry each other? These and other questions are not about homosexuality but about the rest of the population. Perhaps in the genes of heterosexuals we will find the answers we seek!

Chapter Summary: Key Learning Points

1. Even as we approach the 21st century, some scientific research continues to seek a clear-cut biological basis for explaining differences in intellectual functioning and derivative effects (e.g., income differentials, crime statistics) between blacks and whites.

2. The so-called IQ debates have pitted one group of scientists who insist on finding a predominantly biological basis for racial differences against another group (comprising both social and biological scientists) who have countered with their own arguments:

    a. Race is a highly controversial social construct by which the world's peoples have been divided; race is not a natural manner for organizing humankind into groupings of black, white, Asian, or whatever.

    b. Sociocultural analyses suggest that any simple biological explanation for group differences among blacks and whites ignores the clear-cut environmental determinants of both intelligence and other aspects of one's life chances.

    c. According to the bidirectional model, biology and environment work much too interdependently ever to make bold conclusions about the dominating effects of biology, especially on such complex matters as intelligence and social status.

3. In addition to racial differences having caught the eye of both the public and certain scientific investigators, differences in human

sexuality have also become significant issues of contemporary study. Again, the tendency has been for certain scientists to seek a biological basis for human sexuality and a public often all too eager to join this new yet familiar bandwagon.

4. We suggested caution in simply accepting the latest and well publicized finding of a biological basis for any kinds of group differences. The history of biological determinism plus some of its current usages urge this caution and a healthy skepticism.

S E C 3 T I O N

Explaining Prejudice: Characteristics of the Prejudiced Person

The scheme we first considered in the opening of Section 2 contrasted two ways of understanding prejudice. We have just completed our examination of the first way: examining the characteristics of targeted groups to see if there is something about them that would explain why prejudiced attitudes and behavior directed toward them might be better understood. Now in Section 3, we focus on the second perspective: examining the characteristics of those persons who harbor prejudice.

This shift can be quickly summarized as a move from examining characteristics of different racial and ethnic groups to probing racism and the mind of the racist; from examining gender differences to studying sexism and the sexist person; from looking at homosexuality to trying to understand homophobia.

This shift of focus from Section 2 to Section 3—from how target groups' characteristics help us understand the prejudice directed toward them to efforts to understand people who are themselves prejudiced—is not simply a convenient way to organize our study. It also marks an important shift in the social psychological investigation of prejudice (e.g., Duckitt, 1994; Kitzinger, 1987; Samelson, 1976). As we have seen from the work we considered in Chapters 4 and 5, however, this shift is not quite as neat at it once appeared. In spite of the growing significance of the bidirectional model of scientific understanding (see Chapter 4), attempts to discover biological and genetic properties of the groups targeted for prejudice have continued to capture both public and scientific attention. Yet, in spite of these headline-grabbing survivals of the past, considerable work continues to be directed toward studying the prejudiced person—his or her personality and values, as well as the manner in which this person thinks. There are some very good social, demographic, and historical reasons for the shift of interest from target characteristics to the characteristics of the person who harbors prejudice. We will consider four such reasons:

First, as the face of social psychology began to change its own color, ethnicity, and gender from lily white and primarily male to highly mixed in terms of these variables, it became less likely that researchers—who themselves might be Jewish or African American or female—would try to explain people's prejudicial responses to their own people by seeking qualities of their group that evoked such reactions. More likely, they would conduct their search for prejudice by probing qualities that made the prejudiced person so biased.

In the second place, after having passed through World War II, noteworthy for its genocidal horrors, it would be almost obscene to seek an explanation for the anti-Semetic excesses of the death camps in the characteristics that Jews as a people possessed. To do this would be to engage in the very same race science that marked the Nazi regime. How much more likely, therefore, to seek answers to the riddle of prejudice in the qualities of those persons who harbored such intense anti-Semitic beliefs.

A third reason for the shift in focus is sociopolitical. During the 1960s, a series of movements erupted within the United States and worldwide, seeking a dramatic change in the nature of majority-minority relations. Around the world, even well before the 1960s, dominant European nations that held colonial power (e.g., England, France, and Spain, among others) were to see that power eroded as colony after colony sought independence from its European "mother" country. Meanwhile in the United States and in several other Western nations, the 1960s saw the emergence of a variety of civil rights movements on behalf of gaining equality for African Americans, women, and other groups. Under such conditions, it would be difficult to insist that the prejudices that had kept these groups in their subservient places were a function of the characteristics describing the members of these groups. It was far more compatible with these freedom movements to explain prejudice by probing the characteristics of those who resisted their group's claims for equality.

And finally, though not conclusively in itself, certain theories and methodologies emerged within social psychology that increasingly permitted the focus on the prejudiced person to gain a foothold. The key concept of *attitude* and a variety of techniques permitting its refined measurement, for example, emerged in the 1940s and 1950s as a central idea within social psychology. This not only permitted the systematic study of the public's prejudiced attitudes, but also correlated these attitudes with individual personality traits (e.g., Did highly prejudiced people have a particular set of personality traits that distinguished them from people with less or no prejudice?). Today, the onslaught of interest in cognition (i.e., thinking and reasoning), often called the *cognitive revolution,* has made it important to seek some of the roots of prejudice within the mind of the prejudiced person.

The four chapters in Section 3 take up three main approaches to the study of the prejudiced person.

Chapter 6 begins with what to many remains the core of our commonsense belief that prejudiced people have some sort of disturbed or defective personality. We consider the early efforts to uncover the so-called authoritarian personality. We continue with the legacy of this earlier work, focusing on two of its more recent offshoots: (1) the examination of right wing authoritarianism and its relation to prejudiced beliefs, and (2) work that follows up the authoritarian's preference for an orderly world and how this preference is related to prejudiced views of others.

Chapter 7 centers its concern on the values that people hold and how these are related to prejudice. We follow two directions of theory and research. First, we examine the relation between the adoption of core American values and prejudice. Second, we look at the oft-touted but highly complex relationship between an individual's religious values and prejudice.

Chapters 8 and 9 take us headlong into the current cognitive core of research on prejudice, examining how basic mental processes can produce prejudiced attitudes and actions. In Chapter 8, we introduce the idea of categorization as a basic process involved in all human thinking, and of stereotyping—those pictures in our heads about various groups—that have been shown to be related to prejudiced attitudes and behaviors toward members of those groups.

Chapter 9 continues our cognitive study, but now focusing on how the stereotypes we hold shape our interactions in ways that often confirm those very stereotypes and so contribute to both prejudiced attitudes and behaviors.

Chapter 6

Personality and Prejudice: Authoritarianism and Its Current Legacy

When we refer to personality, we are looking for a set of traits or characteristics that describe individuals and that affect how they behave in the numerous situations of their lives. For example, some people are characteristically optimistic, while others are pessimistic (e.g., Peterson, Seligman, & Vaillant, 1988). In a wide variety of situations, the former tend to experience and act differently from the latter. As the old joke says, if you give the optimist an 8-ounce glass with 4 ounces of water in it, she will tell you that it is half full; to the pessimist, the same glass appears to be half empty. In short, because of these individual differences in personality, the same situation is experienced differently. In the context of prejudice, our question asks, "Is there something such as a prejudiced personality, a certain kind of person who is prone to adopt prejudiced attitudes and to act in a prejudicial manner toward others?"

For a variety of reasons (possibly having to do with my own personality!), I have often been skeptical of the role of personality in affecting a person's behavior, especially in the area of prejudice. That skepticism faded somewhat, however, after a personal encounter with rabid prejudice that impressed me for the way it operated. Let me share a bit of this personal encounter and then tell you how it led me to adopt a more charitable view of the relation between personality and prejudice.

A Personal Example

The event occurred in 1968. I was a psychology professor on the Berkeley campus of the University of California. Somehow, I found myself as one of four faculty sponsors of a course on prejudice. One, I repeat, *one* of the guest speakers scheduled for that course was to be Eldridge Cleaver, at that time a major figure in the much reviled Black Panther Party. Many white citizens of California viewed the Black Panthers as a dangerous group of urban guerrillas complete with guns and bands of ammunition strapped across their chests, who made no bones about their intention to usurp power from the whites in whatever way necessary.

The four faculty sponsors of this course, myself included, thought it would be valuable to have someone such as Cleaver make a few guest appearances so that we and our students could learn about his perspective on prejudice. The governor of California, later to become the president of the United States, Ronald Reagan, thought otherwise.

Reagan had built a reputation as a militant conservative who would never allow any armed rebel such as Cleaver access to the classroom where he could "poison the minds of California's youth." In that the governor of the state occupies a key position on the governing board of the university (the Board of Regents), he is influential in getting his views adopted. Not surprisingly, therefore, the board issued an order to the chancellor of the Berkeley campus forbidding this course with Cleaver as a guest lecturer.

In the sociopolitical climate of the 1960s, a command issued from any authority became fighting words, especially in an academic context where professors feel free to structure courses in the manner they believe to be essential. The board's demand, in other words, was tantamount to challenging those time-honored professorial rights. And so, the directive was met with defiance. We were going to teach the course and that was that! We did. And Cleaver lectured to our students.

As it turned out I became the public spokesperson for the group of defiant faculty, and so became fairly well known statewide for the position we had adopted. Appearances on television, radio, and in newspapers ensured that our defiance would be known to all, the governor included, and that I would also become widely known as the defiant one.

All of this is a long introduction to what then occurred and how this pushed me toward taking seriously the role of personality in the understanding of prejudice. Hardly a day would pass without my mailbox being filled with threatening hate mail. To be honest, I was frightened. After all, professors are usually unaccustomed to such intense anger from the public (occasionally, a few students—but that is another story for another time). But being a social psychologist, I found my curiosity about the mail even greater than my fear, and so began to examine the letters for clues about prejudice.

Consider that the event that triggered the hate mail involved faculty inviting a well known but generally feared and hated black speaker to the campus to deliver several guest lectures in a course on prejudice in defiance of the Board of Regents and the governor's directive that he not be permitted to speak. That was the information the public had to inspire this outburst of hate mail. I felt like one of those proverbial inkblots, open to whatever projections resided in the fertile minds of people angered by this event. Here is a sampling of a few of these letters, edited by me but only in order to give them more coherence than the typical letter often had:

> Dear Queer. Well, you've done it again! Having Cleaver appear at the university must be the high spot of your career. Is Cleaver one of your sweethearts too?

> I read of your determination to keep Cleaver alive at Cal. Did someone throw salt on your Matzos? Did you find out at NYU [New York University, a "well known" hotbed of Jews and Communists] that you are androgynous?

> So a stamp I'll waste on a dirty rotten sheenie pig who should be slaughtered by the bres meeler [the mohel, which I think is the reference here, is the person who performs the bris, or ritual circumcision of Jewish male infants] . . . so vy don't you go to Russia . . . you sheenies are at the bottom of all the filth in the U.S. I wish I could get my hands on you. I'll give you a snuff out.

> Time now to clean out those Communist professors and all those stinking long-haired APES and BLACK GERMS that are causing all of the trouble. It turns my stomach to think of that stinking NIGGER talking to the students. When he is on TV you can smell him right through the tube.

As I reflected back then and again today on those letters, I continue to be struck by the fascinating merger of racial hatred toward a black man with anti-Jewish, anti-Communist, and anti-homosexual references. Where did this coalescence of elements come from? Surely not the event itself. This is where personality enters the picture.

This otherwise puzzling merger of various elements that produces a kind of all-purpose hate is the very sign we look for if we are trying to discover the prejudiced personality. Elements that do not necessarily interconnect out there in the world are joined together into one global hate; the connection is made deeply inside the individual's psyche. In other words, in order to understand how this merger of anti-black, anti-Jew and anti-gay came together into a *system* of hate, we must turn to something deeply within the personality of the individuals who wrote those letters. The actual events to which they were responding could not otherwise explain why these several elements came together for them.

The Authoritarian Personality

It was also at Berkeley, but this time almost two decades earlier, in 1950, that one of the first major studies was undertaken seeking to fathom the personality of the prejudiced individual (Adorno, Frenkel-Brunswik, Levinson, & Sanford, 1964/1950). This study's findings revealed

> the rise of an "anthropological" species we call the authoritarian type of man. . . . He is at the same time enlightened and superstitious, proud to be an

individualist and in constant fear of not being like all the others, jealous of his independence and inclined to submit blindly to power and authority. (p. ix)

The research was governed by a central hypothesis (which we have already seen displayed in the several hate letters presented earlier in this chapter), as follows:

> The political, economic, and social convictions of an individual often form a broad and coherent pattern, as if bound together by a "mentality" or "spirit." . . . This pattern is an expression of deep-lying trends in his personality. (p. 1)

What were these deep-lying trends in personality that produced this merger of what might otherwise seem to be the unrelated elements of politics, economics, and social views with anti-Semitism and other forms of prejudice? By joining survey research techniques with in-depth personal interviews, Adorno and his colleagues located key qualities of the authoritarian's unconscious world, and then related those attributes of the unconscious to the family dynamics that produced them. Because several of the major contributors to the study were trained in Freudian psychoanalysis, it should not be surprising to find them emphasizing the family, the unconscious, and forbidden and dangerous impulses revolving around authority, aggression, and sex.

Let us suppose that a person is reared in a family that is highly structured and focused around the traditional authority of the father. This powerful figure controls almost every aspect of the family's life, and controls it primarily through fear: Everyone fears the consequences of failing to comply with his stern rule. One deeply seated result of this family pattern is likely to be a combination of near blind obedience to authority joined with an angry, deep resentment toward all authority. That anger, however, cannot be safely expressed toward its source (the father) and so gains its expression by taking it out on those who are weak and defenseless—that is, people who occupy the same powerless position in the world that the powerless child occupies in the traditional family.

According to Adorno and his colleagues, one of the central qualities of the prejudiced personality involves this deeply seated fear of authority, which produces excessive, blind obedience combined with a rage against authority that is directed toward "safe" targets. Adorno and his associates refer to this aspect by saying that the authoritarian has a *bicyclist's personality*, bowing down on top and kicking from below. That is, authoritarians submit to those who have positions of power over them while acting in an aggressive manner toward those below them.

The authoritarian personality's unconscious world is also filled with concerns over sex and sexuality. If authoritarians are fearful of their aggressive impulses, they are equally fearful of their sexual impulses. The stern and threatening father once again plays a central role in stifling the individual's sexual desires. The youngster learns not only to repress forbidden and thus dangerous sexual longings but also to project them outwards onto others: These others have the impulses that individuals cannot tolerate in themselves. And so, authoritarians come to inhabit a world filled with sexual excesses and wild goings on—a projection of their own inner turmoil.

One manner by which authoritarians manage this inner turmoil is by advocating support for a firm external structure of rules and control. After all, what better way to manage oneself than by living in a well structured environment that manages what the individual cannot personally accomplish? And so, the politics of the authoritarian leans toward structure and control, rules and laws that keep everyone in their place and the dangerous world under control.

The argument is that these deep-lying, unconscious aspects of the authoritarian's personality produce the peculiar merger of elements that would otherwise be puzzling to understand. This is the merger of the person's political attitudes (where authoritarians tend to favor conservative politics), economic attitudes (where authoritarians tend to believe that everyone in this competitive jungle in which we live should take care of themselves), and social attitudes (where authoritarians believe that there is a normal, conventional way to live one's life and that those who deviate from convention should be punished severely).

In turn, these trends in their personality lead the authoritarian to be highly prejudiced. The authoritarian personality is openly anti-Semetic (e.g., "One trouble with Jewish businessmen is that they stick together and connive, so that a Gentile doesn't have a fair chance in competition"), anti-black (e.g., "The Negroes would solve many of their social problems by not being so irresponsible, lazy, and ignorant"), and anti-homosexual (e.g., "Homosexuals are hardly better than criminals and ought to be severely punished"). Had feminism been as vigorous at the time of the original research (late 1940s), there is no doubt that the authoritarian would also have been strongly anti-feminist, for the authoritarian viewpoint holds that woman's place is at home, not at work. Figure 6.1 summarizes the original theory.

Is all of this true? That is, do people characterized in this manner actually exist and function in such a prejudicial way? If you were to ask those who

Figure 6.1

The authoritarian personality: Original theory and outcomes

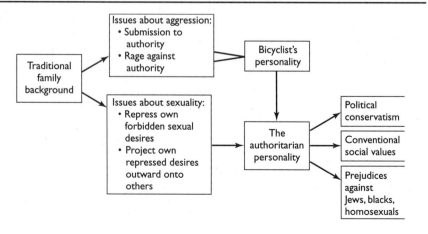

produced the research in 1950, they would answer with a clear affirmative. But at that time, not everyone agreed.

Criticisms of the Original Study

Rather rapidly after its publication in 1950, the study of the authoritarian personality evoked both great praise and nearly as much criticism (e.g., Christie & Jahoda, 1954; Rokeach, 1960; Shils, 1954). Not only were the critics concerned with some of the methodological flaws in the original study, but also with what many felt to be its political bias. In the original study, for example, persons with politically conservative points of view were considered to be authoritarian. But what about radical leftists? Several felt that the study's bias against conservatives was not only unfair but decidedly wrong (e.g., Rokeach, 1960; Shils, 1954). After all, they argued, surely there are people with some of the same traits as the authoritarian personality who have extremely leftist political and economic views and who are just as prejudiced as the authoritarians on the right.

Milton Rokeach was one of the first to examine this point by developing a test of *dogmatism*. Dogmatic personalities were defined as people who were inflexible in their beliefs, whatever the particular slant of their politics. Someone on the far left or someone on the far right could be equally dogmatic. And with dogmatism came a general tendency to be prejudiced toward others. The only difference involved who those others were. The out-groups for the left and right might differ, but their prejudice toward out-groups was equally strong, because they tended to think in dogmatic, rigid, and inflexible ways and to be closed to points of view that differed from their own.

Even critics have their own critics. And in matters of politics, you can be certain that those who criticized the original researchers for their political bias soon found their position under critical scrutiny. Thus, if both left and right political extremes were said to be equally dogmatic and prejudiced, didn't this imply that the only people without prejudice held political views somewhere in the middle? Several challenged this conclusion (e.g., Bay, 1967; Ezekiel, 1995; Sidanius, 1988). Ezekiel, for example, suggested that right and left are *not* similar to one another, implying that the original authoritarian personality was appropriately considered to be aligned with the right political extreme: "Left and right attract different character types; there is a distinction that has to do with openness and closedness, with inclusion and exclusion" (Ezekiel, 1995, p. 25).

What Ezekiel is saying is that prejudiced people tend to be closed-minded and exclusionary in their worldview, more interested in keeping the world pure than including everyone under the same tent. While Ezekiel's view here is similar to Rokeach's view of closed-mindedness and its relation to prejudice, Rokeach argued that both political extremes were closed, dogmatic, and prejudiced, while Ezekiel insisted that this described the far right politically, but not the far left.

Sidanius (1988) joined in this debate by questioning the so-called virtue of being middle-of-the-road. He argued that people may adopt middle positions in order to avoid conflicts; they are primarily interested in achieving acceptance by everyone. Such people may actually be very ill-informed about the issues that are at stake. In Sidanius's view, therefore, people with extremely held political views (left or right) should be the most well informed and self-confident, qualities we usually do not associate with prejudice. On the other hand, the middle-of-the-roader's concern with acceptance may very well lead to prejudiced attitudes, especially in settings in which acceptance means going along with the crowd—and the crowd is prejudiced.

The Current Legacy of Authoritarianism

Because of the success of the original critiques, both methodological and political, as well as the changing face of world politics (e.g., see Stone, 1995), work on the authoritarian personality began to fade somewhat from the center stage of psychological interest. And yet, to fade a bit does not mean to disappear entirely. During the 30-year period from 1950 to 1980, for example, more than 45,000 people worldwide had been measured for their authoritarianism and their prejudice (e.g., Meloen, Hagendoorn, Raaijmakers, & Visser, 1988), suggesting that interest in authoritarianism has remained vigorous at least through 1980 and, as we will next see, even beyond to the present day.

Renewed interest in the nature of the prejudiced person has recently breathed new life into the study of authoritarianism. Two directions have emerged. The first is represented in the research program on right wing authoritarians developed by a Canadian psychologist, Robert Altemeyer (1981, 1988, 1994). The second follows up the cognitive dimension discovered in the original work, involving intolerance of ambiguity.

Altemeyer and Right Wing Authoritarianism

With the vision of 20–20 hindsight to guide him, Altemeyer wisely avoided some of the pitfalls of the original study of authoritarianism; he developed a methodologically more sophisticated way of evaluating this personality type. Through careful statistical techniques that were unavailable to the original investigators back in 1950, Altemeyer was able to reduce the many components of authoritarianism to three central qualities: *submission* (the tendency to yield to persons occupying positions of legitimate authority), *aggression* (the tendency to be aggressive toward others), and *conventionalism* (the tendency to follow the social conventions approved by society). These three qualities, argued Altemeyer, described the personality of the right wing authoritarian

(RWA). It is clear from his naming of the concept that Altemeyer suggests that authoritarianism is linked with right wing or conservative political views.

Having developed an effective way to measure RWA traits, Altemeyer next proceeded to look for the social views and prejudices of high scorers. Not surprisingly, high RWAs tended to support their own government even when that government acted in an unlawful and unjust manner (authoritarian submission to authority). For example, Altemeyer found that high RWAs believed illegal searches carried out to apprehend criminals are appropriate actions for the government. High scorers likewise favored the harsh treatment of criminals and others who break the law. Both of these suggested the continuing relevance of aggression in describing the authoritarian personality.

In their politics, Altemeyer's research showed high RWAs to be highly conservative (favoring the Republican Party in the United States and the Progressive Conservatives in Canada), a trait associated with the conventionalism of the authoritarian personality. High scorers also worried that there is already too much freedom in their nation: They favored denying the right of protesters to protest, even peacefully—and in the United States, they also favored repealing the Bill of Rights!

Central to our own interests in prejudice, the high RWAs had prejudiced attitudes toward almost every known target group, leading Altemeyer to refer to them as "equal opportunity bigots." They were hostile toward homosexuals, blacks, Jews, and all other nonwhite ethnic immigrant groups. In short, Altemeyer offers some compelling evidence that links right wing authoritarianism as a personality pattern with a variety of social, economic, and political attitudes as well as with definite prejudices toward specific groups.

Unlike the original view, in which the seedbed for the development of the authoritarian personality was said to be found in the traditional family, Altemeyer argued that the high RWAs had very strong in-group identifications and a profound fear of all out-groups. High RWAs saw all out-groups to be potential threats to the security of their own people. High RWAs felt that they lived in a dangerous world that could be made safe only by sticking to their own kind and rejecting all who are different.

In one small demonstration of this idea, during the first or second meeting of his introductory psychology class, Altemeyer gave two different sections of students a test that was said to measure their logical reasoning. He then asked the students to predict which of the two sections would score higher on this test. Since the test had been given early in the term, well before students had formed any sense of their class as a special group of people, this might seem to be a ridiculous question. Even so, there were students who said that "my section will do better than the other section." Twice as many high as low RWAs felt this way; that is, more high RWAs than low RWAs favored their in-group over the out-group. This revealed a rather strong in-group favoritism effect for high RWAs, even when the group to which they attached their loyalty was hardly a group with any longevity in their lives. Perhaps it is as Altemeyer suggested: High RWAs need a strong in-group with which to identify and need to feel that their group is better than others. And, this is the basis for their prejudice toward all who do not belong to their in-group—an exclusionary emphasis that we first encountered earlier in the chapter in considering Ezekiel's views of the distinction between authoritarians of the right, who are exclusionary, and of the left, who tend to be more inclusive of other people and hence less prejudiced overall.

Authoritarianism's Cognitive Turn

We will wait until Chapters 8 and 9 for an in-depth examination of the cognitive analysis of prejudice. At this juncture, however, it will be useful to follow up the second direction of more recent work on authoritarianism, building on a lead suggested in the original study. That lead involves a particular cognitive trait that describes high authoritarians: their tendency to be intolerant of ambiguity.

First of all, what does this mean? Suppose you were to confront an ambiguous situation whose meaning is open to many different interpretations. Some people find ambiguity of this sort tantalizing; it gives them the freedom to construct whatever meaning they wish with minimal constraints. Others, however, are fearful of such unlimited freedom and would vastly prefer things to be more clear-cut. The latter are said to be intolerant of ambiguity: They find anything that is open to several meanings not to their liking and so tend to eliminate the ambiguity as quickly as possible. They collapse nuances of difference into an either-or, black-or-white formulation. Shades of gray are not on their agenda.

To say that high authoritarians are intolerant of ambiguity, then, is to say two things about them. First, when confronted by an ambiguous situation, one allowing for a variety of meanings or shades of gray, they feel discomfort. Second, they deal with this discomfort by seeking a quick and easy solution that minimizes the subtleties that exist. In short, they make their world into simple black or simple white. From time to time, all of us show aspects of this intolerance. The mark of the high authoritarian, however, is the tendency to deal uncharitably with ambiguity most of the time.

This quality of authoritarians' thinking should make them especially prone to prejudice for at least two related reasons. First, diversity is like ambiguity for them: It provides too many options and alternatives. They show a preference for getting rid of diversity and muting differences. This is the very quality that fits persons who want to keep their own family, neighborhood, community, and nation pure by not allowing various outside groups to gain entry. Second, we all form quick impressions of others, usually based on the simple stereotypes we hold about them. Some people, however, allow later knowledge to recast their first impressions. Those who are highly intolerant of ambiguity, by contrast, do not take kindly to new information that does not fit the impression they have already formed. Thus, they may persist in maintaining their first impressions of others and disregard conflicting new information.

Some recent work has followed up these ideas, defining a concept that parallels intolerance for ambiguity. This parallel concept has been termed PNS, or *personal need for structure* (e.g., Schaller, Boyd, Yohannes, & O'Brien, 1995), as well as the *need for closure* (Webster & Kruglanski, 1994). According to Schaller and his colleagues, the personal need for structure is a characteristic of an individual's personality and involves a need to simplify the complexities of the world in order to make it more manageable. People are said to differ in the intensity of this need: Some require more structure and greater simplicity than others.

Research reported by Schaller and associates indicates that persons high in PNS tend to engage in simplistic reasoning and to form erroneous stereotypes of out-groups. In particular, persons high in PNS form simplistic systems for processing information about other people, preferring a two-category system, for example, thus erasing the range of differences within any group. As we will see in Chapters 8 and 9 and again in Chapter 11, this can result in a tendency to see the members of out-groups as more similar than they actually are (e.g., "they all look alike to me").

Webster and Kruglanski's (1994) similar work adds to this emerging picture. They find that people who demand structure and the quick closure of ambiguous situations tend to make rapid assessments of others—usually based on minimal, stereotypic information—and to stick to those initial impressions by rejecting new information that might disconfirm their first judgment. In short, persons who are highly intolerant of ambiguity, high in PNS, or high in the need for closure (1) quickly categorize people into the minimal number of groupings that will reduce their own anxieties, in an attempt to erase frightening diversity from their world, and (2) rarely modify their first impressions on the basis of new information they receive, as though new information would upset their existing worldview and introduce just the kind of ambiguity of which they are intolerant.

The Mind That Hates

To this point, we have considered the array of personality traits that have been linked with prejudice and that have been derived from the pioneering work on the authoritarian personality. Our question now turns to another facet of contemporary prejudice, asking, "Is there a specific personality linked with hate and hate crimes?" In other words, we wish to determine whether there is a personality pattern that helps us better understand *the racist mind* (e.g., Ezekiel, 1995).

Ever since the atrocities of World War II, several groups in the United States have monitored so-called hate crimes, crimes that one group commits against another group simply because of who that other group is. In addition to official governmental agencies (e.g., the FBI), several private organizations have taken the lead in evaluating the frequency of hate crimes, determining who are the preferred targets and developing a portrait of the perpetrators. The Anti-Defamation League (ADL), for example, has been especially interested in crimes against Jews. The Klanwatch Project of the Southern Poverty Law Center (SPLC) has been interested in groups that have targeted African Americans. With the sudden presence of numerous "patriot militia" groups (e.g., the Vipers, the Freeman, the Phineas Priesthood), the SPLC has also established a special section—the Militia Project—to monitor the activities of these new varieties of hate groups. The National Gay and Lesbian Task Force has also joined in these efforts, focusing its major attention on hate crimes directed toward people because of their sexual orientation.

All of these agencies, both governmental and private, have recorded an alarming increase in the number of hate crimes during the last few years. For example, the ADL recorded some 6 killings between 1987 to 1990 committed by Skinheads; since 1990, that figure has risen to 22 additional killings, in which most of the victims were Hispanics, Blacks, Asians, homosexuals, and homeless persons. In addition to these actual killings, thousands of hate crimes have been attributed to the Skinheads, including beatings, thefts, synagogue destruction, and so forth.

Hate crime figures reported in 1995 for the state of California also reveal a discouragingly high number: some 2,600 persons were victims of crimes motivated by their race, their religion, or their sexual orientation. More than 69% of these hateful acts were based on the victim's race or ethnicity, another 18% based on sexual orientation, and 12% attributed to the victim's religion (Rojas, 1996).

Accurate records are difficult to obtain. The determination of whether a crime is a hate crime or just another criminal act is often a judgment call made by officials, many of whom may be eager to deny the prejudicial nature of the crime (e.g., were the spate of African American church bombings during 1995 and 1996 hate crimes or some other kind of criminal act?). Officials are sometimes reluctant to consider a crime against several black churches, for example, as a conspiracy motivated by the race of the victims, because these officials operate under an old definition of conspiracy. For them, a conspiracy can exist only if there is some organization that directs the action.

For example, in 1996 President Clinton created the National Church Arson Task Force to investigate the rash of church burnings in the United States. In early 1997, the task force issued its report. The report concluded that of the 328 documented cases of attacks against churches in 1995 and 1996, just 138 were directed toward primarily African American congregations. These data plus other materials the task force collected led to the conclusion that while some of the burnings undoubtedly were motivated by racism, a complex set of motivations going beyond racism was also involved. Furthermore, the report suggested that there was no evidence of a conspiracy or some overarching national plan to spread fires across the United States.

It is possible that the task force overlooked the "newer" forms that define a conspiracy. As other investigations of hate groups teach us, conspiracy may

Figure 6.2

Some familiar symbols of current hate groups

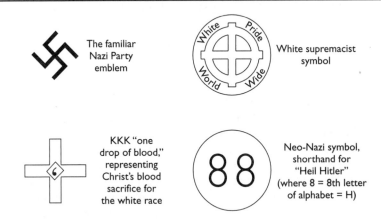

not require any organization whatsoever. All it needs is a sense on the part of various hate groups that the atmosphere is ripe for putting on their hoods and riding out at midnight once again—or more typically today, putting on their old army fatigues and combat boots, collecting their automatic weapons and bomb-making equipment, and heading out to blow up a federal building in Oklahoma City, derail a train in Arizona, or rob some banks in Washington and in the Midwest.

A growing number and variety of hate groups are now being monitored by these public and private agencies, including Klansmen, Skinheads, neo-Nazis, Militiamen, Aryan Nation, the Order, White Aryan Resistance, National Alliance, and so forth. (See Figure 6.2 for a sampling of these groups' symbols.) One of the best studies of the leadership and members of several of these hate groups was conducted by psychologist Raphael Ezekiel (1995), who sought to uncover some of the basic features of what he referred to as *the racist mind.*

Ezekiel spent about 10 years with several of these well known hate groups, interviewing both leaders and members, attending national rallies and local meetings, and keeping himself informed as best he could about their ideas and what made them tick. He did not administer batteries of psychological tests to these individuals. Thus we cannot report scores on standardized tests and compare them with scores of nonmembers, as would be required for the usual scientific study. Nor did Ezekiel tape-record and systematically transcribe every single encounter. Rather, he was a highly skilled observer who spent time talking with the people, observing their meetings and forming his impressions.

I should note here that Ezekiel is not only Jewish, but also a psychology professor—two categories that are especially disturbing to most of these hate groups. And indeed, in his 10 years of research, Ezekiel did run into some incidents that would have frightened off most of us from continuing with this work. Undaunted, however, he continued, never disguising who he was. In spite of their hate for his people, hate group leaders and members more often than not accepted him into their meetings, permitted him to conduct his interviews, and in general provided him an open door to their innermost anxieties and concerns.

Christian Identity

We must begin our own study of hate groups with one of Ezekiel's major findings: the importance to these groups of the ideology of Christian Identity. This ideology was central to almost every hate group that Ezekiel studied. I do not mean that each and every member of these groups adopted the set of beliefs of Christian Identity. Rather, Identity ideas were easily mouthed by most members and were a central element in all their meetings. Members acted as though Christian Identity gave them their very purpose for being in the movement and for striking out with hate against so many others.

The importance of Identity ideology to hate groups has not only been observed by Ezekiel, but has also become a central element in the analyses provided by the SPLC's several projects focusing on the Klan, neo-Nazis, and patriot militia. All seem to be energized by the beliefs of Christian Identity.

According to Michael Barkun's (1994) historical study, the Christian Identity movement began in England in the 1870s under the name "British Israelism." Although strictly speaking neither anti-Semetic nor generally filled with hate until the movement arrived in the United States, the original movement's ideology held that the lost tribes of Israel had migrated from the Near East to Europe, and that in fact, as ascertained by careful historical and linguistic analysis (or so argued its founders), the truly chosen people were British!

In crossing from England to the United States, some of these ideas took on the more virulent anti-Semitic cast that marks Christian Identity in the United States today. I might add that the idea that they too were the truly chosen people also emerged in Germany, where some influential Germans felt that the German people had been chosen to lead the world from darkness.

The essential message of Christian Identity is its insistence that the white races are the chosen people, even if most of them, other than the members of these various groups, do not yet know it. Excluded from the white races are both Jews, who are the sons and daughters of Satan (recall this earlier theme), and the Mud people, people of color who are the offspring of the mating between humans and beasts. Only the white races are the true children of God. It is their destiny to engage in an unending battle with the forces of evil for final control of the world.

The opposing sides are sharply drawn: The children of God, the Christian Identity believers, versus the children of Satan, the Jews. The Mud people are simply dupes of the Jews, under their control, doing what they command. Mud people may often serve as the frontline troops in this war; but the true villains are the Jews. Christian Identity members are so insistent in their beliefs about Jewish control over the forces of evil that they even have a name for the government of the United States: ZOG (or Zionist Occupation Government), a government that in being controlled by the Jews must be fought and brought down so that the children of God can take their rightful place in a truly Christian world. Bombing of governmental buildings or in other ways refusing to accept the legitimacy of governmental authority are reflections of these beliefs.

It is clear that both anti-Semites as well as patriot militia groups can find a common theme within these views. After all, if the Jews are the people behind the federal government, and if that government is a threat to human liberty that genuine patriots must combat, it makes sense to seek the destruction of Jews and all things Jewish, including, in this manner of thinking, the government of the United States itself (or ZOG, in their terms). Just as obviously, people of color, the so-called Mud people, who are the dupes of those in control, must likewise be eliminated so that the world can be made safe by making it pure—pure white, that is.

Followers of this ideology hold meetings in their own churches around the United States and listen as their own preachers deliver the message of Christian Identity both in the churches and now especially on the Internet. They see themselves as the true patriots in a battle of good against evil. It is a battle they are waging on behalf of all the white people of the world, including the majority who continue to misbelieve in the Bible and so fail to see who are the rightful inheritors of the world. Believers of Christian Identity are willing to sacrifice themselves (in principle, if often not in fact) in this battle against true evil and for the truth of their movement.

Membership Types

Ezekiel's 10-year sojourn with these various hate groups, loosely united by their common belief in Christian Identity, led him on a search for a personality type that might underlie these beliefs. Was there something about their personality that made certain people especially prone to accept the ideology of Christian Identity? While he was able to discern various membership types (he identified four), he was less successful in discovering any unifying personality type. Let us examine his conclusions.

The four membership types Ezekiel identified include (1) national leaders and their immediate aides, who have a lifetime of involvement and whose energy and perseverance keeps the groups alive even when few others are around to listen or follow; (2) ordinary followers, who tend not to be fanatical devotees of the movement and who have no wish to do prison time or to seriously harm others, but who take pleasure in belonging and, as Ezekiel puts it, who find a thrill in carrying a membership card in their wallet; (3) loose cannons, whose membership is unpredictable, who are literalists in believing the messages of Christian Identity, and who are, in Ezekiel's words, like tinder waiting for the spark that will set them on fire; and (4) terrorists and guerrillas, who hold a deep belief in the ideology that the enemy is evil and must be destroyed, and who thereby engage in underground violent actions, anchoring their deeds loosely in the umbrella of the movement.

These latter two types (the loose cannons and the terrorists and guerillas) have been identified by the SPLC's Militia Project as comprising the Phineas Priesthood. According to the SPLC's account, the Phineas Priesthood is a group of highly dedicated and dangerously armed individuals who rarely if ever meet together but who share a common belief that gives them their name, Phineas, after the figure from the Old Testament who provided biblical justification for killing in order to restore God's law. The strength of this belief is documented in the work of one of the Identity church leaders, Richard Hoskins, who argued that "violence, murder and robbery are biblically and historically justified when employed to restore 'God's Law' " (*Klanwatch Intelligence Report*, 1996).

Personality

As for the personality traits of the hard-core members, Ezekiel's only conclusion bears quoting:

> The white racist movement is about an idea. . . . There is no simple and overpowering psychological "explanation": There are many ways to be a racist, just as there are many ways to be a nurse or a professor or a grocer. . . . With hesitation, I will suggest that I hear one voice repeatedly, a voice that puts me in mind of the very early teenager—a rebellious youngster, very frightened about himself, utterly self-absorbed. With one or two ideas in his head. (p. xxix)

For those who want some kind of simplistic and unifying story line, a definitive personality to describe the extreme racist—comforting in that it would allow us to say "at least I'm not one"—Ezekiel's conclusion cannot be pleasing.

We came in the hopes of finding an evil person or a classic authoritarian and instead discovered a frightened rebel easily captured by the ideology of Christian Identity and the feelings of security that come with membership in fringe groups. These frightened and angry rebels are not sympathetic figures; they are dangerous. The hate crimes that issue from their beliefs have brought misery and death to many who have done nothing more than to be different.

Christian Identity's doctrine of war between good and evil may give purpose to individuals caught up within these hate groups, and may even make their hateful actions somewhat understandable to us, but, as one ex-member proclaimed, nothing of this sort excuses their actions:

> I can't justify anything I've done. . . . People can say, "Look how he was raised. He had no choices. He was only a kid." Well, bull! I'm responsible. I didn't have to walk down every path that was given to me. (Strong, 1995, p. 89)

Chapter Summary: Key Learning Points

1. Personality refers to traits or characteristics of an individual that affect her or his behavior in a variety of different situations.

2. The search for a uniquely prejudiced personality uncovered a type of individual, the authoritarian, who has problems in managing his or her unconscious impulses of sex and aggression and who finds an outlet in prejudice toward others.

3. When questions were raised about both its methodology and its political bias, research on authoritarianism faded for awhile.

4. Newer approaches, however, gave renewed life to the study of authoritarianism and its relationship with prejudice.

5. A newly identified personality type, the right wing authoritarian (RWA), was assessed and found to be an "equal opportunity bigot." This person was less driven by deep-lying unconscious impulses than by a concern with belonging to an in-group and feeling secure insofar as that in-group could be protected from real or imagined threats from others.

6. Intolerance of ambiguity, the cognitive component discovered in the original study of authoritarianism, reappeared in a new guise as a personal need for structure or a need for closure.

7. This cognitive component was found to be related to prejudice in two ways:
   a. People who are intolerant of ambiguity tend to be intolerant of human diversity.
   b. Such persons tend to stick doggedly with stereotypic first impressions and minimize the impact of new information that might disconfirm those first impressions.

8. We ended the chapter by considering efforts to discover the mind and personality of the extreme racist, one who is involved in hate groups and who commits hate crimes. We found that the many hate groups around today seem united only by a commonly shared ideology, Christian Identity.

9. As we explored this ideology further, we discovered that one of its basic arguments is that we are now engaged in a final battle between good and evil, where Jews especially, but people of color and homosexuals as well, represent evil.

Chapter 7

Values and Prejudice

Our examination of the prejudiced person turns next to the study of values and their relation to prejudice. In many respects, the work on the authoritarian personality we just considered (Chapter 6) has already taken us into the world of values. Probing people's political, economic, and social beliefs necessarily touch on the values that people hold. Unlike the work to which we now turn our attention, however, the values examined in regard to the authoritarian personality were usually not seen as determinants of a person's prejudices; rather, these values were seen to be the outcomes of deeper-lying personality traits that characterized the individual. In this chapter, we will focus our attention on a group of investigators for whom values, in and of themselves, play a central role in prejudice. But first, what do we mean when we refer to "values"?

Values: A Definition

Most of us have a variety of *opinions* on a wide range of issues. We can respond positively or negatively to questions about the kinds of music we like, food we enjoy, films we favor, political candidates we prefer, and positions we hold on public issues such as abortion, same-sex marriage, and so forth. *Values,* however, lie deeper and spread farther than those specific opinions. It is said that our values underlie and determine many of the specific positions on issues that we adopt as well as our preferences and priorities (e.g., Mayton, Ball-Rokeach, & Loges, 1994).

For example, one person may strongly value independence and personal freedom, while for another, loyalty and commitment to the family are more highly valued. We would expect these two people to differ in the specific opinions they hold on a variety of issues, in the preferences they have, and in the priorities they establish for their lives. To value independence, for example, may include the belief that neither the government nor anyone else, even members of the person's own family, should intrude in his or her life. These people make their own decisions and go their own way. By contrast, the person for whom family loyalty is a prime value is unlikely to consider it an infringement of personal freedom if she or he yields to family pressures in decisions about schooling, automobile purchases, or even marriage.

A Latina student in one of my classes told of a time her Anglo friends wanted her to join them for an evening out, but she declined because it was her job to stay home and take care of her grandmother. The student complained that her Anglo friends simply did not understand the high value she placed on the family: Her family came first. The Anglos chided her on still being a "baby" who had no independent life of her own. She complained that because they were not from the same background as she, with the same underlying values and moral beliefs that she had, they simply could not understand her way. She enjoyed being with her grandmother and never felt it to be an infringement on her own autonomy.

The preceding scenario teaches that one of the central, defining features of values is that they are deeper-lying than specific attitudes and so tend to have a wider spread in our lives. In addition, values also operate as standards against which we measure our own and others' actions. Values thereby have a moral tone to them. We approve or disapprove of our own as well as others' actions in light of the underlying values we hold.

Because they valued autonomy over family loyalty, the Anglo students in our example felt that their Latina friend was being foolish to stay home with her grandmother when an evening of great fun was being offered to her. Yet from her perspective, they were insensitive to family loyalties and more concerned about their own personal pleasures. The different underlying values served as standards for judging each other's behaviors.

Further Aspects of the Value Concept

Before we can begin our examination of the role that people's values play in their prejudices, we must first expand a bit further on our understanding of the concept of value. Most psychologists who have examined values (1) develop a list of what they consider to be basic or core human values, (2) ask people to rank the items on this list from most to least important to them, and (3) look for some underlying structure or organizing principle to a person's value system.

The Structure of the Value System: Rokeach's View

Psychologist Milton Rokeach (1973, 1979), one of the major contributors to the study of values, had something to say about all three of the preceding points. Rokeach first reasoned that is important to distinguish between *instrumental values* (i.e., values we hold that specify a mode of conduct or way of behaving, such as being respectful to others) and *terminal values* (i.e., the ends or goals that the value involves—for example, achieving world peace). He next argued that some values are personal (e.g., a comfortable life) while others are social (e.g., national security, equality).

Some of these preliminary distinctions did not stand up to empirical research, and so are generally no longer considered central. It quickly became apparent, for example, that what was an instrumental value at one moment could be a terminal value at another, making the distinction not as useful as Rokeach originally thought. Nevertheless, using these distinctions, Rokeach generated a list of values that prominently included the following: (1) a comfortable life, (2) a meaningful life, (3) a world at peace, (4) equality, (5) freedom, (6) maturity, (7) national security, (8) respect for others, (9) respect from others, (10) salvation, (11) true friendship, and (12) wisdom. (For a similar list, see Altemeyer, 1994.)

This list sometimes grew in number for specific purposes or contracted for other purposes. For our own purposes, these 12 items give a good sense of Rokeach's view of basic human values. By presenting this list to various people and asking them to rank-order each item with respect to its importance to them, Rokeach was able not only to determine people's value priorities but also to check on the stability of values in the population over time.

Rokeach and Ball-Rokeach (1989), for example, report results from several national surveys held in the United States during the period from 1968 to 1981, from which it was possible to see which values held stable throughout that period and which values changed, moving either up or down. They found both impressive stability among the population as well as some disturbing changes. First, they noted that during this time, value priorities had shifted away from the social and toward the personal. Second, and related to this overall shift, they noted that the value of freedom maintained high importance, but equality as a value dropped. This shift led Rokeach and Ball-Rokeach to describe it as a shift from "thee" to "me" (p. 783). In other words, they observed people moving away from a concern with others' well-being, as seen in the high ranking they had given earlier to social values, especially the value of equality, to a greater concern with their own personal well-being, as seen in the high ranking they gave to various personal values, especially freedom. We will shortly return to this point, as data repeatedly suggest an important connection between unprejudiced attitudes and ranking equality higher than freedom. The decrease in the rank of equality over this time period suggests a corresponding rise in prejudice in 1981 as compared with 1968.

Based on these findings, Rokeach made two assumptions about a person's value system. First, the system has an underlying structure in which some values occupy a central position while others occupy a peripheral position. Central values are intimately connected to most aspects of the person's life, while peripheral values have a more limited connection. Rokeach's second assumption argued that changing the values that are most central to the person (i.e., ranked most highly) would produce a more extensive shift in all other aspects of his or her life; by contrast, changing peripheral values would have only a limited impact.

For example, if a person says that freedom tops her list of values, she is telling us that it influences almost everything she does or tries to accomplish:

This person's concern with personal freedom affects how she evaluates other people, social policies, and her own actions. If this most central value could be changed, dropping it, for example, from the top of the list to somewhere in the middle, this would not only make room for another value to move into the central position (because the entire rank-ordering of values would be changed), but in addition would have the greatest overall impact on the person given the intimate connection between freedom and everything else in that person's life. Before we examine how this assumption of value centrality became a prominent part of Rokeach's efforts to change values and thereby attack the heart of prejudice, we will consider another approach that has attempted to look at the underlying structure of the value system.

The Structure of the Value System: Schwartz's View

Shalom Schwartz wondered if a wide variety of human values, including those proposed by Rokeach as well as other possibilities, could be organized on the basis of a small set of fundamental principles (Sagiv & Schwartz, 1995; Schwartz, 1992, 1994; Schwartz & Bilsky, 1987, 1990). Schwartz and his colleagues first argued that all human beings, whenever they may have lived and from whatever culture they may come, confront three universal requirements for living. These requirements are based on our being (1) biological organisms, (2) who must engage in cooperative social interaction with others, and (3) who must learn to achieve relatively smooth functioning together so that the social groupings in which we live can survive.

From this listing of three requirements, Schwartz derived his own list of values. His list included (among others) such values as hedonism, stimulation, self-direction, security, conformity, tradition, achievement, power, universalism, and benevolence. He asked people to rank these values and then used statistical techniques to reveal an underlying structure to the entire system. Two major value structures emerged from this analysis:

1. *Openness to change versus conservation:* The specific values involved were hedonism, stimulation, and self-direction, which reflected greater openness, while security, conformity, and tradition reflected conservation. This would mean that a person who rated hedonism very highly would be more open to change in his or her life than someone for whom tradition or security were a highly ranked value.

2. *Self-enhancement versus self-transcendence:* The specific values involved were hedonism, achievement, and power, which reflected self-enhancement, while universalism and benevolence reflected self-transcendence. For example, a person who ranked achievement as a high value would more likely favor policies and actions that were self-enhancing, that focused on personal achievements and success;

persons for whom universalism was the highest value would be more concerned with transcending their own personal lives and doing work on behalf of others.

We now have before us two approaches to understanding the underlying structure of people's value systems: One is based on Rokeach's work; the other on Schwartz's. At this point, we are ready to examine the relationship between values and prejudice.

The Rokeach Program: Freedom, Equality, and Prejudice

Of all the items on his listing of values, Rokeach argued that the two most reflective of whether a person would relate in an unprejudiced or a prejudiced manner toward others were that person's ranking of freedom compared with his or her ranking of equality. Thus, these two values became central to Rokeach's efforts to reduce prejudice, as he sought to change the priorities attached to these two core values. Let us first examine the reasoning behind this argument. That is, why should we expect a connection between freedom and prejudice or between equality and the absence of prejudice?

Why Freedom and Equality Are So Central

In order to understand the connection between freedom and high prejudice and equality and low prejudice, we need to turn to an analysis proposed by Katz and Hass (1988). They suggested that there is a built-in conflict between two sets of basic American values. On the one hand, we all learn the importance of equality—being fair to all people by treating everyone equally, showing no particular bias toward persons simply because of who they are, their background, their social class, their gender, their race, and so forth. This involves an underlying belief in the value of equality.

The Protestant Ethic   On the other hand, we also have learned to highly value what Katz and Hass call, borrowing a leaf from Max Weber's (1930) analysis, the "Protestant Ethic." This is intimately connected with how much a person values individual freedom—that is, the right to make one's own way in life and to succeed or fail on the basis of one's own individual merit.

Many years ago, Weber suggested that the capitalist economic system, with its competitive market economy and private enterprise, required a particular religious ethic in order to take hold and blossom. This supportive religious ethic came from Protestantism. According to this ethic, certain persons are destined for eternal salvation, while others are not. Although it is not possible simply to look at another individual or even oneself and know which it will be, salvation or damnation, we can make some reasonable predictions based on an examination of a person's worldly achievements. Those who are successful in this world are very likely part of the saved; those who are failures here are likely to be eternally damned.

Weber argued that this religious view provided the psychological basis for capitalism by encouraging people to work hard to succeed in this world so that they could know their fate in the next world. This standard, referred to as the Protestant Ethic, the work ethic, or the individual achievement ethic, served the competitive market economy of capitalism quite well. But what does this Protestant Ethic have to do with the basic conflict in American values that Katz and Hass suggested?

The basic value conflict noted by Katz and Hass among others (e.g., Sniderman & Tetlock, 1986; Weigel & Howes, 1985) lies between equality on the one hand and individual freedom or the Protestant Ethic on the other. The idea is that if people are free enough to shape their own destiny and then fail to do so, perhaps they do not necessarily deserve to be treated the same in all respects as those who do well. That is, whereas equality would tend to value a society of equals, individual freedom would tend to value a society ranked according to individual merit and achievement.

Ranking vs. linking   Another way of describing the value conflict involves two contrasting ideals—one based on ranking, the other on linking (e.g. Sidanius, Pratto, & Bobo, 1994, 1996). To honor *ranking* is to think of society in terms of hierarchical relations among various people, where a person's rank is based on individual merit or achievement. This is the heart of the Protestant Ethic and connects both with Rokeach's concern with freedom as a value and with Schwartz's underlying theme of self-enhancement.

In other words, if I believe that the ideal society is comprised of people of different ranks, some higher than others, and that this arrangement is based on what each individual personally achieves, I am likely to rank Rokeach's value of freedom and Schwartz's value-cluster involving self-enhancement near the top of my list of value priorities. To think in this manner is to accept the Protestant Ethic's worldview, to believe that people individually shape their own destiny and are located as they are on society's ladder of success because of what they personally have accomplished. As Katz and Haas remind us, this belief is as American as apple pie: It is one of the central values of current American society.

But, we are also reminded that there is another slice of this same pie, and this slice involves a contrasting value that is also central to current American thinking. This is the concept captured by Rokeach's value of equality, Schwartz's value-cluster involving self-transcendence, and the whole notion of *linking*. Linking favors a less hierarchical and flatter society comprised of connections and interconnections. Equality rather than hierarchical relations are predominant. (Table 7.1 summarizes these several relationships.)

Table 7.1

Relations Among Several Theorists' Values

Rokeach	Sidanius	Schwartz	Katz & Hass		Outcomes for Prejudice
Freedom	Ranking	Self-enhancement	Protestant Ethic	→	High prejudice
Equality	Linking	Self-transcendence	Egalitarianism	→	Low prejudice

Research on Freedom vs. Equality *and Prejudice*

Katz and Hass developed a series of tests designed to examine the two contrasting and often conflicting ideals of freedom and equality. One test measured people's support for the Protestant Ethic, indicated by opinions such as these:

> Our society would have fewer problems if people had less leisure.
>
> Most people who don't succeed in life are just plain lazy.
>
> People who fail at a job have usually not tried hard enough.

A second test was designed to measure people's support for egalitarianism, indicated by statements like these:

> One should be kind to all people.
>
> Because we are all human beings, there should be equality for everyone.
>
> Prosperous nations have a moral obligation to share some of their wealth with poor nations.

In addition to assessing which ideals are most important to an individual, Katz and Haas also assessed each person's pro-black and anti-black attitudes, determined by asking people to respond to statements such as the following:

> Black people do not have the same employment opportunities that whites do.
>
> Many whites show a real lack of understanding of the problems that blacks face.
>
> On the whole, black people don't stress education and training.
>
> Blacks should take the jobs that are available and then work their way up to better jobs.

The next step in their research program was to relate people's views regarding equality (the test of egalitarianism) and the Protestant Ethic with their pro-black or anti-black attitudes. Results suggested that equality was correlated with pro-black attitudes, while the Protestant Ethic position was correlated with anti-black attitudes. In other words, Katz and Hass found that people who felt that egalitarian ideals are important tended to be more supportive of blacks, while people who felt that Protestant Ethic ideals supporting individual freedom take priority tended to be more anti-black in their attitudes.

Research reported by Sidanius and his colleagues (e.g., 1994, 1996) tends to confirm these same findings: People who favor a ranking view of society tend to harbor the strongest prejudice toward out-groups, including a tendency to be both sexist and racist.

Back to Rokeach: The Value Confrontation Approach

At this point, it should be clear why Rokeach selected the two central values of freedom (his version of the Protestant Ethic, ranking, or self-enhancement) and equality (his version of egalitarianism, linking, or self-transcendence). Rokeach reasoned that if people valued freedom more than equality, then they might be less likely to support policies designed to improve the lot of blacks and other minorities. On the other hand, if they ranked equality higher than freedom, or if they could be induced to change in this direction, then their prejudicial views toward blacks and other minorities might well be reduced.

Armed with this idea, Rokeach developed what has been referred to as his *value confrontation* model of change, which utilizes the following steps:

1. People are given a list of values and are asked to rank-order them from most to least important to them. People usually rank freedom significantly higher than equality, with an average discrepancy of some 5 to 7 ranks.
2. People are then given some information in a brief lecture that informs them about their own rankings and those of other people like themselves. They are told about the finding that freedom is typically ranked higher than equality.
3. People are then told that in general, those who rank freedom higher than equality are more interested in freedom for themselves than for others.
4. Finally, after the preceding three steps have been completed, their attitudes on a variety of issues involving race relations, minority relations, and prejudice are assessed, usually at time points varying from about a week to up to a year or even more.

Some 27 studies have been conducted employing this value confrontation technique (see Grube, Mayton, & Ball-Rokeach, 1994), including research conducted both in the laboratory and at least in one case on a television program entitled "The Great American Values Test" that was broadcast in eastern Washington State. A consideration of these 27 studies as discussed by Grube and his colleagues (1994) suggests that the value confrontation technique successfully changed people's value rankings (96% success), their attitudes toward minorities (73% success), and their actual behaviors (56% success). Although changing either prejudiced attitudes or prejudiced behavior was less successful than changing the value rankings themselves (e.g., 73% and 56% versus 96%, respectively), the value confrontation approach is nevertheless an impressive demonstration of how a change in certain key values can have an impact, however modest in some cases, on people's views of minorities and in their actions (e.g., enrolling in ethnic studies courses; joining political action groups seeking to improve interracial relations). As Grube and his fellow researchers note, the changes they describe occurred not just immediately after the value confrontation procedure—but endured for months or in some cases years afterwards (e.g., 21 months or nearly 2 years later).

Altemeyer's Research With Value Confrontation

Using this same value confrontation approach, Altemeyer (1994) reports comparable findings. For example, in September 1989, his introductory psychology students at a Canadian university initially ranked freedom higher than equality. Several months later, in March 1990, Altemeyer introduced the value confrontation lecture. Seven weeks afterwards, he both reassessed their value rankings and evaluated their attitudes toward a minority relations issue confronting their campus: providing special scholarships each year to native students.

Altemeyer found a significant improvement in the students' willingness to agree with this proposal, even among those who had been assessed to be high in authoritarianism. In other words, even high authoritarians moderated their views about this minority group relations issue. In December 1990, Altemeyer did a further follow-up with the same students. Were the effects originally obtained still present? They were! Being suspicious, however, Altemeyer replicated the entire procedure with another group of students the next year, finding confirmation for the same effect: Value confrontation changed students' rankings of the values of freedom (it dropped) and equality (it increased); and most significantly, with these value changes came changes of a lasting nature in the students' prejudices. They too decreased.

Sagiv and Schwartz: Willingness for Contact

Recall that Schwartz proposed a model of value organization that had several important similarities with the Rokeach model we have been considering, as well as an important difference. Both Schwartz and Rokeach suggested the importance of the distinction between personal values and social values. Rokeach referred to the former as freedom and the latter as equality, while Schwartz referred to the former as self-enhancement and the latter as self-transcendence.

Unlike Rokeach, however, Schwartz also uncovered a second value-cluster involving, as he termed it, openness to change versus conservation: The former expressed an individual's willingness to take risks and seek stimulation, while the latter emphasized the high priority individuals placed on security.

Sagiv and Schwartz (1995) used this two-structure model to examine the nature of prejudicial relations between groups. They reasoned that people's value priorities would either increase or decrease their likelihood of favoring contact between themselves and members of a group with which they otherwise had a hostile relationship—for example, the willingness of Israeli Jews to have contact with Israeli Arabs.

Specifically, they predicted that Israeli Jews who value openness to change would be more likely to welcome the potentially unsettling contact with Israeli Arabs than those who strongly value conservation. Their research generally supported this prediction: Those Israeli Jews who ranked the openness values more highly than the conservation values expressed a greater willingness to have contacts with the Israeli Arabs.

Sagiv and Schwartz next reasoned that those who highly value self-enhancement might either favor contact, because it would enlarge the number of people they could control, or oppose contact, because it would dilute their own powerful social positions. Thus no clear prediction could be made. On the other hand, those who highly valued self-transcendence should clearly favor contact. Again, their data for Israeli Jews supported this prediction.

Sagiv and Schwartz also compared their findings with some that Rokeach (1973) reported earlier involving the willingness of American whites to invite or to avoid contact with American blacks. Although as we have seen, Rokeach's list of values differs in certain ways from Schwartz's, there are sufficient parallels to permit comparisons to be made. For example, Rokeach's value of equality corresponds to Schwartz's value-cluster of self-transcendence; Rokeach's value of security corresponds with Schwartz's value-cluster of conservation.

According to Sagiv and Schwartz, their own and Rokeach's findings are quite similar. Both Israeli Jews and American whites who favor self-transcendence and equality tend to be more open to interethnic or interracial contacts than those who favor freedom and self-enhancement.

To this point, we have examined the role of values in either supporting or challenging prejudiced attitudes and discriminatory practices. We have seen that the systems of values described by Rokeach, by Altemeyer, and by Schwartz, while differing in certain respects, offer parallel predictions about the role of values in prejudice. Both Rokeach and Altemeyer used a value confrontation technique to challenge people's ranking of the two central values, freedom and equality. They found not only that the relative ranking of these values could be changed, but that with such change came a reduction in prejudice (e.g., when equality increases as a priority and freedom decreases, prejudice decreases). From Schwartz and his associates, we learn that certain values—especially those favoring both openness to change and self-transcendence—improve the willingness of persons who hold these values to be open to intergroup contacts of the sort that might reduce prejudicial relations. In contrast, those who favor values of conservation are less interested in having these contacts with differences.

Religious Values and Prejudice

It has become a near truism in our current era that people who are highly religious tend to use that religion in very uncharitable and exclusionary ways to deny rights to others. We have already glimpsed this possibility when we examined the role of Protestant Ethic values in supporting racism and anti-black sentiments among white Americans; when we presented Schwartz's finding that Israelis who favor tradition, including religious tradition, tend not to want intergroup contact; and when we discussed the connection between Christian Identity ideology and extreme hatred of Jews, blacks, and homosexuals. And, as even a cursory consideration of history teaches us, many wars have been fought because the followers of one religion want theirs to dominate all others, even if it demands the brutal destruction of all "nonbelievers."

As we further examine the connection between religious values and prejudice, however, we will see that the situation is a bit more complex than the preceding explanation suggests. Religion is neither simply related to affirming prejudice nor to challenging it. (Figure 7.1 previews and summarizes the

Figure 7.1
Religious values and prejudice: A complex story

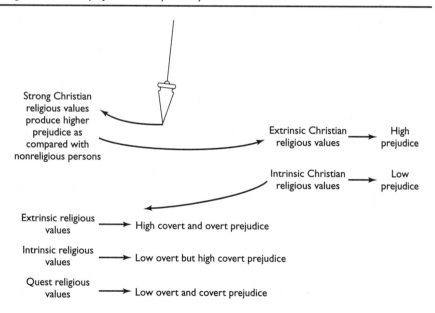

relationships between religious values and prejudice.) Let us now look more closely at both the theory and the data that make this picture complex.

Take One

Gordon Allport was one of the first to document a relationship between religious values and prejudiced attitudes. In their pioneering study, for example, Allport and Kramer (1946) found that students with a strong religious orientation (Protestant or Catholic) were more prejudiced against blacks than those without any strong religious affiliation or interest.

Reporting several decades later in 1982, Batson and Ventis (see Batson & Burris, 1994) found that results from 34 of 44 separate investigations support Allport and Kramer's finding of a positive relationship between prejudice and a person's involvement in religion. These data make it appear reasonable to conclude that religious values do not follow the Golden Rule—that is, not love and acceptance, but increased intolerance and prejudice go along with strongly held religious values.

Take Two

But, even Allport had some doubts about the meaning of this relationship. He suggested that perhaps there were different *ways* of being religious. He offered two: A person could be *extrinsically religious,* using religion less as something deeply believed in than as something to serve useful social purposes. Or, a person could be *intrinsically religious* because of deeply held faith.

People who value religion extrinsically use it as a tool to some other ends. For example, going to church for them means being seen as good, upstanding citizens engaging in civic responsibilities essential for business and social life. People who value religion intrinsically, by contrast, hold their faith as an end in itself, as central to the very person they are. If research could be shown to demonstrate that the extrinsics are prejudiced while the intrinsics are not, then religion as a way of approaching the world might be saved from the bad press it had originally received and the negative light in which it is often currently seen.

In their review of the relevant literature, Batson and Ventis (see Batson & Burris, 1994) find support for this expectation. Extrinsically religious people were more prejudiced than intrinsically religious people. Batson and Burris, however, remained unconvinced even by these findings. They wondered if perhaps something else might be operating here to make the intrinsics appear less prejudiced. And the search for that "something else" leads us to a further complication in the relationship between prejudice and religious values.

Seeking Social Approval

Batson and Burris suggested that in addition to the *way* in which people hold religious values, it might also be important to examine the *kinds of belief* that their religions advocate. Some religions, for example, are very clear in their condemnation of any and all kinds of prejudice, while other religions teach that because certain groups engage in so-called unnatural acts (e.g., homosexuals) or are clearly anti-God (e.g., communists), prejudice against such groups is appropriate. Batson and Burris wondered if perhaps people who are intrinsically religious merely seek to conform to their church's teachings so as to appear to be good church members. In short, perhaps the apparently unprejudiced viewpoint of intrinsically religious people is less a genuine tolerance for others than it is a desire to appear to be whatever kind of good person their particular church requires (i.e., social approval rather than genuine tolerance might be involved).

Batson and Burris evaluated several direct and indirect ways of examining this possibility. In one investigation, for example, they report a conformity effect rather than a genuine absence of prejudice on the part of the intrinsics: They were prejudiced when their church gave them permission to be prejudiced; they were unprejudiced when being unprejudiced was favored by their church.

Batson and Burris next wondered if the true colors of the intrinsics would show up even more clearly if there were a more subtle way of assessing prejudice. That is, if intrinsics are concerned with social approval—but if you measure prejudice in such a way that they have no clues about what is expected of them and thus no clues about how they are supposed to look in order to be socially approved—they might reveal the prejudices they really feel. Batson and Burris find support for this argument using a complex measure of prejudice involving *attributional ambiguity*.

Consider the following situation. Your behavior in a given situation is being observed by others, thus making you especially concerned about how you will appear to these observers. The situation, however, permits you to behave in a prejudicial manner and get away with it, because it does not appear to be motivated by prejudice but by something more reasonable that the observer will surely understand. What specifically occurred was to invite subjects to select a film to watch, showing in one of two theaters. For half of the subjects, both theaters were showing the same film; for the other half, a different film was being shown in each theater. For half, a black person was already sitting in the theater; for the other half, a white person was already sitting in the theater.

Now, let us suppose that you are sufficiently prejudiced not to want to sit in the same theater with a black person, but do not wish to appear to be prejudiced. If each theater is showing a different film, then you can claim that your decision to avoid the theater with the black person is not because a black person is there, but rather because you prefer the film in the other theater. In other words, the situation is sufficiently ambiguous that your choice might not mean prejudice, but rather, film preference.

Employing this design, Batson, Flink, Schoenrade, Fultz, and Pych (1986) found that when both theaters show the same film, and thus when the excuse is unavailable and so your prejudice will show clearly to everyone, intrinsically oriented religious people reveal no preference for theaters. However, when each theater shows a different film, and thus genuinely prejudiced persons can conceal their prejudice in the guise of a film preference, the religiously intrinsic people clearly reveal a preference for the film showing in the theater with a fellow white person already seated. This led Batson and his colleagues to conclude that rather than considering intrinsics to be the truly unprejudiced among the religious folks, they are in fact also highly prejudiced but careful to cover their prejudices so as to appear in conformity with whatever policies their religion advocates.

Any Hope for Religion?

Where does all of this leave us? Is there no hope of redeeming religion from the clutches of prejudice? A third way of being religious offers the hope some seek. This third way (extrinsic and intrinsic are the first two) is referred to as the *quest orientation,* which research reveals to be genuinely both religious and unprejudiced (e.g., see Batson & Schoenrade, 1991a, 1991b; Hunsberger, 1995). Quest people take their religion as an ongoing challenge, a search for answers. Unlike the extrinsics, quests do not use their religion to accomplish other goals; unlike the intrinsics, quests do not find the answers to all of life's issues in their religion. Rather, religion for quests is just that—a quest, a search, a process of exploration.

On closer inspection, quests turn out to be more open to experience (a familiar value dimension) and generally less in search of some absolute truth to guide them. They are involved in a never-ending search process. They are seeking answers wherever they may find them. In short, quests seem to take their religion both seriously and yet in an open and inquiring manner. They are not captured by a single set of unfailing beliefs, but remain open to exploration, challenge, discernment, and change. Research evidence suggests that quests are significantly less prejudiced than the other forms of religious orientation we have considered.

What can we fairly conclude, then, about the link between religion and prejudice? Well, the story is quite complex and undoubtedly in need of even more research than has thus far been conducted. The initial finding that highly religious people are also highly prejudiced required modification, because only some of these highly religious people were found to be highly prejudiced (the extrinsics); others (the intrinsics) seemed not to be prejudiced. In time, however, even that position had to be modified in light of research indicating that intrinsics are not tolerant people, but rather are driven by their need for social approval, and so take on the coloring of whatever their church requires of them. In terms of the values presented by most world religions, therefore, such people are not truly tolerant. This leaves only one group—those for whom religion is a quest—as open, tolerant, and unprejudiced.

Chapter Summary: Key Learning Points

1. Values involve principled beliefs that lie deeper and spread more broadly than a person's specific attitudes and that operate as standards by which people measure their own and others' actions.

2. Two key values identified by Rokeach have been found to be connected to prejudiced attitudes: freedom and equality.

3. Freedom fits a general tendency to value a hierarchical or ranking model of society (Sidanius) or a tendency toward self-enhancement (Schwartz), whereas equality better fits an egalitarian or linking view of society (Sidanius) or a tendency toward self-transcendence (Schwartz).

4. A person's preference for freedom over equality has been found to be connected with prejudiced attitudes toward various other groups in society; a preference for equality over freedom has been found to be connected with the absence of such prejudiced attitudes toward others.

5. Rokeach and Altemeyer have used a value confrontation technique to change people's value preferences, shifting freedom lower and equality higher. The technique first helps people discover their own value priorities, with evidence suggesting that most people initially tend to rank freedom higher than equality. A brief explanation helps people see how in ranking freedom higher than equality they are engaging in a selfish pursuit of freedom for themselves at the expense of others. After this confrontation with their own value preferences, people tend to show a lessening of earlier prejudices they held toward various typical targeted groups.

6. Religious values, primarily Christian religious beliefs, have been found to have a complex relationship with prejudice.

   a. Allport originally found a positive relationship between strongly held religious beliefs and prejudiced attitudes toward several out-groups.

   b. Allport later modified his understanding of religion, distinguishing between those whose religion was primarily extrinsic (i.e., their religion was a means to other, nonreligious ends) and those whose religion was primarily intrinsic (i.e., their religion was an end in itself). Data suggested that it was the extrinsics, but not the intrinsics who were most prejudiced.

   c. Other investigators (e.g., Batson) challenged this understanding of intrinsics, arguing and generally finding that intrinsics were motivated to be accepted by their religious community and so would appear overtly to be without prejudice while covertly harboring strong prejudices.

d. Batson introduced a third form by which people might hold religious values, terming this third possibility quest (i.e., adopting religious values as an ongoing search for meaning and commitment). His data suggested that those for whom religion was a quest (and so neither extrinsic or intrinsic) tended to be both highly religious and yet without prejudice toward others.

Chapter 8

Cognition and Prejudice, I: Categorization and Stereotyping

The study of cognition has become of monumental importance in all of psychology today, including in the study of prejudice. When I speak of cognition, I am asking us to focus on *how* people think and process information, on *how* the human mind operates in dealing with the many tasks we confront in our daily lives.

From the moment we awaken in the morning until we go to bed at night, and perhaps even during our sleep, our minds actively process information, helping us make choices and providing meaning to our world. Was that the alarm ringing or the telephone? Was that a dangerous or a comforting sound at the door? Is that a friend or a stranger approaching from down the street? How can I tell if it's safer to fly or to drive? How do I know which car is the best one to buy? Which stereo?

This interest in cognition accomplishes a real about-face from the focus of Section 2, which sought answers to our questions about prejudice by looking at the nature of the stimulus object—that is, the characteristics of the targets of prejudice. The cognitive focus, on the other hand, directs us away from the stimulus itself and toward the way people define that stimulus. Cognition asks us to attend to the manner by which people's minds transform the stimuli around them into knowledge and understanding of the world in which they live.

Categorization: The Key to Cognitive Information Processing

If there is a key to understanding the role that cognition plays in prejudice, it lies in one central concept: categorization. Several examples of categorization will give us a general sense of this concept before we apply it to the study of prejudice. George Lakoff (1987) provocatively entitled one of his major books *Women, Fire and Dangerous Things,* in order to introduce us to the importance of categorization as a basic cognitive process:

> The title of this book was inspired by the Australian aboriginal language Dyirbal, which has a category, *balan,* that actually includes women, fire, and dangerous things. (p. 5)

What Lakoff's title tells us is that there is a place in the world in which three items that to us may appear to have no common bond are lumped together into one category; items we would never group together are so classified in Dyirbal. And to consider women, fire, and dangerous things as elements of the same category is to treat them all in similar ways.

Here is another example, from another place and time, but illustrative nevertheless of the importance of the central cognitive process of categorization. The example was reported by the famous Russian psychologist A. R. Luria (1976). Luria conducted some of his studies among the peasant peoples living in the distant hinterlands of Russia in order to see if the conditions of their living influenced the way they came to think and categorize.

In one of the tasks he used, people were given a set of common objects and asked to say which ones went together and which were the "odd object out." For example, which of these four objects—a hammer, saw, log, and hatchet—fit together and which do not? A typical peasant argued that they *all* fit together because they are all needed. In other words, whereas we might exclude the log from our listing of "tools," for this peasant all four items fit the same category: He experienced them as all part of the same project.

Another subject was given the same type of classification task, but this time with a human grouping consisting of three adults and one child. Rather than doing as we might , excluding the child from the category of adult, this person insisted that they all go together because the child must stay with the others in order to help them out. Another peasant was given three wheels and a pair of pliers. We might lump the wheels into one category and the pliers into its own. Not the peasants studied by Luria, for whom the pliers, as different appearing as they might seem to us, are nevertheless said to part of the same category as wheels because pliers may be needed in order to repair any loose wheels!

The point of the preceding examples is to demonstrate that how people categorize things, making one group out of some items and distinguishing them from items they categorize as different, is a basic—some would argue (e.g., Lakoff, 1987) *the* basic—process of human cognition. To understand how categorization occurs is to understand how the human mind operates in processing information; it is also to understand how we behave in the world based on how we have grouped or categorized the objects of that world. And, as Allport (1954), Tajfel (1969), and Hirschfeld (1996) remind us, categorization is not only a fundamental cognitive process, but also the basis for stereotyping and prejudice.

Three Points About Categorization

Before we proceed, three points need to be made about categorization.

Activity of the mind   First, categorization is an activity of the mind; it is not a principle by which the world itself comes organized. That is, if women, fire, and dangerous things seem to fit together into the same category, it is not because the world has ordained it. In fact, the natural world does not lump things very much at all (although the *cognitive* world of Dyirbal speakers does). In like manner, whether adults comprise a separate category from children or tools a separate category from logs is not determined because of the way the world is arranged, but rather because of the way the mind operates to group some things together and to separate those things from other groupings. We create the groupings and categories of our world (see Rosch & Lloyd, 1978). And thus, because it is the person doing the categorizing—rather than the nature of the objects being categorized—that is important, we must probe the cognitive processes by which categorization is accomplished.

Culturally shared process   Second, the methods used in categorization tend to be culturally shared rather than peculiar to an individual person. To combine women, fire, and dangerous things into one category is not the solo act of an individual, but rather the act of a language community and thus is culturally shared among the speakers of that language. Likewise, what Luria hoped to demonstrate in comparing the way Russian peasants categorize objects with the way more literate Russians do was to show how the social and cultural environment organizes our understandings in ways we share with others within that same environment.

When we apply the idea of categorization to the study of prejudice, we will see that the way people group other people into categories of "similar" and "different" is less a matter of their own peculiar worldview than of the way in which their culture accomplishes such groupings.

An intriguing example that illustrates the foregoing point is now emerging as an issue in the United States. Assume that a black man marries a white woman and they have a child. That child grows up and goes to school where she is asked to check off her racial category on a form she is to complete. Which category does she check? Is she black or white? Many would argue that she is expected to check black, for that is what she really is. In fact, what she "really" is represents a cultural decision about people's racial groupings, a decision that most of us share with others in our culture (see Hirschfeld, 1996).

This issue is now becoming somewhat contentious. A growing number of multiracial couples demand that in responding to official requests (e.g. census forms) they not be required to make a choice between options that do not fit their children's situation. They want another category introduced: "interracial." If that option is someday provided, this again will demonstrate the culturally shared quality of all category systems.

As you might anticipate, there is even a political side to this issue of cate-gorization. Some groups are concerned that the use of a new "interracial" cate-gory will dilute the influence of specific ethnic categories in shaping public policy and in allocating resources. For example, if all the offspring of black-white couples are currently classified as black, and if certain government bene-fits are provided as a function of the percentage of blacks within a given area, then those benefits will be lost if the new category of interracial (replacing the category of black) becomes the one used to describe their offspring.

Hirschfeld (1996) has conducted some intriguing research, designed to de-termine the age by which children acquire their culture's system for categoriz-ing people by race. He assumes that racial categories (e.g., the sorting of peo-ple by skin color) are not based on something natural but rather are, as we earlier maintained (in Chapter 2), a product of culture. What would children of various ages say if you presented them with either a monoracial couple (e.g., white man and white woman; black man and black woman) or a biracial cou-ple (e.g., white man and black woman; black man and white woman) and asked them to choose, from an array of possibilities, the "type" of child the couple would produce? How would each age group respond?

Hirschfeld reported that "not surprisingly, the overwhelming majority of children (90% of the second graders, 92.3% of the sixth graders) and all of the adults expected the white couple to have a white child and the black couple to have a black child" (p. 168). The interesting findings, however, involved the ways in which the children dealt with the interracial couple's offspring:

Second graders showed no particular bias toward assuming that a mixed-race couple would produce either a black or a white child.

Second graders, however, did reveal a gender bias: They assumed that a white mother and black father would produce a white baby, whereas a black mother and white father would produce a black baby.

Unlike the adults, sixth graders seemed to assume that the infant produced by an interracial couple would be white.

Adults tended to select black as the interracial couple's offspring, conform-ing in general to the old one-drop rule (i.e., one drop of black blood makes the person black; see Chapter 2).

Overall, Hirschfeld's data suggest that as children mature within a culture, they begin to behave more and more like the adults in that culture in their manner of sorting people by race. The research also helps us better see that racial categories are determined less by the visual inspection of the other per-son than by applying culturally learned rules to others: In other words, race is more a matter of culture than nature.

Assimilation vs. differentiation   A third key feature of categorization that is central to our interest in the relation between cognition and prejudice involves the dual processes of assimilation and contrast (or differentiation). Items that are grouped together tend to take on the appearance of being more alike than they may actually be; this is referred to as *assimilation*. Items that are placed in different categories tend to have their differences exaggerated; this is referred to as *contrast* or *differentiation*. Another way of putting this is to say that if we categorize hammer, saw, and hatchet together into one group we call "tools," then we are likely not only to emphasize the ways in which they are similar, but also to exaggerate their differences from items we have classified as "materials on which tools operate" (logs, lumber, wallboard, etc.). In other words, things grouped together are generally experienced as more similar to one another than they would otherwise be, and things not classified together appear to be more different than they would otherwise be.

Suppose we categorize into one grouping all people who have brownish-tinted eyes and into another grouping all people who have bluish-tinted eyes. Assimilation tells us that we will tend to see a greater similarity among those we have grouped together as brown-eyed, and contrast tells us that we will exaggerate the differences between them and those we have grouped together as blue-eyed. We do this not because items within a category are *in fact* similar or because items between categories are *in fact* different, but rather because once we organize our world into categories, the tendency is to increase the similarity among things within a category and to exaggerate the contrast with things from a different category.

Now that we have in mind some of the essentials of the cognitive process of categorization, we can move directly into examining the relationship between categorization and the process that most of us intuitively know is related to prejudice—namely, stereotyping.

Stereotypes and Categorization

In 1922, journalist Walter Lippmann used a technical term from printing—stereotype (printing from a form that reproduced an endlessly unchanging product)—to refer to those "pictures we carry in our heads" about various groups of people. A stereotype was said to conform "very little to the facts it pretends to represent and results from our defining first and observing second" (Katz & Braly, 1952/1933, p. 68). Both the idea and the term caught on. The concept captured a growing awareness of the way people deal with differences by forming ready-made judgments about others and then using these judgments "to categorize people into social groups" (Stephan, 1985, p. 600). Stereotypes clearly involve categorization: People place other people into groups or categories and then relate to them as reflections of the category. Much of the early work on stereotypes focused on their content. That is, what descriptions of others did these pictures in our heads contain?

Stereotype Content

In 1933, Katz and Braly provided one of the earliest systematic investigations of stereotype content. They asked Princeton undergraduates for their ideas about 10 ethnic groups: Americans, English, Germans, Irish, Italians, Japanese, Jews, Chinese, Turks, and Negroes (the preferred term at the time). Their research method involved a *checklist technique,* whereby people were asked to select from a list of descriptive terms those they believe best describe the group in question.

Katz and Braly found both general agreement about these pictures in people's heads as well as differences among the students' judgments. For example, 78% of their sample said that Germans were scientifically minded, while 65% described Germans as industrious. Some other widely shared stereotypes included these: Italians are artistic (53%); the English are sportsmanlike (53%); Jews are shrewd (79%); Negroes are superstitious (84%) and lazy (75%); and Turks are cruel (54%).

An important point to be made about this original study is that the Princeton undergraduates had very little, if any, actual contact with the groups about whom they held these stereotypes. This suggests how important the general cultural climate is in "instructing" people in the content of group stereotypes. We know others less by actual contact with them than by contact with widely shared stereotypes about them.

As others have commented, however (e.g., Gardner, 1994), although 120 attributes were presented in the Katz and Braly (1952/1933) study, agreement by 50% or more of the subjects was not overwhelming—specifically, only 8 attributes were selected by more than 50% of the subjects. In other words, agreement about each group's stereotype was not uniformly high, opening questions about just how widely shared these pictures in our heads really are.

Later replications of Katz and Braly's original work—reported by Gilbert in 1951 and by Karlins, Coffman, and Walters in 1969—found a degree of consistency in each group's stereotype over time. Yet, Karlins and colleagues also found at least two new twists. First of all, many students protested against being asked to apply stereotypic labels, seeing these to be unwarranted generalizations about a group's characteristics. (Of course, this was 1969, when protests and defiance of authority and labeling were very high!) And secondly, while stereotypes did persist over time (from 1933 to 1969), some changes in their content were noteworthy. For example:

1. The stereotype for the subjects' own group, Americans, became somewhat less positive. The year 1969 was not a good one in terms of Americans feeling positively about their nation and its people.
2. The two groups against whom the United States fought in World War II—Germans and Japanese—produced some shifts in stereotypes. The Germans continued to be seen as industrious and scientifically minded, but a few more negative terms crept in, tempered, however, by a generally positive view overall. The Japanese stereotype revealed some

transformations over this time period. In 1933, the Japanese were seen in generally positive ways; this perception declined during the war years (they became sly and treacherous), but became positive again in the 1969 study.

3. Read what Karlins and associates describe as their findings for African Americans: "The most dramatic and consistent trend over the 25-year period has been the more favorable characterization of the Negro" (p. 8). In 1933, for example, 84% of the subjects described the Negro as superstitious; this declined to 13% in the 1969 study.

As Gardner is quick to note, however, "the majority of the students in all three studies did not subscribe to the stereotypes listed" (p. 5). Again, this suggests that those pictures in our heads may not be as commonly shared as was once thought.

Stephan, Ageyev, Stephan, Abalakina, Stefanenko, and Coates-Shrider (1993) suggest that this low level of general agreement cannot be blamed on the use of the checklist methodology. They find that different ways of assessing stereotypes produce roughly comparable judgments. Thus, our first conclusion about stereotype content based on this body of research is that these pictures in our heads are not as uniformly shared as we might otherwise suppose. Some group characteristics are widely shared within the larger culture; others are not.

A third finding of Katz and Braly's original studies demonstrated that not all stereotypes contain negative qualities; many are also positive. If we consider only those characteristics that Katz and Braly reported with more than 50% agreement, for example, we find that sportsmanlike, scientifically minded, industrious, and artistic are generally considered positive qualities, whereas superstitious, lazy, shrewd, or cruel tend to be more negative. The point, however, is that simply having a stereotype about a group does not necessarily mean that we think poorly of them. As the research has consistently demonstrated, stereotypes can be positive as well as negative. And, if we recall the definition of prejudice presented in Chapter 1, prejudices can and do involve both a positive as well as a negative biasing.

A further finding of the original Katz and Braly work was a general, though not perfect, consistency between the positive quality of the stereotype and the ranking of the group. Not surprisingly, their subjects preferred those groups who they believed possessed more positive than negative traits. On the other hand, when a measure of the clarity with which a group is stereotyped was correlated with these preferential rankings, the picture changed somewhat. The clearest group stereotype (for Negroes) and the most vague group stereotype (for Turks) were both related to low preferential rankings: Students said that both groups were "least desirable as companions or friends" (Katz & Braly, 1952/1933, p. 73). In other words, there is no simple correspondence between the clarity of those pictures in our heads and our preferences for various groups.

Cognitive and Behavioral Consequences of Stereotypes

The preceding work has focused primarily on the content of stereotypes. As noted, this was the primary interest of the early work, and for many it continues to be of substantial interest. With the cognitive turn in psychology, however, interest has shifted from stereotype content to (1) the consequences that follow once persons hold stereotypes, (2) the conditions under which people are likely to use stereotypes, and (3) the conditions under which stereotypes change and more accurate judgments about others are formed. The first issue asks us to consider the various effects that follow from categorizing people as members of groups with specific traits.

The Functions of Stereotypes for the Individual

Snyder and Meine (1994) argue that stereotypes serve three distinct functions for the individual:

1. In their cognitive function of categorizing persons into groups, stereotypes make our daily transactions with others easier. Some have described this role that stereotypes play in our lives by referring to stereotypes as the sluggard's best friend (Gilbert & Hixon, 1991, p. 509). In short, stereotypes are energy-saving devices (Macrae, Milne, & Bodenhausen, 1994).

2. In their ego-defensive function, stereotyping others negatively may help us feel better about ourselves. If blacks are lazy, then not only are my people hard workers, but this laziness explains their lesser standing in society compared to my group's standing.

3. Finally "stereotypes serve the social function of helping people fit in and identify with their own social and cultural in-groups" (Snyder & Meine, 1994, p. 36). Stereotypes help make my people different from your people (contrast effects) and so help solidify my in-group identification. We will have more to say on this idea in Section 4, when we deal directly with intergroup relations and prejudice.

It is the role of stereotypes in information processing (i.e., function 1), however, that has garnered the greatest interest among cognitive social psychologists.

Hamilton, Sherman, and Ruvolo (1990) offer a useful way of examining these cognitive consequences of stereotypes. They focus on three questions: (1) How do stereotypes influence our information processing? (2) How do stereotypes influence our information seeking and hypothesis testing? (3) How do stereotypes influence our social interaction? (Figure 8.1 summarizes the first two questions and the directions that answers have taken.)

The cognitive model is our guide in this chapter. According to that model, our task is to examine how people categorize items in their world—that is,

Figure 8.1

Some effects of stereotypes on cognition

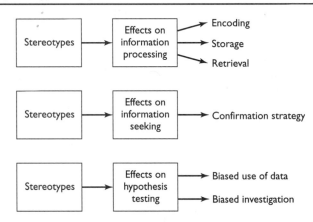

how people process information by categorizing it and then proceed to think and then to act on the basis of that now-categorized information. The *cognitive miser hypothesis* summarizes one of the central roles that stereotypes play in categorization and in thereby simplifying information processing.

The Cognitive Miser Hypothesis

I previously hinted at the cognitive miser hypothesis and the role that stereotypes play in this process when I described stereotypes as the sluggard's best friend. The argument is that because there is too much information in the world, we can never adequately deal with it without help. Stereotypes provide this help for us. By quickly and effortlessly categorizing people according to the stereotypes we hold about them, we cut down on the potential overload of stimuli that we would otherwise confront, and so make our everyday dealings with others move forward more easily.

In this view, therefore, to stereotype others is a normal and natural part of the very fact of being a human being who must use shorthand ways of processing information or suffer from overload. Even though stereotyping other people can interfere with getting to know them as individuals, and tends also to contribute to maintaining prejudice and discrimination, these negative outcomes are not the result of a pathological or sick mind; rather, they are the normal outcomes of normal minds processing information in a most economical manner.

Bodenhausen (1990) provides an interesting illustration of this miserly role that stereotypes serve. First, he determined whether individuals were morning or evening people. If you are a morning person, you are most alive and alert before noon; on the other hand, if you are an evening person, you come alive much later in the day. If stereotypes serve as energy-saving devices, which type of person do you think is more likely to use stereotypes in the morning? The morning or the evening person? And, which type is more likely to use stereotypes in the evening? The morning or the evening person?

Research results show that morning people, who are at their best before noon, tend to stereotype less in the mornings than later in the day. On the other hand, evening people, who come to life later in the day, seem to reserve their stereotyping for the morning. In other words, if it is true that stereotypes provide us with shorthand ways to process information about others, then presumably the less alert we are, the more likely we will be to employ these shorthand tools, while the more alert we are, the less likely we are to use them.

A similar argument was developed in the research reported by Macrae, Milne, and Bodenhausen (1994). They demonstrated how stereotypes simplify our interaction with others and make us more efficient information processors. Their research showed how using stereotypes helped people improve their performance on various other kinds of activities. This lends credence to the view that stereotypes are normal labor-saving devices that all of us routinely use to simplify our lives and free us up to take on other tasks efficiently. Without stereotypes, we would be less efficient in our daily activities: "Through the deployment of social stereotypes, perceivers are able to free up limited cognitive resources for the execution of other necessary or desirable activities" (p. 45).

While agreeing that stereotypes are the lazy person's tool, Gilbert and Hixon (1991) also suggest that laziness alone will not invariably produce stereotyping. They argue that we need to distinguish between *holding* a stereotype and *activating* that stereotype. They describe this difference as somewhat comparable to owning a tool that one can use (holding) versus actually locating that tool so that it will be used (activating). All of us have various stereotypes we hold about others stored away in our cognitive toolboxes. But if these stereotypes are not activated during a given encounter, they will not affect that encounter.

Gilbert and Hixon's research suggests that *cognitively busy individuals,* whom we might expect to be most likely to use stereotypes, do not invariably employ them because their very busyness interferes with their activating the stereotypes they hold. In other words, such people have stereotypes available, but in being so busy, they fail to activate them. In this case, busyness interferes with using the stereotypes that people have.

And so what would be a reasonable first conclusion? According to the cognitive miser hypothesis, stereotypes are a normal part of the human mind confronting a complex world. Stereotypes help to simplify this complexity and allow us to function more efficiently in the world. Yet, simply because we have stereotypes does not necessarily mean we will use them.

Interpreting Ambiguous Events

While the cognitive miser's view gives stereotypes a normal and even beneficial quality, those who have examined the role of stereotypes in shaping our interpretation of ambiguous events return quickly to their biasing functions. Research has repeatedly demonstrated that stereotypes lead us to interpret otherwise ambiguous events in a manner consistent with the stereotype.

Duncan (1976), for example, presented a group of white students with a videotape showing either a black student shoving a white student or another white student doing the shoving. These white observers saw the same action very differently depending on who did the shoving. Commonly shared stereotypes that blacks are violent apparently influenced how these white students interpreted the shoving. They "saw" the same shove as more violent when a black person did it than when a white student did the same act.

If we consider the several processes that take place in our perception of an event, we can better appreciate how stereotypes play a role at several different points. It is common to divide the process into three parts:

1. Encoding—how an event is taken in and perceived by the individual
2. Storage—how the perceived event is stored in memory
3. Retrieval—how the perceived and stored event is brought back at a later time

In any specific case, it is not always clear as to just what part of the process is implicated. What is clear, however, is that stereotypes can and do play a role in all three phases. Duncan's research, for example, suggests that the white students' stereotypes (that blacks were violence-prone) led them to encode the same act quite differently depending on whether a white or a black student was the perpetrator. Had the study been arranged differently, it is also likely that both storage and retrieval would also have been affected by the white students' stereotypes. Other research offers further demonstration of the effects of stereotypes on encoding as well as the other parts of this overall process.

Another study on the interpretation of ambiguity, primarily concerned with the spread of rumors, was undertaken by Allport and Postman (1952/1945), who examined the psychological processes that produced distortions in the accurate reporting of an event. Their description of the process of *assimilation* is quite similar to our understanding of the role that stereotypes play in encoding information. They described it as "the powerful attractive force exerted upon rumor by habits, interests, and sentiments existing in the listener's mind" (p. 167). Of all the many striking effects they observed, one of the most fascinating involved the following occurrence.

The initial experimental subject saw a complex picture. The picture showed a group of people standing or seated on a subway train. In one part of the picture, a white man and a black man were standing and talking to one another. The white man's left hand, which was resting on his hip, held an open straight razor, though not in a menacing way. The first subject saw this picture and gave a verbal description to the second subject, who had never seen it; the second subject then gave a description, now based on what he heard, to a third subject, and so on down the line. Here is the authors' statement about what happened to that razor in these repeated tellings:

> The most spectacular of all our assimilative distortions is the finding that, in more than half of our experiments, a razor moves (in the telling) from a white man's hand to a Negro's hand. . . . This result is a clear instance of assimilation to stereotyped expectancy. Black men are "supposed" to carry razors, white men not. (p. 168)

As noted, it is not simply in the encoding of information, but in its storage and especially in its retrieval, that we see the further biasing effects of stereotypes. Snyder (1982) reported an interesting study of this effect. Students first read a fictitious biography of a woman. The biography was intentionally ambiguous regarding the woman's sexuality. For example, it was reported that she rarely dated in high school but did have a steady boyfriend; in college, her steady was a friend rather than a lover.

A week after reading this biography, some of the students were told that the woman was living in a lesbian relationship with another woman, while others were told that she was now living with her husband. All were then asked about her life history. Although they all had read the same biography, those who were led to believe she was a lesbian *reconstructed* a biography for her that was consistent with their view of what a lesbian is like: In short, they "recalled" in ways that fit the stereotype they held about lesbians. For example, those who thought she was now a lesbian recalled that she never did have a steady boyfriend in college, thereby confirming their suspicions about her.

Work reported by Elizabeth Loftus (e.g., Loftus, 1979; Loftus & Hoffman, 1989) is perhaps the clearest in demonstrating what Loftus terms *reconstructive memory:* how the retrieval of stored information is profoundly influenced by events that occur *after* the event has occurred. We consider some of this work in the next section.

Information Seeking and Hypothesis Testing

The role of stereotypes in our information seeking and hypothesis testing activities is also fairly well known and predictable. If we hold a stereotype about someone, we are likely to employ that stereotype to guide the kinds of information we seek as well as the way we proceed to test the hypotheses we form about other people.

The Confirmation Strategy

Darley and Gross (1983) effectively demonstrated what they refer to as the *confirmation strategy* by which the stereotypes we hold lead us to seek primarily confirmatory evidence that will support rather than refute those already-formed pictures in our heads. In short, given our stereotyped expectations about others, we seek information about them that fits the stereotype. We can then leave our encounter feeling confident that our stereotype was indeed accurate.

Darley and Gross describe a two-stage process. Initially, the stereotype gives us a tentative hypothesis about what we are likely to find. The second stage involves our checking that hypothesis against our observations. However, insofar as those observations are guided by a confirmation strategy, we will "discover" information that supports rather than refutes the stereotype.

Darley and Gross presented subjects with a videotape of a fourth grade girl responding to problems on an achievement test. The subjects were asked to evaluate her academic performance. The videotape, however, was ambiguous about her actual performance. Half of the subjects were given information about the young girl that would lead them to see her as coming from a lower-class background, while the other half received information that would lead them to consider her as coming from a middle-class background. The idea was that the knowledge of the girl's social class would establish stereotyped expectations about her likely performance: poor performance expected for lower class; good expected for middle class.

Results were quite informative about the role that stereotypes play in each stage of the two-stage process. Those subjects who had been presented with the stereotype only—that is, were told only her social class background and were not shown the part of the tape in which they could observe her taking the test items—revealed very little impact of the stereotype on their judgments of her abilities. On the other hand, subjects who had received information on *both* her background and her performance were affected in their judgments about her academic ability. Specifically, those who expected her to do poorly rated her performance as lower than those expecting her to do well, but only when they saw her performance on the test items. In short, what happened was the use of a confirmation strategy in which subjects interpreted her performance in a manner that fit their stereotyped expectations. The same performance was rated differently to fit the expectations. This clearly also illustrates the same encoding effect we previously considered.

Biased Use of Data for Testing Hypotheses

Although the context was quite different, the results of another study also revealed people's preferences for a confirmation strategy. Crocker (1981) found that people prefer the kinds of information that will confirm rather than challenge their expectations. Suppose you are asked to obtain information that will test the hypothesis that the amount of tennis practice will influence the outcome of a match. What kinds of information might you wish to obtain? Crocker discovered that people preferred hypothesis-confirming information: They wanted information that would let them know whether a great deal of practice resulted in success while little practice resulted in failure. They did not want information that would provide a fair test of the actual relationship between practice and success. This would involve also learning about how many matches were won by people who had practiced very little and how many were lost by people who had practiced a great deal. In other words, people seem to prefer information that will confirm rather than test their hypotheses.

Schaller (1992) adds further to this picture by demonstrating how stereotypes about a particular group are confirmed by the manner in which we interpret data. Suppose, for example, you observe a large corporation in which men occupy more leadership positions than women, and you infer, therefore, that men make better leaders than women. Here you have two events that co-occur: one involves the category of gender (male or female), the other pertains to the person's position in the organization (leadership or not). There is a real correlation between these two. But if you fail to probe further to determine why that co-occurrence is present, you may be led to confirm your gender stereotypes rather than test them.

In a series of experiments, Schaller was able to demonstrate this effect. In one study, for example, both men and women were presented with an organizational chart with a built-in correlation between employees' gender and their leadership status in the organization. Subjects were then asked to develop some conclusions about the relation between gender and leadership ability and to indicate the basis on which they reached their conclusions. Results indicated that males were especially likely to use the correlational information without probing it further. For example, fewer than 10% of the male subjects said that they considered situational constraints or discriminatory hiring and promotion practices in reaching their conclusions about women's lack of leadership ability. On the other hand, a much greater percentage of women did not use this simple co-occurrence to infer a lesser ability on the part of women. We will return to this idea in the final section of this chapter when we explore what has been termed "the kernel of truth" hypothesis.

Biased Investigation

Let us now take a slightly different angle on many of these same processes. In the previous cases, we examined how observers are guided by the stereotypes they hold of others to use a confirmation strategy. In the next several cases, we consider how stereotypes can guide the kinds of questions that a person investigating a situation might ask. Here we will see how asking leading questions or providing subtle suggestions can lead an investigator to construct a stereotype-confirming "truth" rather than conduct an unbiased test designed to discover the truth.

Work on eyewitness identification as well as some suggestions about what is involved in the recovered memory debate both suggest how biased information-seeking strategies might be implicated. Recall Elizabeth Loftus's idea that memory is a reconstructive process affected by what occurs after an event has taken place. Loftus (1992) has demonstrated how witnesses may be led to confirm the investigator's hypothesis by the manner in which they are interviewed. For example, people are shown photos of a simulated traffic situation and are asked to report what they see. Some, however, are "misled" by the investigator's manner of asking questions. People say that a car is going much faster when the investigator uses phrases such as "running a stop sign" or "smashing into the other car," rather than some other, more neutral phrasing. In other words, the biased phrasing of the questions leads people to reconstruct what they report having taken place so as to fit the bias of the questions.

Loftus also reports that the more subtle the leading question, the more effect it will have in distorting witness responses. Compare the phrasing in the following two questions: (1) Was the mustache worn by the tall intruder light or dark brown? (2) Did the intruder who was tall and had a mustache say anything to the professor? By "hiding" the mustache in a more complex phrase (i.e., question 2), more people are likely to report that the actually clean-shaven person they saw had a mustache.

Although neither of Loftus's studies involves the direct influence of stereotypes on an investigator's information-seeking activities, it is easy to see how an investigator who has particular stereotypes about racial groups, for example, might ask leading questions of witnesses that confirm stereotype-generated hypotheses. Therefore, an investigator—who may not even be aware of how the phrasing of questions shapes the answers obtained—might confirm beliefs about blacks as shoplifters or criminals, obtaining confirmation from well-meaning witnesses whose testimony about what they saw is reconstructed in response to the way questions were asked.

Loftus (1993) employed much this same form of analysis in her accounts of what might be taking place in the debates over the reality or distortive quality of so-called recovered memories. Perhaps the most striking case of this involved the conviction of George Franklin (it was later reversed) for a crime he supposedly committed some 20 years earlier, based primarily on the testimony of his own daughter, who had "recovered" a memory of her father killing a young friend of hers; this memory had been confirmed during her therapy sessions. Similar recoverings during therapy have led to others being accused of abuse, incest, and even satanic rituals.

The issue that Loftus addressed is whether such recovered memories are memories of actual events that occurred (as supporters and their therapists maintain) or reconstructions created out of biased information seeking and question phrasing. Loftus's own position, based on her years of research on question asking that is designed less to obtain the truth than to confirm a hypothesis, is one of skepticism.

For our own purposes, this work suggests that biased information seeking can *create* memories, even with rich details, of events that never took place. As Loftus says, "New, postevent information often becomes incorporated into memory, supplementing and altering a person's recollection" (1993, p. 530). In other words, the way an inquiry is conducted may lead people to recall past events with great conviction about their truth, even if nothing of the sort recalled ever actually occurred. A therapist who profoundly believes that satanic abuse is rampant, for example, may make inquiries of patients that creates memories of such abuse even when it was absent. The confirmation strategy can thereby play itself out in a context, as the George Franklin case indicates, with very serious consequences.

The Kernel of Truth Hypothesis

We must now address a troublesome question: Is it not possible that many stereotypes (e.g., Germans are a highly efficient and well organized people; Japanese are truly gifted in math and science; Jews are genuinely good in business; blacks are good in sports; homosexual men are effeminate) contain a kernel of truth to them? The kernel of truth hypothesis, then, asks whether those stereotypes that people commonly hold about their own and other groups may in fact be partially accurate. If this is the case, then perhaps it follows that stereotypes do not reflect a prejudiced understanding as much as a reasonably accurate perception of real group differences.

In his pioneering work on the psychology of prejudice, Gordon Allport (1950, 1954) proposed two critical questions about this hypothesis. The first question suggests that the hypothesis may involve a faulty causal interpretation of the facts. The second challenges the tendency to look inside the individual in order to explain behavior. Let us examine both ideas separately first before we combine them into a clear-cut challenge to the whole idea of "kernel of truth." (Figure 8.2 summarizes these issues.)

Faulty Causal Interpretations

The first issue raised by Allport tells us that while a stereotype about a group's characteristics may turn out to be reasonably accurate, the causal interpretation of these facts introduces some serious questions. For example, Swim (1994) reports that people's stereotypes about men and women tend to be more true than false. To establish this, Swim compared people's stereotyped images of men and women with research findings that described the actual scores of men and women on tests measuring their traits. People turned out to

Figure 8.2

The kernel of truth hypothesis

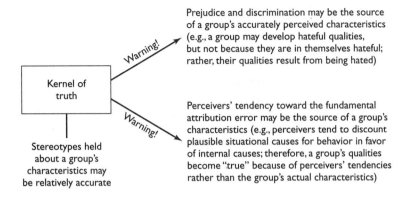

be reasonably good judges of male and female characteristics. In other words, there is a kernel of truth to people's judgments about what men and women are like. And so, if systematic studies reveal that men are indeed more assertive and women more passive and if, as Swim demonstrated, people accurately perceive these to be qualities that men and women possess, then we would have to say that there is a kernel of truth to their perceptions. They are seeing accurately and not in a distorted or biased manner. Surely no prejudice here!

The question of causal interpretation that Allport noted enters at this point. How did those traits, now accurately perceived, get to be characteristics of men and women? Are men assertive and women passive because that is simply the way each gender is, in some fundamental and essential way? Or, is male assertiveness and female passivity better understood as a *consequence* of particular life experiences that produce passivity in one group and assertiveness in the other?

In a paper exploring just this issue of the causal interpretation of the "facts" of sex differences, Riger (1997) raised much this same point. She described what she termed the "differently situated" argument: While there are male-female differences of the sort that many social stereotypes accurately capture, these may better be seen as the result of the typical social status of men (dominant) and women (subordinate) rather than anything more fundamental about their essential character.

The question of causal interpretation that both Allport and Riger raise is one involving the direction of causality. Do the traits of men and women that may be accurately perceived cause the different destinies they face, or is the direction of causality reversed? That is, perhaps men's and women's destiny in life causes the kinds of stereotypic descriptions that they come to have.

Allport readily recognized that the causal direction of interpreting the "facts" was a central issue when he observed, for example, that people in minority groups might have developed "certain defensive characteristics simply because people in the dominant group persistently refuse to treat them as individuals according to their personal merits" (1950, p. 8). Under these conditions, the stereotypic traits that a group comes to have may not be the *cause* of any prejudice directed toward them, but rather may be a *consequence* of that very prejudice.

Eagly's social role interpretation   Alice Eagly (1987, 1995; Eagly & Steffen, 1984; Eagly, Karau, & Makhijani, 1995) has devoted a considerable amount of her professional work to examining the issue of cause versus consequence in the case of stereotypes about women and men. Her arguments are equally informative about other group differences we may encounter.

Eagly refers to her theory as the *social-role theory of sex differences.* She makes two key points. First, before we assume that the stereotypic characteristics we observe about a group involve something basic or essential about the members of that group, we should pause to consider the kinds of social roles that these group members have typically occupied. And so, for example, before we assume that men are skilled leaders while women are not, we might do well to consider the frequency with which men have occupied leadership positions and the infrequency with which such roles have been occupied by women. This tells us that the differences we observe may not be about essential characteristics of men and women as much as about social discrimination that leads people to take on certain roles and not others and to acquire the characteristics most suitable to those roles.

This then brings us to her second point: "As a general tendency people are expected to engage in activities that are consistent with their culturally defined gender roles" (Eagly et al., 1995, p. 126). What this means is that all of us are under social pressure to behave in ways that are congruent with our social roles. Insofar as many leadership roles are said to require stereotypically masculine characteristics of aggressiveness and assertiveness, women who occupy leadership positions may receive negative responses for acting in role-congruent but gender-incongruent ways. This involves the well known tendency to describe a meeting of men as a discussion and of women as gossip, to describe forceful men as being assertive and forceful women as pushy and bitchy.

Eagly's social role theory thereby tells us that while a group's characteristics may fit the cultural stereotype—there is a kernel of truth to them—this is the consequence of certain social processes that very likely involve prejudice and discrimination. A well known legal case captures much of this point and takes us one further step toward understanding the idea of cause versus consequence.

Sears vs. EEOC   This case involved a question of possible employment discrimination and opposed Sears Department Stores against the EEOC, the Equal Employment Opportunity Commission (see Scott, 1988). Did Sears engage in discrimination by not hiring women for the relatively lucrative commission sales jobs? Or, was it as Sears claimed, that women were less interested than men in such positions and that is why so few women were in commission sales? The EEOC called it discrimination, arguing that any differences between men and women in their expressed interests did not exist because of something fundamental about men and women, but rather resulted from years of discrimination that shaped women's interests.

This case highlights the cause-consequence issue involved in different interpretations of the same factual observations. Women are in fact hired far less often than men for the better paying jobs in commission sales. But, what does this mean? One possibility, argued by Sears's attorneys, is that this is not prejudice but rather reflects the real differences between men's and women's interests: Women are simply less interested than men in sales work. In other words, characteristics of the targeted groups *cause* the pattern of hiring that Sears's opponents label as discriminatory.

The other possibility, argued by the EEOC's attorneys, is that these differences in preferences are themselves the outcome of a long history of discriminatory hiring practices. In other words, the differences in male-female interests did not in any simple way cause the differential hiring rates, but were a consequence of differential hiring practices. To continue to follow preferences that are a consequence of prejudice, therefore, is to perpetuate a prejudicial and discriminatory policy.

As you can already tell, the matter is never simple. The point to be kept in mind from this chapter, however, is that even if a given judgment about a group's characteristics is found to be relatively accurate (i.e., contains a kernel of truth), these characteristics may be less the cause of discriminatory policies than the result or consequence of such policies.

Correspondence Bias: Fundamental Errors in Explanation

Let us now look at Allport's second idea. He noted that most of us tend to attribute our observations about other people to something about the people's characteristics rather than to their situation:

> For example, in deteriorated residential districts we are far more likely to see the Negro who lives there as disfiguring the district, than to perceive the district as disfiguring the Negro. (1950, p. 9)

This well known effect has been referred to as the *correspondence bias* (Gilbert & Malone, 1995) or the *fundamental attribution error* (e.g., Jones, 1990; Ross, 1977; Ross & Nisbett, 1990). It involves people's tendency to make inferences from their observations about someone's behavior to qualities that the person possesses rather than to circumstances. We will return to other forms of what have been referred to as attributional or explanatory biases again in Chapter 11. For now, the point to be kept in mind is that there is a general tendency, at least within U.S. culture, for people to attribute the causes of others' behaviors to something inside the other persons—that is, qualities, traits, or characteristics they possess—rather than to the situations they happen to be in.

A classic study has illustrated this biasing tendency (e.g., Ross, Amabile, & Steinmetz, 1977). People were asked to judge the skill of basketball players who had been randomly assigned to shoot free throws under poor lighting. The people tended to judge them as relatively less capable than players making free throws under good lighting conditions. In other words, although it would seem obvious that lighting (i.e., the situation) would influence a person's performance, observers nevertheless insisted that poor shooting meant less capable players!

Causal Interpretation and Attributional Bias: A Dangerous Combination

Let us now combine the interpretative problem with the correspondence bias in order to see just what we are up against. We will do this by leaving our basketball players in the background and returning to the case central to Eagly's argument. We observe men behaving more assertively than women. We attribute this trait to something about men and women, ignoring or discounting the circumstances of their lives that have produced this trait—the fact, for example, that women (like basketball players shooting in the dark) have been kept in the shadows for so long that they do not have the kinds of experiences that produce assertiveness.

Our tendency to discount people's circumstances and attribute their behavior to traits they possess—the correspondence bias or fundamental attribution error—produces the very error of interpretation that gives the kernel of truth hypothesis its appearance of validity. That validity, however, lies elsewhere. Where prejudicial attitudes and discriminatory behaviors are concerned, we can see how the kernel of truth about a given group, which we claim causes the destiny those people have, is a consequence of both their destiny and our search for internal causes. Prejudice and discrimination are thereby part of a vicious circle that cannot be broken as long as we rest comfortably and uncritically with what our observations tell us. Those observations require further examination.

Chapter Summary: Key Learning Points

1. Categorization is a basic cognitive process by which people learn how to sort the various objects in their world into groups or categories, leading them to perceive some things in their world as going together and being distinct from other things in their world. This describes a

feature of the mind at work rather than a feature of the world as such. That is, it is an activity of the mind, not a principle by which the world itself comes already organized.

2. As we grow up in a culture, we learn its primary ways of sorting people and things—including, for example, its way of sorting people by race. These are socially created, widely shared ways within a given culture of organizing its perceptions.

3. Items that fall within a category tend to be seen as more alike than they may actually be (referred to as assimilation), while items in different categories tend to have their differences exaggerated and so are seen as more different than they may actually be (referred to as contrast, or differentiation).

4. Categorization and stereotyping go together. Stereotypes refer to the "pictures in our heads," our mental images and descriptions of various groups of people.

    a. Initially, major interest focused on the content of social stereotypes of various groups.

    b. More recent work has been directed toward examining the role that stereotypes play in how we (1) process information, including its initial recording as well as later retrieval from memory; (2) seek information; (3) test hypotheses about our world; and (4) interpret what we discover. In each case, stereotypes tend to bias our understandings toward the confirmation of the stereotyped beliefs.

5. Stereotypes are said to play an important role in simplifying our understanding of others, acting as a kind of shorthand for categorizing the people we meet. This has been termed the cognitive miser hypothesis.

6. Stereotypes tend to be resistant to change. How we perceive, remember, and examine new information tends to conform to verifying existing stereotypes we hold rather than testing or challenging those stereotypes.

7. The kernel of truth hypothesis suggests that although many of our social stereotypes about others may have a degree of truth to them, some rather difficult interpretative work remains before we can justifiably act on the basis of even accurately held stereotypes.

    a. A stereotype may be true and yet be the consequence of prejudicial attitudes or actions, not the cause. To continue to act in light of the stereotype, therefore, is to succumb to faulty causal interpretations and thus to perpetuate the effects of prejudice rather than to challenge them.

b. The well known tendency of people to attribute or explain another's actions by seeking some intrinsic characteristic that the other possesses (termed the fundamental attribution error) increases the probability that we will fail to attend to the role that circumstances have played in causing the behavior, thereby confirming stereotyped judgments rather than testing or challenging them.

Chapter 9

Cognition and Prejudice, II: Stereotypes, Social Interaction, and Change

To this point, we have focused most of our attention on the role that stereotypes play in shaping our information processing—that is, how we encode, store, and retrieve information in conformity with the stereotypes we hold. But stereotypes also have important consequences for the way in which we interact with those people about whom we hold stereotypes. This chapter examines some of these effects on social interaction, especially, how the stereotypes we maintain about others often lead us to interact with them in prejudiced ways.

Let us begin with a benign situation before moving into more troubling territory. Clever Hans was a horse who reputedly could do simple arithmetic problems. If asked to multiply 2 times 3, the horse would use his foot to tap out the answer, 6. This would occur even when the owner was not present and presumably "giving" the horse the answer. How did this happen?

A group of reputable experts examined the horse and concluded that he must truly have an unusual ability, at least for a horse. It took another investigator, however, to uncover the real story. What was actually taking place was that those who believed that Hans was indeed clever and able to solve problems inadvertently gave him the answer. True believers would ask the question of Hans—"What is 2 times 3?"—and then turn their heads and eyes downward to gaze intently at his feet. In anticipation of hearing the correct answer, as the horse approached tapping out "6," they would lift up their heads very slightly. Hans's cleverness was in being able to "read" these head moves. He was clever all right, but not in simple arithmetic. Hans had been taught to stop tapping once he saw a head move up slightly in expectation of the correct answer.

The Self-Fulfilling Prophecy

Robert Rosenthal (1994, 1995; Rosenthal & Jacobson, 1968) took this idea and applied it in a real classroom situation (with people, not horses), testing whether teachers who had information given to them about some of their students would inadvertently act on that information to produce the effects that they had expected to come true. This effect is referred to as the *self-fulfilling prophecy.* It demonstrates how potent stereotypes can be in leading people to behave in ways that confirm their stereotyped expectations. (See Figure 9.1.)

In the original study, Rosenthal and his associate, Jacobson, gave a test to the children in one school, saying that the test was designed to measure a student's potential to succeed in school. Some of the students were then *randomly* chosen to be in the experimental group. Teachers were told that these students had scored high on the test (they actually scored no differently from other students) and so were expected to blossom intellectually during the term. No information was provided to the teachers about the other students. At the end of the school year, some 8 months later, all children were tested for their intelligence. Rosenthal and Jacobson discovered that the students whom the teachers had expected to succeed actually had a significant gain in their intelligence when compared with the other children! In other words, the teacher's expectancies had been fulfilled.

In spite of some critiques raised about that original study (e.g., Snow, 1995), Rosenthal reports that some 345 experiments using a similar approach have demonstrated repeated support for this same effect. In other words, expecting that someone will do well or poorly actually influences the way we interact with that person, so as to create an outcome that is consistent with our expectancy.

Figure 9.1
Some effects of stereotypes on social interaction

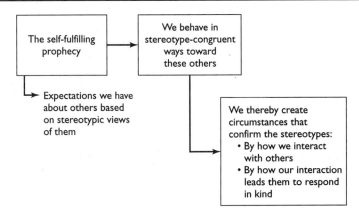

Imagine a teacher who has a classroom of mixed racial groupings and who holds stereotypes that black and Latino students are not likely to do well but that Asian and white students will succeed. Is it possible that the teacher's stereotyped expectations could subtly shape his behavior so as to produce the effects he anticipates? Yes, says Rosenthal. But how does this work?

Rosenthal has spent considerable time examining the mechanisms by which the expectancies are fulfilled, uncovering four major factors: (1) The emotional climate for the chosen students is much warmer, as communicated nonverbally by the teachers, than the climate created for the unchosen students. (2) Teachers appear to try to teach more material and more difficult material to the chosen students than to the others. (3) Teachers not only pay more attention to the chosen students, but also give them more time to respond to questions. (4) Finally, teachers give the chosen students more feedback designed to improve their performance. The first two factors have been found to be especially important.

Interaction Is a Two-Way Street

Here, then, we have a rather striking and indeed frightening look at how stereotyped expectancies concerning other people can shape how we behave with those other people, and so produce effects that fit the stereotype in the first place. But, the story here is complicated by the other side of the equation—namely, the other person. Snyder (1984; Snyder, Tanke, & Berscheid, 1977) reports some intriguing findings that demonstrate how holding a stereotype not only influences the way in which the holder behaves toward the target, but in turn, how the target also behaves.

In one of his studies, for example, Snyder paired off college-age men and women who were to get acquainted with one another via a telephone conversation. Before chatting, however, each man was shown a recent photo, presumably of the woman with whom he was about to talk. Half of the men were shown a photo of a very attractive woman; the other half, a woman judged to be less attractive. Before chatting, in other words, the men's stereotypes about attractive and unattractive women had been activated. But what effect did this have on (1) how the men interacted over the telephone with the women, and (2) how the women behaved in response to the men's actions toward them?

On both counts, Snyder found a significant effect of the stereotype. Men who anticipated talking with an attractive woman not only formed a stereotyped expectation of someone who was sociable, poised, and humorous, but they themselves were judged to interact in a warm and friendly manner. In turn, this behavior on the part of the men elicited behavior from the women that was in fact friendly and sociable. On the other hand, men who anticipated talking with an unattractive woman formed a stereotype of someone who would be awkward, serious, and socially inept; these men behaved toward them in a more cold and reserved manner, and in turn elicited a more aloof and distant response from these women. In short, the stereotype influenced both how the men interacted with the women and in turn how the women interacted in response to these differences in men's behavior. Snyder also reports that in a replication, women do much the same!

Other findings paralleling these but involving racial stereotypes have also been reported. By secretly videotaping interviews between white and black job applicants, for example, Snyder demonstrated that when talking with black applicants, white interviewers displayed grammatical speech errors and errors in pronunciation, as though they were talking down to the black applicant. In addition, they were generally less friendly and less outgoing with black as compared with white job applicants. This is the first step of the now familiar effect of stereotypes on people's way of interacting with others. The second step was also revealed in a related study. Here it was found that the blacks who had been treated stereotypically by the white interviewers responded by being more aloof and more nervous. This all translated into the simple fact that the blacks did not have a real chance to show their best qualifications, having been disrupted in their own behavior by being treated stereotypically by white interviewers. In their turn, the blacks' behavior confirmed the white interviewers' stereotypes about blacks, thereby justifying white-held stereotypes.

Stereotype Threat

Some recent research reported by Steele and Aronson (1995; also Steele, 1997) takes this process one step further in exploring what they describe as *stereotype threat:* the tendency of people who have been stereotyped to be fearful that they will fulfill the stereotype and who thereby fulfill it because of the disruption in their performance generated by their anxiety. In the study we just considered, black interviewees were made nervous by the white interviewers' behavior toward them and so did not perform as well as they might otherwise have. On the other hand, in the case of stereotype threat, it is not being made anxious by what the other person does, but rather being made anxious by one's own worries about confirming a stereotype.

To study this effect, Steele and Aronson had a group of both white and black students take a brief test based on items from the Graduate Record Exam. Half of each group took the test believing that it was a serious measure of their intellectual ability; the other half took the test believing that it was a general problem-solving exercise. When thinking that the test was a measure of their intellectual ability, blacks scored considerably lower than whites; on the other hand, when considering the test as a problem-solving exercise, blacks scored as well and at times better than the whites.

The interpretation of these and related results uses the idea of stereotype threat. Blacks have learned the cultural stereotype that blacks are not very sharp intellectually. If that stereotype is triggered whenever they are placed into a test-taking situation, they may become fearful of confirming the stereotype. This anxiety over their performance might interfere with their doing well, just as Steele and Aronson found. When the threat is diminished, however, their performance at a high level appears.

Steele (1997) has demonstrated a similar effect for other groups for whom the anxiety over fulfilling the stereotypes held about their group may interfere with their actual performances. For example, women and men who were good at math and identified themselves as being good participated in a study in which they were presented with a very difficult math test. Women scored lower than men on this difficult test, even though they were as equally qualified as the men. Steele suggests that this lowering of female performance occurred because of "the impairing effects of stereotype threat" (1997, p. 619). In other words, it was women's anxiety over fulfilling the stereotype that produced their lower performance. On the other hand, there was no difference in the math performance of men and women on a literature test. Steele's argument is that whereas math evokes the stereotype that women are poor performers and so produces the threat effect, because literature does not evoke any stereotype there is no comparable performance interference.

In another variation of this same approach, Steele represented the math test differently to equally qualified men and women. In one condition, for example, everyone was told that the test was a good device for assessing gender differences in math ability. In the other condition, everyone was told that no gender differences had been found on this test. It was assumed that the former instructions would evoke stereotype threat for women, negatively impacting their test scores, whereas there would not be any similar threat in the latter condition, leading them to score as well as men. Steele's findings clearly showed support for these ideas: Women scored lower than men when told that the test revealed gender differences but no differently from men when they believed that the test was not a measure of gender differences. These findings parallel the earlier findings we considered involving the effects of stereotype threat on the test performance of African Americans, suggesting that this may well be a very general phenomenon.

As he considered his findings for both African Americans and women, Steele (1997) offered some wise counsel to those who have established special programs designed to improve the test scores of both groups. He suggests that many of these efforts may backfire and lead to actual decrements in performances because of people's fears that they will confirm the stereotype held about their group. In short, as long as people worry that they might confirm a stereotype held about their group's abilities, this anxiety could interfere with their doing well. Because most of these educational programs call attention to the importance of the ability being assessed (e.g., math or intelligence), they may trigger the very performance interferences that his own research demonstrates. Steele suggests that perhaps the first task is to work on the stereotypes themselves and their links with performance anxiety before addressing the actual abilities being tested.

Changing Stereotypes: Lots of Resistance and a Little Hope

The work we considered in Chapter 8 suggests that once in place, stereotypes are rather resistant to change (e.g., stereotypes bias people in their encoding of information, their storage and retrieval of information, their information-seeking strategies). In addition to these sources of resistance, however, there are still other cognitive processes by which stereotypes may be sustained. The process of *subtyping* (e.g., Maurer, Park, & Rothbart, 1995) is another possibility: "Subtyping refers to the process by which group members who disconfirm, or are at odds with, the group stereotype are mentally clustered together and essentially set aside as 'exceptions to the rule' " (p. 812). In short, the stereotype of a group is preserved by figuratively saying that this person whose behavior is incongruent with the stereotype doesn't count, is different from the others, is an exception. The process is one that is not only generally well demonstrated by social psychological research, but is also something familiar to most of us from our daily lives. We hold a particular group stereotype, for example, that blacks are dangerous and prone to violence, but then have several very good black friends who we happen to know are not violent or dangerous: We subtype them as exceptions that permit us to maintain the group stereotype about blacks even with the disconfirming evidence from our friends. Subtyping thereby offers yet another way in which stereotypes resist change.

In the study that confirmed the process of subtyping, Maurer, Park, and Rothbart also found a different kind of response that they termed *subgrouping*. According to Maurer and associates, subgrouping involves a kind of *recategorization* of the larger group into a series of subgroups. The result of this recategorization into subgroups is a modification of the group stereotype itself. Let me provide a personal example.

In late June of 1996, I attended the Gay Pride parade in San Francisco, lugging along my camera to take "interesting" photographs. What I ended up filming was the great diversity of subgroups within the larger category, homosexual. The undifferentiated (i.e., unsubgrouped) category originally included simply male homosexuals and female lesbians. The parade produced a much more highly differentiated picture. I saw police officers, firefighters, university students, public employees, park service workers, medical personnel, hearing and visually impaired people, persons representing both the political right and left, as well as political moderates. On and on went the diversity. In short, homosexuality was a category that included within it such a diversity of subgroups that no single stereotype about the group as a whole could reasonably be maintained. And so, as the research of Maurer and colleagues suggests, while subtyping sustains a group stereotype, subgrouping forces us to change the stereotypes we hold about a particular group.

Let us return to the Gay Pride parade and make a couple of assumptions. Let us suppose that I decided not to remain for the entire parade, but left the after the first 5 minutes. All I would have seen at that time was the group known as "Dykes on Bikes" riding down Market Street on their Harleys. Let us also assume (incorrectly in my own case) that my stereotype is that all lesbians are rather mannish in their dress and demeanor. Had I left after 5 minutes, my judgment would have been confirmed by seeing this one group. Of course, had I waited around to see the entire parade (as I did), the highly variable sampling of people would have made it almost impossible to retain any single, simple stereotype about homosexuals.

This point is made rather clearly in Park and Hastie's (1987) suggestion about how to change stereotypes. They first comment that if we hope to change stereotypes by getting people to stop categorizing others, we might as well give up now, because of the "propensity of human beings to group objects into categories and to label them with perceived characteristics" (p. 634). On the other hand, if we can educate people to see the great diversity within any one group, as happened with the Gay Pride parade, we can be more effective in breaking the hold of stereotypes. Park and Hastie encourage us to change stereotypes by impacting on people's knowledge of group variability or diversity, the subgrouping effect previously illustrated.

Just Say No

Another approach to breaking the hold of stereotypes involves efforts documented by both Devine (1989) and Monteith (1993). Each adopted a similar argument. Both first remind us that since stereotypes are a normal part of the human repertoire for dealing with the complexities of life, rather than trying to get rid of them our task should be to help people learn to control them and inhibit their automatic activation. In other words, our goal should be to help people learn how to impose counterstereotypic thoughts that challenge the stereotype.

For example, in a context in which she could assess both prejudice and stereotyping, Monteith discovered that while both high- and low-prejudiced students tended to stereotype homosexuals, the low-prejudiced students could be taught more readily than the highly prejudiced to control their tendency automatically to think in terms of the stereotype. The effect of this control was to reduce the otherwise compelling hold of the stereotype on their judgments. The more prejudiced students were less successful in inhibiting the stereotype.

Yet, as Macrae, Bodenhausen, Milne, and Jetten (1994) demonstrate, "saying no" might not always work out as the preceding suggests. There exists in psychology a well known effect sometimes called the "white bear" effect that shows what I mean (e.g., Wegner, 1989; Wegner & Erber, 1992).

If you are asked not to think about white bears, what is one of the first thoughts you are likely to have? Thoughts about white bears, of course! In other words, when asked to suppress thinking about something, we are likely to think about that very thing. As applied to the "nay-saying" approach to inhibiting stereotypic thoughts, it is possible for this same effect to occur. In order to reject the hold of a stereotype, we must first think about that stereotype. Is it not possible that in just thinking about the stereotype, its hold over us might be increased rather than diminished?

This is the conclusion that Macrae and his associates reached from their own research. Rather than reducing the impact of a stereotype on people's judgments of others, the researchers found that "saying no" had a rebound effect and so influenced those judgments: "Out of sight, then, does not necessarily mean out of mind, at least where unwanted thoughts are concerned" (Macrae, Bodenhausen, Milne, and Jetten, 1994, p. 814).

Nothing in this business comes easy. Just when we think we have a seemingly intractable problem solved, along comes some research that throws a monkey wrench into the picture. This does not mean that we should just give up trying to undo the hold of stereotypes. It does mean that we should not believe that simply "saying no" works in as direct a manner as we were initially led to believe, and indeed, may even backfire and intensify the effects of stereotypes on our judgments.

Implicit Stereotyping

The preceding work leads us directly into our next topic, both intriguing and a bit unsettling. The topic is *implicit stereotyping:* "the unconscious or automatic operation of stereotypes" (Greenwald & Banaji, 1995). We often think that people willfully and consciously use stereotypes, and thus that the prejudicial attitudes and discriminatory actions that follow are either intentional or the symptoms of a bad person. By now, however, we should be accustomed to seeing how cognitive psychologists argue that stereotyping is part of categorization processes that characterize the normal individual. The case of implicit stereotyping adds to this picture of normalcy the idea that stereotyping often involves processes of which the person is not even aware. Let us turn to Devine's (1989) research, which we briefly considered in the previous section, and look more closely at how unconscious stereotyping is revealed.

Devine first asked her subjects to identify the location of various words that were presented to them at the edge of their visual field—that is, presented such that they could not consciously identify the words. She had two different experimental conditions. In one, 20% of the words were related to a racial stereotype about African Americans; in the other, 80% of the words were related to this racial stereotype. For example, words related to the stereotype included *nigger, poor, afro, jazz, slavery, musical, Harlem, busing, minority, oppressed, athletic, prejudice, ghetto, welfare, basketball, unemployed,* and *plantation.* As a control, Devine presented a listing of stereotype-unrelated words, including *number, considered, what, that, however, remember, example, called, said, animal, sentences,* and *important.*

The real purpose of this first part of the study was to activate or *prime* the stereotype that people held about African Americans, but to do so in a manner that was outside a person's conscious awareness. The assumption was that those who unconsciously experienced 80% stereotype-related words would have their stereotypes about African Americans primed or activated and that this would affect their behavior in the second part of the study, even though they were unaware that a stereotype they held had been activated or that once activated it would influence their subsequent behavior.

After this initial priming task, subjects were then introduced to a second study, presumably unrelated to the first one. In that second study, they were presented with a paragraph describing a typical day in the life of an individual, Donald, about whom they were asked to form an impression. Donald's day brought him into a variety of ambiguously hostile encounters (e.g., he demands his money back from a store clerk; he refuses to pay his rent until his apartment is repainted). At the conclusion of reading about Donald's day, subjects were to make a series of judgments about him. Half of the items on which they were to rate Donald involved assessments of his level of hostility. Some of the items would describe a person who was hostile (e.g., hostile, dislikable, unfriendly); some would not (e.g. thoughtful, kind, considerate).

Now the results. First of all, Devine's experimental subjects were quite unaware of any connection between the two studies in which they had just participated. In addition, they were unaware of the actual content of the words that they had been presented with in the first study. They made very few accurate guesses at what a word might have been; less than 2% of their guesses were correct. And yet, being exposed to this initial task had a rather striking effect on their impressions of Donald. Those who had been exposed to 80% stereotype-related words saw Donald as significantly more hostile than those who had been exposed to only 20% stereotype-related words. In short, what Devine demonstrated is that when a stereotype is activated unconsciously, it still influences the judgments that people make, even though they are unaware of the influence of the stereotype on their judgments. At work is an unconscious or implicit stereotyping effect.

Devine's research is but one of numerous studies that have demonstrated this same or a very similar effect in a variety of stereotype-related contexts including racial stereotyping as well as gender stereotyping. Banaji, Hardin, and Rothman (1993), for example, showed how the stereotype that males are aggressive but females are dependent would unconsciously affect the kinds of judgments that people make about males and females. As with Devine's study, all subjects were involved in two ostensibly different research projects: the first would activate the stereotype in an unconscious manner, and the second would examine the consequences of this activation.

In the first part of the study, then, Banaji and his colleagues presented their subjects with sentences that they were asked to unscramble. In the second part, subjects were asked to describe a target person, either Donald or Donna, about whom they had just read a story. The unscrambling task unconsciously primed or activated the gender stereotype. For some subjects, the unscrambled sentences contained many aggression-related references (e.g., threatens other people; belongs to the National Rifle Association); for others, they contained many dependency-related references (e.g., can't make decisions; never leaves home).

There is a clear parallel between the priming approach used here and in Devine's study. In both cases (and in most other cognitive priming efforts), an initial task primes a stereotype even while the individual is unaware that this is what is taking place. And so, if you are a subject and are busily engaged in trying to unscramble sentences, you may be oblivious to the fact that most of the sentences involve hostility. Yet, having completed this task, you have now been primed to be sensitive to hostile and aggressive ideation in your later judgments.

In this case, results indicated that subjects who had the stereotype activated by aggression-related words described Donald, but not Donna, as aggressive; those who had the stereotyped primed by dependency-related words described Donna, but not Donald, as dependent. These effects occurred beyond the subjects' awareness. They were not aware that a gender stereotype had influenced them.

But notice the kind of unconscious effect that was found. Only stereotype-congruent effects were noted: That is, Donald, but not Donna, was seen as more aggressive because the stereotype is of males, but not females, as aggressive. Meanwhile, Donna, but not Donald, was seen as more dependent, again because dependency is congruent with the female, but not the male, stereotype. Finally, both male and female subjects showed this effect and in a similar manner.

Similar findings have been reported by Banaji and Greenwald (1994) for a variety of other gender-related judgments. For example, without any awareness that they were engaged in stereotyping, both male and female subjects recalled more names of men associated with fame than names of women associated with fame after a preliminary procedure that, as in the preceding research, primed or activated the social stereotype that linked men, but not women, with fame.

In their thoughtful review of much of the research on these implicit stereotyping effects, Greenwald and Banaji (1995) report similar effects in many contexts that are usually not associated with implicit stereotyping—for example, in research involving the well known *halo effect.* The halo effect is the tendency to judge an unknown characteristic of a target person in terms of an already-known characteristic the person possesses—for example, generalizing from the person's attractiveness (the known quality) to being cheerful, sociable, and intelligent (other qualities), and to do this without any awareness that the person's attractiveness is guiding these other judgments (e.g., see Dion, Berscheid, & Walster, 1972).

An especially intriguing study that Greenwald and Banaji (1995) point out was originally reported by Wilson (1968). A group of undergraduates was introduced to an individual who was presumably going to be involved at some later point in their instruction. The individual's status varied for each group of students who met him: He was variously described as a student from Cambridge, a lab assistant in psychology from Cambridge, a lecturer from Cambridge, a senior lecturer from Cambridge, or a Cambridge professor. Each group was asked to estimate his height. The interesting findings were the effects of status on judgments of height. The higher the status, the taller he appeared! For example, when introduced as a student, he was judged to be 139.7 inches tall; when a full professor, his height was estimated to be 144.6 inches. In other words, subjects used the status of the person (the known quality) to generate a halo onto an unknown quality (e.g., height). And all of this occurred without their awareness.

Some Implications

Before we leave this work on implicit stereotyping, it is important to examine some of the implications that Greenwald and Banaji have suggested about this phenomenon. For the most part, we still tend to think poorly of people who engage in stereotyping and to believe that they are responsible for such "bad" behavior. Cognitive psychologists, however, have taught us that we all engage in categorizing others and that it is more of a normal than an abnormal process. And now Banaji and Greenwald tell us that implicit stereotyping makes much of the process occur behind our backs and out of our awareness. This makes it somewhat unreasonable to hold individuals responsible either for stereotyping or for not stereotyping. Actually, how can they be responsible for something of which they are not even aware?

In short, how can we hold people responsible for their unconsciously driven actions—in this case, their unconscious use of social stereotypes to sustain prejudicial treatment of others—when they are doing so not willfully or even maliciously, but well beyond their own awareness? But responsibility is only one of the issues involved once we enter this world of implicit stereotyping.

A second issue involves how to get people to stop doing something they don't even realize they are doing. It is hard enough to help people stop doing something when they know they are doing it. Imagine how much more difficult to help them stop doing something they are not even aware of! In this case, the task may require altering the social conditions that encourage stereotyping in the first place. And here, Greenwald and Banaji (1995) recommend three approaches: (1) blinding, (2) consciousness raising, and (3) affirmative action. Their argument is clear, even if their solutions raise still other questions: Stereotyping that operates unconsciously must be addressed by modifying the conditions that encourage stereotypes in the first place (e.g., by making it difficult to use stereotypes in decision-making processes).

Blinding, for example, involves making selections of people without any awareness of the particular social category to which they belong. It is difficult to unconsciously stereotype the selections if they are made in the absence of any knowledge of the person's group memberships. The problem with blinding, however, as Greenwald and Banaji point out, is that it does not make up for past discriminations that place people on an unequal footing in competing for given positions. That is, even if the decision process is blind to a person's group memberships, if those memberships have placed some people at an advantage over others, no matter how blind one is to the evaluation, it will still reflect these past differences.

Consciousness raising turns us in a direction that is more like the approaches suggested by Devine and Monteith. This approach tries to attack unconscious stereotyping and prejudice by increasing people's awareness that stereotypes may operate unconsciously, and so encourage people to remain forever vigilant of their operation.

Finally, *affirmative action* policies are designed to compensate for past discriminations and to prevent their perpetuation in the future. In the long run, policies that place people on a more equal footing may reduce the very stereotypes that would otherwise operate unconsciously. We revisit these and other approaches in Chapters 15 and 16.

It should be clear that there is no perfect approach for dealing with stereotypes. The implications of work on implicit stereotyping and its role in shaping the judgments we make of others, however, adds a new dimension to our understanding of the nature of the cognitive processes involved in maintaining prejudices. In this case, because these processes are beyond our awareness, even those who are well intentioned and otherwise without prejudice may find themselves inadvertently in its hold.

I am reminded here of the interesting, though imperfect, study (see Swim, Borgida, Maruyama, & Myers, 1989, for a critique) reported some years ago by Goldberg (1968), in which presumably well intentioned readers said that an essay was of better quality when they thought it was written by a man than when the same essay was said to be written by a woman. If we can assume that the reviewers were not consciously sexist or intentionally out to "get" women (the reviewers were female!), then we see the insidious operation of social stereotypes in perpetuating prejudice on the part of people who, if push came to shove, would never wish to be caught doing what they nevertheless have done. Many of us are in that same boat. The only way out according to those who have investigated implicit stereotyping involves challenging the very social bases of these pernicious stereotypes.

Chapter Summary: Key Learning Points

1. Stereotypes not only affect how we process and recall information, but also how we interact with other people.

    a. The self-fulfilling prophecy describes the role that stereotyped expectations may play in shaping how we inadvertently interact with others so as to make those expectations come true. For instance, we saw how teachers who anticipated teaching students they expected to do well related differently to these students, actually helping to improve their classroom performances. We also saw how men's and women's stereotypes about attractive and less attractive partners influenced both how they related to the partner as well as how the partner responded, confirming the stereotypes by shaping the partner's behavior.

b. We saw the operation of stereotype threat, how stereotypes may even affect how we "interact" with ourselves (e.g., how people's fears that they will confirm a negative stereotype held about their group can interfere with their performances and so confirm that very stereotype).

2. We also considered several ways designed to modify those stereotypes that influence both our processing of information and our social interactions.

a. We considered the process of subtyping—which, rather than modifying the stereotype, actually helps to confirm it by making an exception out of those whose actions to not fit the stereotypes we hold about members of their group.

b. We considered the process of subgrouping—which, unlike subtyping, helps to challenge stereotypes by revealing the diversity of people within a stereotyped group, making it difficult to maintain any one stereotyped image of that group.

c. We examined attempts to challenge stereotypes by seeking to negate their effects through a conscious effort to impose counterstereotypic thoughts.

3. We also saw the importance of unconscious or implicit stereotyping in shaping our views of others. By priming stereotypic associations (e.g., presenting stereotype-related ideas that unconsciously trigger stereotypic thoughts), people's judgments of others are influenced well below their conscious awareness.

4. We also considered several attempts to alter the hold of implicit stereotypes on both our judgments and our social interaction, as follows:

a. Blinding: This approach involves making decisions or judgments blind to the group memberships of the persons involved.

b. Consciousness raising: This approach attempts to help people become aware of their tendencies to stereotype in order to increase their vigilance to such tendencies.

c. Affirmative action: This approach seeks to alter the social conditions that give rise to stereotypes in the first place.

Explaining Prejudice: Intergroup Relations

At this point it should be apparent that whichever lens we use to examine prejudice—whether focusing on the characteristics of those targeted for prejudice or on the characteristics of those who are prejudiced—prejudice is first and foremost an intergroup phenomenon concerned with the way that people from one group feel about and relate to members of other groups. While we intuitively recognize this quality of prejudice, most of us who have been reared in highly individualistic societies such as the United States often resist considering one another as anything other than distinct individuals whose group memberships are not considered central to the kind of person we are or might yet be (e.g., Hofstede, 1980, 1991; Sampson, 1977, 1988; Triandis, 1995, 1996).

On meeting another person, for example, we say that we simply want to relate to that individual as a fellow human being, not as a member of a social category defined by race, ethnicity, gender, and so forth. Often we believe that if people only learned to get along better as individuals, then all the problems of prejudice and discrimination would quickly fade.

However, author and critic Benjamin De Mott (1995) has challenged this idea. He argues that by trying to relate to one another on a personal or interpersonal basis, as friends, rather than on an intergroup basis, as members of social categories, we may be heading down the wrong road if we want to solve those social problems that stem from prejudice. De Mott observes, for example, how the media—television and films in particular—play up the idea that all of our problems involving differences can be resolved if we can only forget these differences and become friends. Audiences readily learn "that racism is *nothing but* personal hatred, and that when hatred ends, racism ends" (p. 23). De Mott not only rejects this thesis, but argues that its very hold on the American imagination thwarts real solutions, which, he argues, require changing intergroup rather than interpersonal relations.

I am reminded here of a film clip I recently saw depicting a multiracial group of men who were meeting to discuss issues of race relations. In a particularly poignant moment, one of the white men looked at one of the black men in the group and said, "I don't want to see you as black, but only as a fellow human being." In response to this plea for shared humanity, the black man rose from his seat, and with his voice growing louder with every syllable he uttered, shouted, "That's bullshit!" He explained: "To be a human being means to be white; that's what you really are saying to me—I want you to be white like me so that we can finally all get along together. Well, buddy, I'll have none of that!" His shouting completed, the black man sat back in his seat, head bowed, arms folded in sadness that this message could not seem to get through to the whites in the room for whom the simple lesson remained: Let us forget black and white and simply be friends.

Although the entire film sought to demonstrate how it was possible to bring together persons from multiracial and multiethnic backgrounds and over time help them better appreciate one another, and in this way reduce their previously prejudiced attitudes, this scene depicted one of the key issues that separate two sides of what is a complex debate: those who believe that by establishing friendships we can overcome years of prejudiced habits and institutionalized practices; those who believe that because prejudice is an intergroup phenomenon, it must be resolved by addressing it on an intergroup rather than interpersonal (friendship) level. The chapters we consider in this section explore both sides of this issue.

Chapter 10 begins our foray into this contentious territory with an examination of the distinction between personal or interpersonal relations on the one hand and intergroup relations on the other.

Chapter 11 takes a closer look at what typically happens when people are formed into groups and begin to relate to one another on the basis of their group memberships, as in-group and out-group members, rather than individual to individual. We will see that many of these effects are less than helpful if our aims are to reduce prejudice.

Finally, in Chapter 12, we examine more closely several theories that have been developed to address intergroup relations and the effects we visited in Chapter 11. We will examine the implications of each theory for understanding prejudice and moving toward its reduction.

Chapter 10

Interpersonal and Intergroup Relations: Friends or Categories?

We begin with an oversimplification, using the fictitious Bob and Jane as examples. Following the lead of the European theorist of intergroup relations Henri Tajfel (1978, 1982; and Brown and Turner, 1981), let us picture a dimension with one end labeled *personal or interpersonal* and the other labeled *intergroup*. Suppose that when Bob and Jane meet, they relate to one another primarily in terms of their gender categorization, as male and female. In this case, we are located on the intergroup end of the dimension. We are there, because when Bob sees Jane, he sees himself as a male encountering a female. On the other hand, suppose that when Bob and Jane meet and get acquainted, they begin to personalize their sense of the other person and of themselves; for example, Jane sees Bob not only as handsome and friendly but also as someone who likes hiking; Bob sees Jane as attractive and intelligent as well as someone who has an extensive shell collection. In this case, we are located on the interpersonal end of the dimension. At the interpersonal end, Bob and Jane relate to one another in more personal terms, as unique individuals with their own particular characteristics rather than simply as members of a particular group.

Social Identity vs. Personal Identity

It is clear that the dimension describes the kind of identity that people adopt for others and for themselves. On the one hand, we can see others as well as ourselves primarily in terms of our social (collective) identities—our group memberships or social categories as men, women, black, white,

Asian, straight, gay, young, old, and so forth. On the other hand, we can see others as well as ourselves primarily in terms of our personal identities—our unique qualities as individuals with our own personal history and special characteristics that make us who we are. Thus there are two contrasting ways in which people may define themselves and others and in turn guide their relationships.

Of course, all of this is too neat. It is a simplification of the more complex ways we all can and do relate with one another. Obviously, we can relate both personally as well as in terms of our group memberships, even shifting back and forth between the two. But, bear with me for a little while longer with this too-neat way of considering human relationships.

A personal experience illustrates this dimension that Tajfel emphasized, while revealing its relevance in our everyday lives. It was my second day in Ann Arbor, Michigan. I had arrived early in order to get settled in before my days as a graduate student were to begin. A tennis partner from California, Alex, and I thought that we might save money by rooming together; and so we set about trying to locate a place. We found what we considered the perfect room: the top floor of a rooming house, a large room with a huge window looking out on a quiet street and a small park. The price was right. The landlady (an intergroup category for her) seemed very pleasant as she showed us the room and gave us some of the details that we potential tenants (another intergroup category) would need to know in making our decision.

We were both extremely pleased to have found something so nice in such a short time. As we walked together down the stairs flanking the landlady and prepared to sign the documents needed to clinch the deal, she casually mentioned her pleasure in having two such fine young Protestant boys renting her rooms. My friend and I looked at one another and then back at her. I had to tell her that I was Jewish and my friend Catholic; neither of us quite fit her category requirements. We departed without any comment, leaving her stumbling over words to express what she had really meant, words we never heard nor really cared to.

As far as my friend and I were concerned, we had arrived simply as two individuals, Ed and Alex, not as Catholic and Jew. She compelled us to see ourselves, however, not as just Alex and Ed, but rather as a Catholic and a Jew—and not merely members of particular religious groups, but (for her) the wrong ones at that.

As this little story suggests, where one is located on the personal-interpersonal dimension is not a trivial matter. In this case, being located on the intergroup end, categorized by our religions, meant that we were not qualified to get the room, no matter how wonderful we were as individuals. In short, where people stand on this dimension makes an important difference in their lives. Let us examine another unfortunately not uncommon situation that illustrates this dimension and some of its more negative consequences.

Tamara has spent years studying, making great grades, and becoming overqualified for the new job she has just been offered. It is her second day at work when her boss invites her into his office for a get-acquainted chat. She is both a little nervous and excited at this early opportunity to meet her new boss. Immediately on entering, she feels a bit tense; something is not quite right. He has her take a seat and then moves his own very near to hers. He offers her some coffee, which she politely accepts, and then leans over a bit too close to chat with her. His gestures soon become moves toward her. His remarks, which began with some informal comments on the weather and the office furniture, shifted noticeably: He began to comment on her clothing, her fine body, her attractive face, his own prowess in bed. Tamara knew what was likely to come next.

What has occurred in this small vignette is also illustrative of the dimension we have just considered. Tamara's boss is relating to her in terms of their group memberships—hers as a woman and his as a man—and not as the uniquely qualified and intelligent person she also is. Her boss has ignored Tamara's personal work talents and has placed her squarely on the intergroup end as fair game for his unwanted advances.

Which One Are We?

Given that there are two contrasting possibilities for defining our own and others' identities, and that sometimes we are one and sometimes the other, what are the *conditions* under which each identity will emerge? That is, when will our personal identity be most salient to ourselves and others, and when will our social identity take precedence? Because social psychologists interested in the roots of prejudice have found the personal-intergroup dimension to be central to their analyses, answers to this question have become important to consider. We will examine five factors that influence which of our identities will emerge:

1. Calling attention to people's group memberships
2. Distinctiveness
3. Status
4. Face-saving
5. Culture and social ideology

As we review these five, ask yourself about how each might lead people to relate to you in terms of your intergroup identity rather than as a unique individual. (Table 10.1 summarizes these five conditions.)

Calling Attention to People's Group Memberships

First, others may call attention to our group memberships and so define us in terms of our intergroup rather than our personal identity. This is what the

Table 10.1

Conditions That Increase the Likelihood of Defining Self by Personal or Social Identity

Condition	Increased Likelihood of Personal Identity	Increased Likelihood of Social Identity
1. Attention is drawn to person's group memberships	No	Yes
No attention is drawn to person's group memberships	Yes	No
2. Person has high distinctiveness in situations with others	No	Yes
Person has low distinctiveness in situations with others	Yes	No
3. Person is member of a high-status group	No	Yes
Person is member of a low-status group	Yes	No
4. Person of high power relates to those of low power	No	Yes
Person of low power relates to those of high power	Yes	No
5. Person's self-esteem is challenged	No	Yes
Person's self-esteem is not challenged	Yes	No
6. Person comes from individualistic culture	Yes	No
Person comes from collectivistic culture	No	Yes
7. Person has high pride in group and seeks political advantage	No	Yes
Person has low pride in group and does not seek political advantage	Yes	No

landlady did to Alex and me. There are other similar ways in which this can occur. A racial slur or some other group-based epithet, for example, brings into sharp relief the fact that we are not simply Jane, Bob, or Tamara, but a bitch, a fag, or a nigger. Similarly, people's stares when we enter a room serve as a reminder that we are not just Jamie, but a person with a leg brace and a strained walk. As a kid growing up, I vaguely knew that I was Jewish, but my first real contact with being identified as a Jew occurred in the second grade when I suddenly became a dirty kike Jew bastard, fair game for punching.

Of course, these are dramatic ways in which we suddenly encounter ourselves in our intergroup guise. Whenever we fill out some official form that asks us to indicate our gender or our ethnic identity, we are made aware of the fact that we are not simply individuals but also members of a particular category. Recall the earlier discussion (see Chapter 8) of the children of interracial couples who are forced to choose one category from a menu of identities, none of which adequately fits them. Even their difficulty suggests how a simple form can force us to consider our group memberships and intergroup identity.

Distinctiveness

A second possibility looks at our distinctiveness in a social setting. The idea is that the more distinct we are in a given setting, the more our social identities (i.e., the intergroup end of the dimension) will become salient to ourselves and others. For example, it is likely that in a situation in which there are five men and one woman, the woman's gender identity will be more salient than in a situation in which the woman does not stand out as a distinctive element. This is exactly what some early research reported by McGuire and his various associates (e.g., McGuire, McGuire, Child, & Fujioka, 1978; McGuire & Padawer-Singer, 1976) generally found.

In one of their studies, for example, McGuire and his colleagues (1978) argued that "we notice in ourselves those aspects that are peculiar in our customary social milieu" (p. 512). Therefore, ethnicity should become noticed when it stands out. McGuire and his associates carried out their research in Connecticut using secondary school students as their subjects. The students were simply asked to "Tell us about yourself." The idea was that when their ethnicity was salient because it stood out as distinct, then they would spontaneously be more likely to mention their ethnicity in response to this question than when it was not distinct.

Because the ethnic composition of the school was already known (it was 82% white, 9% black, and 8% Hispanic), it was assumed that the white majority would not define themselves as much in terms of their ethnicity as would members of the two minority groups. Indeed this is generally what the authors found: Only about 1% of the white students compared with 17% of the black and 14% of the Hispanic students spontaneously commented on their ethnicity in answering the open-ended request to tell about themselves. Although there were several confounding features in this study design, the overall point makes intuitive sense and is consistent with others' work as well: In general, the quality we have that stands out from the background will be salient; and salience in this case leads to our being identified in terms of our group memberships. Minorities, thereby, are usually more sensitive to their racial or ethnic identity than are members of majority groups to theirs.

A personal example again. My wife is a minister who works in a San Francisco church that is about 95% African American and about 95% gay and lesbian. She is white and fairly straight. It has been fascinating to see someone whose distinctiveness based on race and sexual orientation is rarely an issue suddenly find herself in a situation in which her intergroup identity is salient. Distinctiveness does make a difference: For instance, in that setting she is very aware that she is white, whereas in many other settings her "whiteness" is not noted by her or others but is simply part of what is taken for granted (see Chapter 14 for more on this idea).

The effect of distinctiveness in making a person's intergroup identity more salient has been examined in contexts other than race or gender. Here is a typical scenario that Nelson and Miller (1995) presented to their subjects. Ask yourselves how you might respond to this situation. Suppose you were to buy a book as a gift for a friend or a relative who you knew had two interests—skydiving and tennis. Assuming that you could only select one book, would it be on skydiving or on tennis?

Nelson and Miller suggested that only one of these two hobbies is distinctive (i.e., skydiving) and that distinctiveness makes that identity the most salient. And so, you should choose the book on skydiving, the most distinctive identity for your friend. To make a long story short, when given this choice among several others in which one member of the pair was distinctive and the other was nondistinctive, subjects selected the distinctive choice significantly more often than the other. Since skydiving is said to be a more distinctive hobby than tennis, the book choice would favor going with that identity for the friend rather than the nondistinctive one.

Nelson and Miller used many more situations than skydiving versus tennis to test this idea. For example, let us say your friend is a pet lover who owns both snakes and dogs as pets. Again, which book would you be likely to get? Obviously, a book on snakes, since that is the most distinctive category of pets as compared with dogs, which are relatively nondistinctive as pets.

Nelson and Miller also examined how distinctiveness influences the traits people were assumed to have. For example, if you are told that Bob is both a skydiver (distinctive) and a dog owner (nondistinctive) and that skydivers are morning people and dog owners are night people, what type of person do you think that Bob is? Nelson and Miller find that 69% of the time, subjects predicted that Bob would share the qualities of the distinctive category; in this case, therefore, Bob would be a morning person because that is the quality that goes along with the distinctive membership that he has.

The point of Nelson and Miller's research, like that of McGuire, is the demonstration of the important role that distinctiveness plays in emphasizing a person's intergroup identity rather than his or her personal identity. Whereas McGuire and his colleagues examined how distinctiveness shapes a person's own choice of identity, Nelson and Miller's work shows how others base their judgments on distinctiveness as well.

We might conclude from these studies, then, that when a person's characteristics are distinctive in a given social context—either because they are in the minority in that context (McGuire) or because they have a hobby, interest, or point of view that is distinctive (Nelson & Miller)—both we and they are more likely to use that distinctiveness as a basis for defining them in terms of their intergroup identity. As Nelson and Miller observe, their findings complement those of others including McGuire, as well as anecdotal reports on token women in organizations reported by Kanter (1977), who suggests that the more distinctive a person is, the more she will be seen in terms of her intergroup identity as a female who shares the stereotypes held about that group. In other words, since tokens are by definition distinctive, more often than not they are assumed to be just like the group in which they hold membership (i.e., their individuality is lost): Token blacks are assumed to be more black than unique individuals; same for token women, token homosexuals, token whatevers.

The preceding also suggests that we might expect to find what has been referred to as *self-stereotyping* (e.g., Hogg & Turner, 1987; Simon & Hamilton, 1994); that is, persons who experience themselves in terms of their intergroup identity tend to apply to themselves the stereotypes that go along with such membership. Subjects in Hogg and Turner's study, for example, were placed either in four-person discussion groups consisting of two males and two females or in two-person groups of the same sex. The former was said to be a condition in which gender would be salient to persons, and if salient, should result in greater self-stereotyping (i.e., describing oneself in gender terms). The latter, by contrast, was said to mute the relevance of gender and so should result in lesser self-stereotyping. Results generally confirmed these expectations.

Simon and Hamilton also found self-stereotyping based on status: Minorities of high status but not minorities of low status tended to self-stereotype. The introduction of status as a factor determining whether one will be identified personally or in intergroup terms brings us to a third condition to be examined.

Status

In reflecting on the meaning of their findings, Simon and Hamilton suggest that people who are members of high status groups have the very kind of distinctiveness that makes their group memberships salient: They often prefer to be defined in terms of their intergroup or social characteristics. Under these conditions, therefore, their intergroup rather than their personal identity should take precedence.

We are also all aware of those circumstances in which this might not hold. For instance: "I want you to love me for who I am and not because I am about to inherit $20 million from my rich and ailing father." We also recognize fads that lead those in high status to emulate the fashions and music of those in lower status, calling attention to their group identity as one of the gang rather than the elite.

In his original formulation, Tajfel introduced what he referred to as a social identity theory of intergroup relations. (We consider details of this theory in Chapter 12.) According to the theory, group memberships are important to people because they provide them with a sense of personal value and self-worth. By belonging to groups that are held in high esteem, people feel themselves to be held in high esteem as well. Concerns of this sort might shift people away from seeing themselves as unique individuals and toward seeing themselves as members of a group (e.g., Turner et al., 1987). As we noted, when membership confers high status, people will generally want to be seen in terms of their social identity. But, if membership confers low status, people would prefer having their personal rather than their collective identity to take precedence. Research tends to support this analysis (e.g., Brewer, Manzi, & Shaw, 1993; Ellemers, van Knippenberg, de Vries, & Wilke, 1988; Ellemers, Wilke, & van Knippenberg, 1993).

A somewhat different view of the effects of status as a condition that encourages either a social or a personal identity to take precedence comes from the interesting program of research on stereotyping and power reported by Fiske (1993). As we have seen from our earlier consideration (e.g., Chapters 8 and 9), when stereotyping exists we tend to treat individuals in terms of their group memberships rather than their personal characteristics; that is, with stereotyping, people's social identity takes precedence over their personal identity. What Fiske examined was how people's status within an organization, where status involves their power over others, affects the kind of identity (social or personal) that tends to predominate.

Consider first her conclusions: Powerful, high-status people tend to stereotype those of lesser power, whereas they tend not to be stereotyped by those in low-power positions. In other words, whereas powerful people treat those with lesser power in terms of their social identity, the latter tend to treat the powerful in terms of their personal identity.

Fiske has some ideas about why this difference occurs. For one thing, because powerful people have the ability to affect others' lives in often significant ways, those whose lives are affected have a vested interest in forming rather distinct and specific personal impressions of them. This produces the tendency for the lower-status people to individualize their views of those in high-status positions. On the other hand, because low-status persons have little control over their behaviors, high-status people need to pay little attention to them, resulting in the greater tendency to use stereotypic information (i.e., the social identity of the low-status people becomes salient).

Face-Saving

A fourth condition under which our group memberships become salient involves a self-protective, face-saving strategy. A common observation is that some people use their social identity as a device to save face—that is, to avoid having to confront themselves as a personal failure. Crocker and Major (1994) have extensively examined this possibility and offer some useful illustrations and supportive data (as do Ruggiero & Taylor, 1995). Crocker and Major examine both how people use their own intergroup identity to save face and how others often provide support for this face-saving strategy by excusing people from personal responsibility because of their social category.

One experimental demonstration of this effect involved asking a group of women to write an essay that was to be evaluated by a male who was known to be either sexist or nonsexist in his attitudes toward women. These women were then given either positive or negative feedback from this evaluator and were asked to judge how much they felt his attitudes about women influenced his ratings of their essays. Quite unsurprisingly, women who received a negative evaluation from a sexist evaluator were more likely to believe that the evaluation was based on his hostility toward women. Thereby, they saved themselves any attribution of having written a poor essay: "It was his negative attitudes not my poor essay that explains what went on here." On the other hand, when they received negative feedback from a nonsexist male, they could not as readily blame him. They were stuck blaming themselves and overall felt more discouraged than those with the sexist evaluator.

A parallel study was conducted using black and white students who were being judged by a white evaluator who could either see them, and so identify their racial group membership, or not see them. Results indicated that black students were more likely to attribute any negative feedback they received to the evaluator's prejudice against blacks, especially when the evaluator could easily identify them as being black.

Both of these studies illustrate how people's social identity becomes more salient when it can save them from seeing themselves in a less favorable light. In other words, I claim my group membership when it is to my advantage to do so. In these cases, I can save face by seeing your prejudiced treatment of me and my people as the source of my difficulties.

Justifiability: control and legitimacy   The notion of *justifiability* is involved in this face-saving process. Justifiability operates in two ways. The first involves a question about the extent to which people have control over their group memberships. The assumption is that the more in control they are, the less they can claim discrimination in order to save face (i.e., if you made your own bed, then you had better lie in it and accept the consequences). Obviously being female or black is not a condition that one can control. Therefore, both observers and the persons themselves are unlikely to see any negative reaction based on their gender or race as justifiable: It is sexism or racism.

On the other hand, what about people who have been categorized into groups on the basis of factors that either observers or they (or both) believe to be under their own control? For example, if we consider homosexuality to be a choice that a person makes rather than a destiny with which they come prepackaged at birth, then we are likely to consider any negative outcomes they receive to be more justified (i.e., because they choose their sexuality, we should not pity them if all does not go well for them).

Consider the debates in the United States Congress about providing additional funding for AIDS research. Some legislators insist that since homosexuals have "chosen" to be gay and to engage willfully in "unnatural" practices, they should not be rewarded by additional funding to find treatments and a cure for "their" disease. Although it might seem that this kind of argument could not be used against people whose racial-based and gender-based memberships result in negative outcomes, some people continue to reason that although blacks are not responsible for being black, they are *responsible*—that is, in control of what achievements they accomplish. Therefore, any failures are their own doing and are justified, because these unsuccessful people must be lazy.

What does all of this imply for saving face? It would seem that when people are presumably not free to choose their group memberships, the more useful it will be to claim that their social identity is the source of any negative reactions they receive (with the exceptions as noted above). In other words, since my group membership was not of my own choosing, if I experience negative reactions, it is because of your prejudice toward people in my group. On the other hand, the more people are thought to have freely chosen their social identities, the less useful will it be to call attention to them in order to save face. There is an old tale about a child who kills his father and mother and then pleads for mercy from the court because he is an orphan. This illustrates the point and requires little additional comment!

A second way in which justifiability operates to save face involves *legitimacy.* Some of the research reported by Crocker and Major (1994) is suggestive about when a cry of discrimination may backfire and not help the person's face-saving effort after all. For example, in one study, they compared people's responses to a job applicant who was either in a wheelchair or whose face was disfigured because of an auto accident. The applicant was presented as applying for a job as a receptionist, a mover, or a data processor. It was hypothesized that because the scars might interfere with the receptionist's job, observers would feel that it was legitimate to reject the applicant for that position. Likewise, because being in a wheelchair would interfere with the mover's job, it would be legitimate to reject the applicant for that job, but not for either the data processing or receptionist positions.

When presented with several scenarios containing variations on these characters and jobs, subjects responded as hypothesized: They felt that not hiring the scarred person to be a receptionist was justifiable, but it was not legitimate to reject this person for the other two positions; also, not hiring the person in the wheelchair to be a mover was justifiable but was illegitimate for the other jobs.

It would seem, therefore, that if the person in the wheelchair used her identity as a person with a disability to cry foul because she was not hired for the mover's job, this would not help her save face because observers would feel it was legitimate to reject her for this type of work. On the other hand, if she failed to get the data processing job and claimed discrimination, this would be considered legitimate and hence face-saving.

Additional studies have examined much this same idea. One interesting study reported by Crocker and Major involved overweight women who were rejected as either a potential dating partner or a potential work partner. These women felt the former rejection was legitimate, but the latter was not. In the same study, women of normal weight, who were also rejected, felt both rejections were equally unjustified.

Because the overweight women agreed that to be rejected as a potential date because of their weight was justified, they could not claim discrimination in order to save face; not even they would believe this. On the other hand, because they felt that their weight had nothing to do with their ability as an employee, any rejection in this context could be dealt with not as a personal failure but rather as a matter of weight discrimination, thus saving face. Interestingly, the women of normal weight saved face in both contexts, apparently believing that there was no good reason for rejecting them for much of anything.

What, then, can we conclude from the Crocker and Major work? First of all, the research confirms that people can and do use their group memberships defensively to protect themselves and save face when they are rejected or treated negatively. Secondly, it is also important to recognize that observers participate in this face-saving strategy when they agree that certain group memberships count among the conditions that mitigate against holding an individual personally responsible. And finally, the more choice that people have over a given group membership, the less that membership can be effectively used to protect the individuals from any challenges to their self-esteem.

Culture and Social Ideology

The fifth condition that influences whether a person's social identity or personal identity will emerge involves a two-part consideration of the cultural and social environments. First, cultures vary in the degree to which they are individualistic or collectivistic (e.g., Brewer & Gardner, 1996; Markus & Kitayama, 1991; Sampson, 1988; Triandis, 1995, 1996). This should make a difference in determining whether a group or individual identity is *generally* salient, with collectivist cultures being more "we" oriented and individualistic cultures, more "I" oriented (an idea confirmed by Rhee, Uleman, Lee, & Roman, 1995). Secondly, social ideology, including matters of political belief and even political strategy, can play a significant role in determining when and if people's social identities will become salient. We will examine each of these factors.

Individualism, collectivism, and identity as "we" or "me"   By now, it has been generally well established that cultures differ in the degree to which they emphasize individualism, in which the individual is prominent, or collectivism, in which the group is prominent. It is also generally well known that the United States is one of the world's most individualistic cultures (e.g., Ho, 1995; Hofstede, 1991). The implication of this latter finding is that group-based identities might meet a less hospitable reception in the United States than in more collectivistic cultures where thinking in terms of "we" rather than "I or me" is more typical.

It would be reasonable, therefore, to anticipate that culture plays an important role as one of the conditions that can either increase or decrease the salience of a person's intergroup identity (e.g., Brewer & Gardner, 1996; Rhee et al., 1995). In more collectivistic cultures, people are more likely to emphasize their group memberships over what to us would be considered our personal identity, and so define themselves and others predominantly in terms of social categories.

Rhee and colleagues (1995) demonstrated this effect in examining the spontaneous self-descriptions offered by persons from individualistic cultures (e.g., United States, Australia, Britain) compared with those offered by persons from more collectivistic cultures (e.g., China, Japan, Korea). Their data generally support the hypothesis: People from collectivistic cultures tend to call on group-based factors in their spontaneous self-descriptions (e.g., define self in terms of family) as compared with the more abstract categories employed by persons from individualistic cultures (e.g., define self in terms of general traits they individually carry with them apart from any group memberships they may have).

Social ideology and identity   An effect reminiscent of the findings we previously considered as reported by McGuire and his associates, in which majority whites seemed oblivious to their whiteness, whereas racial and ethnic minorities were cognizant of their group identities, is also involved in the research reported by Judd and his colleagues (1995). They found that whites rejected race or ethnicity as a basis for categorizing others, claiming that "race blindness" was preferred—whereas African Americans revealed the opposite tendency, making their race highly salient in their identities. This turns out to be a rather important phenomenon worthy of more careful examination.

The point is that various groups within a complex society such as the United States have learned to think differently about the use of group memberships such as race or ethnicity to categorize themselves and others. Both social history and current politics play an important role in determining whether a person will or will not employ intergroup definitions in identifying self and other. Let us consider the conclusion reached by Judd and associates, based on the several studies they conducted with whites and African Americans:

> Group perceptions are guided not only by the fundamental cognitive processes that we have come to understand reasonably well in our laboratories but are also guided by ideological beliefs that our society has taught us all about the role of ethnicity and the extent to which ethnic differences are to be valued or denied. (p. 479)

In other words, beyond the factors of distinctiveness and status, which contribute to the salience of intergroup identity, current social ideology has taught whites in particular to avoid defining people in terms of their racial group memberships. Simultaneously, however, members of various racial or ethnic groups have begun to take great pride in their group memberships, and so feel resentful when whites decline to grant them even this basis for their pride. Is it possible, wonder Judd and his colleagues, if perhaps this white denial of collective identity is a new form of prejudice toward blacks?

Huo, Smith, Tyler, and Lind (1996) point out another aspect of this same issue. As we are well aware, one of the worries that has motivated white efforts to erase the markings of people's social identities is the fear that emphasizing group memberships will disrupt the smooth functioning of society by highlighting the ways we differ rather than the ways we are all alike. Muting differences through assimilation (which we consider in more detail in Chapter 13) is often touted as the best way to achieve social harmony. Perhaps this is a part of what the whites studied by Judd and his colleagues are doing when they deny the importance of race or ethnicity for defining their own or others' identity.

And so we encounter a situation in which members of one group (e.g., blacks) claim their group identity as a matter of pride, while those of another group (e.g., whites) deny the importance of group identity, fearing that to focus on a person's social identity might undermine social harmony. The former feel it is racist to deny them their blackness, while the latter feel it is fragmenting society when people insist on being accepted in terms of their social identity. Often, they talk past one another, never quite understanding the other's position.

Another aspect of the preceding dilemma is also relevant to consider: the politics of social versus personal identities. People may call attention to their social identity as a strategy in the politics of gaining power and advantage for their own group. Emphasizing that one is a unique individual, for example, may not work effectively in the political area. The voice of the solo protester is often not heard; the collective voices of many can quickly gain an audience.

To call attention to one's ethnicity, therefore, may not simply be pride in group, but also a political strategy designed to gain benefits for people who have long suffered. Approaching the world not as an individual but as a black person, then, might prove nettlesome to the still dominant white majority, but it is a political strategy that may help turn around a bad situation.

In like manner, and starting most noticeably in the United States in the 1960s, various groups have made their claims for equal treatment by calling attention to their group identities rather than seeking to conceal them. Women emphasize their feminism, homosexuals their sexual orientation, and so forth.

Sometimes, I hear my female students making rather nasty comments about the feminist movement, noting how they personally feel very comfortable about themselves and so see no need to change anything in their lives. It seems clear that they have defined themselves primarily in personal terms, which in this case interferes with seeing themselves in intergroup terms as well. Therefore, they are less likely to find the appeals of feminism to their liking because who they are is not rooted in their social identity as a woman. And it may well be that the potential for political action that goes along with seeing oneself in terms of "we" rather than "I or me" is lost on those who reject the social in favor of a uniquely individual self definition (see Lalonde & Cameron, 1994; Taylor, Wright, & Porter, 1994).

These points were brought home to me in one of my group dynamics classes when a readily identified Latino student, in response to a question about the role of culture in affecting people's behavior in the group, bristled with anger. He actively rejected any cultural interpretation, claiming that he was himself, a unique and special individual and should not be identified as Latino. As he put it, he did not want to be treated as just another stereotype.

It seems we have encountered yet another dilemma. Political action may require that people recognize their memberships in social groups. Yet, personal well-being, as in the preceding cases, might lead people to reject those intergroup identities in favor of simply being taken for themselves. As the young man in my group dynamics course said, he was himself, not a Latino. Perhaps the choice of who to be—"me" or "we"—is not always ours to make; but when we have a choice, in this culture at least, we tend to embrace "me."

Chapter Summary: Key Learning Points

1. People can be described as having two major types of identity:

   a. Personal identity refers to their unique identity as an individual.

   b. Social identity refers to their identity as a member of a particular social category or group.

2. Because prejudice typically involves intergroup relations—that is, how people relate to one another in terms of their social identity—it is important to understand the conditions under which a person's social identity or personal identity is more likely to appear.

3. We considered five conditions that encourage either a social or personal identity to take precedence:

   a. A person's social identity is made salient by others' hostile or favorable comments that call attention to that person's group memberships, or by completing official forms that require self-labeling into one of a set of designated social categories.

   b. A person's social identity is made salient when he or she stands out as distinctive in a group—for example, one woman among a group of five men.

   c. A person's social identity is made salient as a function of status. Specifically, high-status people may wish to call attention to this fact and so reap whatever benefits accrue to having high status. It has also been shown that low-power people in a group tend to be concerned about the personal identity of those who exercise power over them, whereas high-power people tend to focus more on low-power people's social identities.

d. A person's social identity is made salient when it serves to help that person save face.

e. A person's social identity is made salient as a function of cultural values and social ideology. Social identity is salient in collectivistic cultures; personal identity, in individualistic cultures. Social identity becomes salient when group pride and political advantage demand collective action.

Chapter 11

Intergroup Effects: In-Groups and Out-Groups

Once people begin to relate primarily in terms of their social identities—in terms of their memberships in specific groups and thus as in-group to out-group—a variety of things begin to happen. These "things" are what I am referring to when I speak of "intergroup effects." What are some of these effects that occur once two people, let us call them Jim and Jamil, engage one another more as white and black than as Jim and Jamil each with his own distinctively individual characteristics? Three major effects have typically been noted. Although they may not exhaust all the possibilities, they cover some of the main consequences of living in a world in which people are identified by their group memberships and relate to one another on an intergroup basis. (Table 11.1 summarizes these effects.)

The first effect involves in-group heterogeneity and out-group homogeneity: People perceive great diversity and variety among members of their own group, while seeing out-group members as pretty much all alike. For example, Jim would not only see Jamil primarily as an African American, but would view him stereotypically as being just like all other African Americans, while considering himself and other whites to be a very diverse lot.

A second effect involves in-group favoritism, accompanied at times with out-group derogation. In this case, Jim would show favoritism to members of his own group and may even go so far as to derogate members of other racial categories even as Jamil does much the same.

The third intergroup effect we will examine involves attributional biases, and particularly what Pettigrew (1979) has called the *ultimate attribution error*. This is related to the in-group favoritism effect, but in this case involves *explaining* the same actions very differently depending on whether they are performed by an in-group or an out-group member. An example of this would involve Jamil's interpreting Jim's standoffishness as a sign of prejudice while interpreting a fellow African American's standoffishness as merely his shyness in social settings.

Table 11.1
Some Commonly Observed Effects Once In-Groups and Out-Groups Are Established

Concept	In-Group	Out-Group
In-group heterogeneity/ Out-group homogeneity	Seen as more diverse	Seen as more alike
Ethnocentrism	Strong in-group favoritism	Less favoritism; may also involve derogation
Ultimate attribution error	Attributions made that enhance the in-group • e.g., positive acts explained in terms of actor's dispositions • e.g., negative acts explained in terms of the circumstances the actor faced	Attributions made that diminish the out-group • e.g., positive acts explained in terms of the circumstances the actor faced • e.g., negative acts explained in terms of the actor's dispositions

Before we examine each of these three effects in more detail, it is important to look at a situation that both reveals all three effects and yet lacks most of the characteristics that real in-groups and out-groups possess. This involves what has been called the *minimal group design.*

The Minimal Group Design

It is most disturbing to learn that each of the three effects briefly summarized here has been observed under the minimal group design—that is, when people are formed into groups using the most trivial of characteristics as the basis for this division (see Brewer, 1979; Cadinu & Rothbart, 1996; Tajfel, Flament, Billig, & Bundy, 1971). In the typical minimal group setting, for example, people are randomly assigned to membership in either group A or group B based on something as trivial as their presumed preferences for an artist's work or their estimates of the number of dots in an array presented to them. The individuals never meet their fellow group members nor have any contact with them whatsoever. In short, what the minimal group design attempts to do is to eliminate nearly every known basis for any intergroup effects: (1) no conflicts of interest between the two groups; (2) no contact between the two groups; (3) no contact among members within each group; (4) no history of rivalry between the two groups; and (5) no loyalties developed over time to one's own group. The term *minimal* should thereby be taken in its most literal sense.

Despite the fact that these minimal arrangements are barely meaningful as groups, research using this design has rather consistently revealed that "the mere categorization of subjects into in-group and out-group is sufficient to trigger intergroup discrimination" (Bourhis, Sachdev, & Gagnon, 1994, p. 209; Brewer, 1979; Brown, 1995; Taylor & Moghaddam, 1987). For example, significant in-group favoritism is found: People allocate more rewards to members of their own in-group than to members of the out-group. This is quite worrisome, considering how much more intense this effect is likely to be when one or more of the other factors found in real-life groups is present—for example, a history of intergroup rivalry and antagonism, an intense identification with and loyalty to one's own group, and so on.

So that the point of all of this is not lost, let me repeat what we have just seen take place. First of all, you create a rather arbitrary division of people into two groups, which in the usual sense of that term are hardly groups at all: "Members" never see one another; they have no history of relationships together. In short, there is hardly any basis for even considering oneself to be a group member—after all, membership was suddenly conferred by some arbitrary decision that was made only moments ago. A truly minimal group!

Now, you give each of these minimal groups some tasks to carry out, at the conclusion of which you have each member allocate rewards and answer some questions. The surprise is that merely categorizing people into two groups produces most of the intergroup effects we briefly introduced at the opening of this chapter. As already noted, in-group favoritism is a typical research finding. That is why the conclusion says that the *mere* categorization of people into two groups produces intergroup discrimination: Without any other factors being present, the mere fact of being categorized as group members leads people to favor their own group over others.

Although this effect is by now well established, as Cadinu and Rothbart (1996) comment, all the reasons for its occurring still remain puzzling. Why would people who suddenly find themselves members of a group about which they know nothing and with whom they have had no contact whatsoever favor that group over any other? Originally, Tajfel suggested that the reason this occurs is that because a significant part of people's social identity is located in groups; thus, they make their own group appear in a positive light so that they can have a positive identity for themselves. In other words, I can feel good about myself insofar as I belong to a group that is thought well of. By making my group's image appear good (e.g., favoring it), I can make my own self-image likewise seem good. An interesting idea, and perhaps meaningful in real groups, but it stretches our credulity to believe that this takes place in the minimal group situation. Are we all so much in need of positive self-regard that we will grasp at any straws in order to make ourselves feel good? Perhaps.

Cadinu and Rothbart, however, were not entirely satisfied with this interpretation and so examined several other possibilities. One of their ideas, generally supported by their research findings, may explain intergroup effects in the minimal setting but may or may not generalize to real world groups as well. Here is their argument. In the absence of any information about the in-group or the out-group (after all, this is a minimal setting), people use themselves as the anchor-point for making their judgments. My suddenly acquired in-group, about which I know absolutely nothing, becomes a kind of copy of the person I am. In turn, the out-group, again about which I know nothing, becomes an opposite image of the person I am. And so, if I think well of myself, I will think well of my in-group, because in the absence of any other information, I use my-self as the framework for judging its qualities.

As Cadinu and Rothbart note, this argument reverses the direction of cause and effect proposed by Tajfel. Tajfel argues that by making the in-group appear good I can appear good. By contrast, Cadinu and Rothbart suggest that because I am good, so too is my in-group. In summarizing their research findings, they observe "that the causal direction is from self to group, rather than from group to self" (p. 675).

What we should keep in mind as we now examine each of the three inter-group effects in more detail is that some of them can be produced in the most minimal of settings, for reasons that undoubtedly involve elements of both Tajfel's original ideas as well as Cadinu and Rothbart's revision. If ethnocentrism (i.e., in-group favoritism) emerges in minimal settings, imagine how much more intense it is likely to be in the real world, where we want to be certain that our own group will shine so that we will shine (Tajfel) and/or when we use our own shine to anchor our judgments about our own groups (Cadinu & Rothbart).

We are now ready to examine each of the three major effects introduced at the beginning of this chapter.

Out-Group Homogeneity/ In-Group Heterogeneity

One of the first consequences of dividing the world of other people into two categories, in-groups and out-groups, involves an often observed perceptual effect: Members of one's own group, the in-group, appear to be a highly diverse collection marked by many different kinds of people, whereas members of the out-group appear to be all of one kind—they all look alike, think alike, behave alike (e.g., Judd & Park, 1988; Judd et al., 1995; Ostrom & Sedikides, 1992). For example, males tend to perceive females as similar to one another while perceiving other males to be very diverse. Females repeat this same effect. Another example: People who are opposed to abortion tend to judge those who favor a women's freedom to choose as similar to one another while judging members of their own group to be different from one another (e.g., Robinson, Keltner, Ward, & Rose, 1995).

One approach to studying the homogeneity-heterogeneity effect looks at the degree to which the group's stereotype is endorsed by in-group and out-group members. To help make this approach easier to follow, let us suppose that the two groups in question are the Wollonians and the Apollonians. The in-group heterogeneity/out-group homogeneity effect should appear if the Wollonians perceive the Apollonians as fitting their stereotype for Apollonians, but see themselves as not quite matching the stereotype held about their own group, the Wollonians. Support for this effect has been found in both laboratory and field investigations (see Ostrom & Sedikides, 1992).

Judd, Ryan, and Park (1991), for example, asked business majors and engineering majors to rate each group on traits chosen so that half fit the common stereotype of business majors (e.g., extroverted) but were counterstereotypic of engineering majors (e.g., impulsive), while the other half were stereotypic of engineering majors (e.g., analytical) but counterstereotypic of business majors (e.g., reserved). Their findings support the out-group homogeneity effect: People said that members of their own group fit the stereotype less often than they said that members of the out-group fit that group's stereotype. For example, business majors were less likely than engineering majors to say that business majors were as extroverted as the stereotype maintained, but would claim that engineers were indeed as analytic as the stereotype of engineers suggested.

A second approach designed to evaluate the out-group homogeneity effect uses measures of dispersion, or *variability*. If the first approach asks people to judge a group's *average* qualities (i.e., the stereotype for the group), this second approach asks people to estimate how *variable* group members are on a given set of traits: For example, tell me where on this scale measuring personality traits the highest group member will fall and where the lowest group member will fall. This provides a measure of the range or variability in the judge's perceptions of the particular group in question. A high number indicates a large discrepancy in their judgments about high and low members, and so reveals greater variability than a low number. Obviously, if there were perfect homogeneity, the judge would claim that the high and low group members are exactly the same (e.g., everyone in that group is highly aggressive without any variation whatsoever). Judd, Ryan, and Park's (1991) study involving business students and engineering students, which we considered a little earlier, also evaluated measures of variability and once again found support for the out-group homogeneity effect; that is, people judged less variability among out-group than among in-group members.

And so, our friendly Wollonian would tell us that on a 10-point scale measuring the trait of helpfulness, the highest Apollonian would score about 4 and the lowest about 2, for a discrepancy of 2 scale points. On the other hand, that same Wollonian would tell us that the highest Wollonian would score about 9 and the lowest about 2, a discrepancy of some 7 scale points. Clearly, for Wollonians, there is greater homogeneity among the Apollonian out-group (a 2-point discrepancy) and greater heterogeneity among the Wollonian in-group (a 7-point discrepancy).

But, why does this effect occur? Several answers have been proposed. As we have seen, Tajfel originally argued that people's group memberships are important to their sense of identity and self-worth. People thereby prefer to belong to groups that bolster their self-worth. One way people accomplish this is to make a sharp distinction between the great variety of people within their own group as opposed to the dearth of variety in the out-group. In short, my people are unique and special while your people are all cut from the same cloth with nothing very special about them.

Familiarity is another possible reason for this effect. It seems likely that people are more familiar with members of their in-group than they are with members of the various out-groups with which they come into contact. In this case, familiarity breeds diverse knowledge about the in-group, and lack of familiarity breeds impoverished knowledge about the out-group. While some research has confirmed this interpretation, other research has not provided clear-cut support. Of course, if this effect is found in the minimal group design (Mullen & Hu, 1989, argue that the effect is found even under minimal conditions; Ostrom & Sedikides, 1992, by contrast, argue that the effect is not found under minimal conditions), then familiarity would hardly count as a meaningful explanation given that people remain anonymous to one another in the minimal situation.

A third possibility is that the effect is used *after the fact* to justify why the out-group should receive such poor treatment. For example, if people argue that all of "them" (the out-group) are uniformly evil people who deserve the kind of harsh treatment they receive, they have used this homogenization of the out-group to justify what will be done to them. This kind of reasoning was quite apparent among the Nazis for whom *all* Jews were exactly alike and none of them was worth saving.

Most of us are familiar with similar usage, even if we prefer not to think of ourselves as succumbing to this way of thinking. For example, having observed that very few women occupy important positions in his organization, Jim thinks that this is because women as a group are too emotionally unstable to be in positions of leadership. Jim homogenizes the out-group (women) in order to justify why women do not gain access to key executive positions.

Before we entirely depart from the examination of the in-group heterogeneity/out-group homogeneity effect, some important caveats are in order. Although out-groups may often be homogenized, in-groups, especially those with minority standing, are not invariably seen by their members to be as heterogeneous as the effect suggests. Consider a situation in which people who belong to an embattled minority benefit from seeing a great deal of in-group homogeneity (i.e., we are all as one in battling the enemy). Under such conditions, a group's power position in the community might lead members to homogenize its own group. When this occurs, the validity of the in-group heterogeneity effect that we have been examining is put into question (for some parallel ideas to this apparent exception to the effect see Fiske, 1993).

We previously considered another complication in reviewing the results from the series of studies reported by Judd and his colleagues (1995). Recall that they compared responses of white Americans with African Americans on various measures. In several of their studies, neither whites nor blacks supported the expected out-group homogeneity effect. If out-group homogeneity were present, we would expect that whites would report greater variability and less stereotypicality for whites, while blacks would report greater variability and less stereotypicality for blacks. Results, however, revealed few if any differences between whites and blacks in this regard.

Judd's research group found one measurement, however, that did reveal the expected effect. All subjects were asked to generate as many subgroups within each white or black category as they could think of. Presumably, if you cannot think of many different types of whites (if you are black) or types of blacks (if you are white)—in other words, few subgroups—this would indicate out-group homogeneity. Support for the out-group homogeneity effect was found for this one measure: That is, whites generated more subgroups for whites and fewer for blacks while blacks generated more for blacks and fewer for whites, just as we would expect if the in-group heterogeneity/out-group homogeneity effect held.

In reviewing these findings, the authors concluded that white Americans do not appear to follow the predictions from intergroup theory, whereas in general black Americans do. We will shortly consider what these ethnic differences might mean.

In-Group Favoritism With and Without Out-Group Derogation

A second major intergroup effect, aspects of which we have already considered in reviewing the minimal group design, involves in-group favoritism with or without out-group derogation. Before we examine this effect further, however, I think it will prove helpful to expand our understanding by considering a dimension of attraction and repulsion. Figure 11.1 represents this dimension. At one extreme we find *ethnocentrism,* the favoring of one's own group: We are the best, the greatest, the most wonderful of all, God's clearly chosen people. In the middle, moving toward the negative end, we find *out-group derogation,* a tendency to demean, diminish, and express hostility toward the out-group: They are dirty, lazy, unnatural in their desires. Finally, at the far other extreme, we leave prejudiced attitudes and move more directly into the behavioral realm of *genocidal actions,* or the systematic attempt to destroy a people as a people, whether defined as a race, a religion, or a culture.

Because much of the research that has examined the in-group favoritism effect has been conducted on short-lived laboratory or experimental groups and has focused primarily on attitudes, it is not typical to include a dimension

Figure 11.1

A continuum of attraction and repulsion

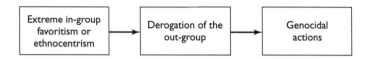

that extends beyond attitudes and especially a dimension that moves into the realm of genocidal actions. Obviously, we would not anticipate genocidal responses in the laboratory! However, as world history continually reminds us, genocide is a phenomenon that has not occurred just once, or twice, or only a half-century ago. Genocide has an unfortunately long history in the world of intergroup relations, with a past as current as today's newspapers. And so I have included genocide at the far end of this dimension that has its innocent beginnings with ethnocentric attitudes.

Ethnocentrism

Ethnocentrism, or in-group favoritism, is something with which most of us are intimately familiar even if we may not call it by that name. For instance, in spite of the number or intensity of conflicts rooted in family life, we often hear people proclaiming that "blood is thicker than water." This describes the loyalty and favoritism often directed toward family members, as difficult as family life may be.

Although a considerable amount of research documents the in-group favoritism effect in minimal group settings as well as in natural groups, recall the contradictory evidence reported by Judd and his colleagues (1995). Their findings suggested that African Americans affirmed the in-group favoritism effect (e.g., by favoring blacks over whites) but the white Americans did not (e.g., they did not show more favoritism to whites than blacks). The one measure on which the effect worked as predicted, however, involved what has been termed *thermometer ratings.* People were asked to use a thermometer to report their warmth toward both African Americans and white Americans. Ratings confirmed the tendency for African Americans to report greater warmth toward other African Americans while white Americans showed the expected greater warmth to other whites.

On other measures of ethnocentrism or in-group favoritism, however, only the African Americans fit the expected pattern; the white Americans did not. If anything, the white Americans showed somewhat greater positive feelings toward African Americans than toward other white Americans, a reversal of the expected in-group favoritism effect!

If you recall our previous discussion of this particular study (see Chapter 10), you will remember that its authors suggested that many whites may be reluctant to emphasize group differences. The authors also suggested that this reluctance is a relatively recent cultural shift. If this is indeed the case, then younger whites should be more reluctant than older whites to focus on group differences, because the former are part of this newer view that favors blindness to ethnicity. The data from the Judd group's (1995) study confirmed this prediction: While older whites revealed the expected in-group favoritism effect, younger whites did not. A parallel analysis for African Americans showed the expected reversal: Younger African Americans, emphasizing group differences, showed more in-group favoritism than older African Americans.

Judd and his colleagues concluded that perhaps we have an important racial split now taking place. It would seem that whites deny the very kinds of interethnic distinctions that blacks find so important to their current need to receive recognition and respect. Color-blindness on the part of whites, argue Judd and his colleagues, may prove to be a blindness to the importance of group identification among minorities who fear that when their group differences are not sustained, they will lose their own identity to the dominant white majority. Sounds a bit like a replay of Boyarin's interpretation of Paul's letter to the Galatians we considered in Chapter 3. Although the cast of characters has shifted, the message remains much the same: The more powerful hope to eliminate differences that the less powerful insist must be maintained.

Derogating the Out-Group

To this point, the focus has been on ethnocentrism, on the favoring of one's in-group. There is no necessary link, however, between favoring the in-group and derogating the out-group. That is, one may show in-group favoritism without necessarily revealing out-group derogation as well. Her review of the literature on intergroup relations led Brewer (1979) to conclude that the evidence on behalf of in-group favoritism was more substantial than the evidence in support of out-group derogation. Brewer is primarily referring to evidence based on controlled laboratory studies rather than the evidence generated by historical experience.

The historical evidence suggests that in many instances, as it seeks to solidify itself through a firmly ethnocentric view of the world, the in-group develops a strong contrast with members of the out-group: They lack the very virtuous qualities possessed by the in-group. The history of intergroup relations we considered, especially in Chapter 3, provides all too many instances of this tendency to build in-group harmony around out-group derogation. The out-group derogation effect was also rather strikingly observed in what is perhaps the best known "natural" study of intergroup relations, as reported by Sherif and Sherif (1953).

Sherif and Sherif: A key study   The Sherifs had the good fortune of being social psychologists who also had access to a summer camp, permitting them to provide an interesting camp experience for young boys aged 11 or 12 as well as an opportunity to conduct some serious research on intergroup relations. Reasonably normal young boys from a similar background who were not acquainted were invited to attend a camp session. They were not informed, however, that they would be subjects in a study nor that the camp personnel were all part of the investigation. Leaving aside ethical issues that would be raised today, the Sherifs were able to conduct their research without the boys suspecting that they were not only campers enjoying a summer of fun but also subjects in a carefully designed study.

After the boys arrived at the camp, they were housed in a large bunkhouse where they spontaneously divided themselves into various friendship groupings. After a few days, when these friendships had been established, the boys were then divided into cabins, placing the initial "best friends" into different cabins. Sherif and his fellow "camp counselors" observed that the boys within each cabin began to form groups with special names not only for their group (e.g., Rattlers for one cabin; Eagles for another) but also for specific members who occupied key leadership roles (e.g., "Baby Face" led one cabin, "Lemon Head" another).

Once these cabins had solidified as groups, the Sherifs began their experimental procedures, all of which were fully integrated into the routine activities of the summer camp. They pitted cabins against one another in a variety of competitive games, discovering rather quickly the degree to which the good feelings that had originally existed within the entire camp soon dissolved into some strongly negative feelings between the groups. Names were used to refer to rivals as "stinkers" or "cheaters"; furthermore, when asked to rate members of their own group and other groups, in-group favoritism was clearly shown; even those kids who had been best friends in the beginning turned on their former friends and derogated them. Intercabin rivalry also extended to attacking the other cabins, seizing their flags, scuffling with them, initiating food fights during meal times, and so forth.

In terms of the effects we are examining, ethnocentrism with out-group derogation and hostility were both clearly found. The boys not only showed favoritism toward their own cabin, but also devoted considerable energy to derogating other cabins through name calling and fighting. In short, the Sherif and Sherif study demonstrates what often occurs in natural groups—a combination of ethnocentrism with out-group derogation and hostility. The research also demonstrated the often short trip between hostile attitudes and aggressive actions, the topic to which we now turn our attention.

Genocide

In opening this examination of in-group favoritism, I suggested a dimension with ethnocentric attitudes at one extreme and genocidal actions at the other. My reasons for putting genocide at the other extreme is so that we might see the possibility hinted at in the Sherifs' work, that as we begin a process of favoring the in-group over the out-group and then move toward derogating the out-group, the next (but by no means inevitable) step might involve a turn toward genocide: the coordinated and planned annihilation of a national, religious, or racial group.

The careful historical examination of numerous cases involving genocide reported by Chalk and Jonassohn (1990) finds but one commonality among the numerous cases studied: "We have no evidence that a genocide was ever performed on a group of equals. The victims must not only not be equals, but also clearly defined as something less than fully human" (p. 28). It seems that the step from derogating the out-group to dehumanizing them and then to considering them as not worthy of sharing the same web of human obligations as other human beings, though a major step, is one that has occurred all too often in human history. We may wish that genocide were a stranger; it is an all too familiar sign of the extremes to which intergroup relations can extend.

Attributional Effects

The third set of intergroup effects that frequently occur once people become defined in terms of their social identities involve *attributions*—that is, the explanations people use to interpret actions (e.g., Kelley, 1973; Ross & Nisbett, 1990). We already encountered an attribution effect when we considered Duncan's study (see Chapter 8) in which white subjects attributed greater violence when a black person shoved a white person than when the shover was white. In other words, the same action was interpreted differently depending on who did it—a fellow group member or an out-group member.

Attribution Theory

Before we can appreciate how intergroup attributions occur, we need to understand a little more about attribution theory. Usually, when we try to explain someone's behavior, we have two different options. We can use an explanation that refers to some personal quality or characteristic that the person has (these are called *internal* or *dispositional* attributions); or our explanation can call on some quality of their circumstance or situation (these are called *external* or *situational* attributions). For example, a friend of ours gets his first midterm exam back and scores rather poorly. How do we explain this misfortune?

If we call on internal attributions, we search for something about our friend that makes failing understandable: for example, "After all, he's not very bright." On the other hand, we may seek our explanations externally, arguing, for example, that this particular professor makes up unfair examinations, which she then grades subjectively and in an unfair manner. This is why our friend did poorly. As this example suggests, since failing is not a desirable event, to explain it via internal attributions (he's stupid) is to portray the person in uncomplimentary terms. External attributions, by contrast, excuse the person. He is but an innocent in this professorial plot to do grievous harm to students' self-esteem.

If we were probing all the ins and outs of attribution, we would spend some time exploring the conditions under which either internal or external attributions are more likely to be made (e.g., see Kelley, 1973). But, in that our main purpose is to examine intergroup attributions, we will stick to those attributions people make for the same behavior when performed by an in-group member as contrasted with an out-group member.

The Ultimate Attribution Error

In our earlier discussion of the kernel of truth hypothesis (Chapter 8), we introduced the idea of the fundamental attribution error (e.g., Ross, 1977; Ross & Nisbett, 1990). We saw this as involving the generally observed tendency for people to discount situational factors that could plausibly explain a person's behavior in favor of dispositional explanations. People seem to prefer explaining why someone did so poorly on an examination, for example, by concluding that the person is stupid rather than the professor's exam is too ambiguous and difficult.

But, as fundamental as this tendency is, in-group and out-group membership seems to override it in a very particular and important manner, resulting in what Pettigrew (1979) has called the *ultimate attribution error:* the tendency to make in-group serving attributions; to attribute the desirable actions of in-group members to something internal and their undesirable actions to something external. This is reversed for out-group members, for whom every positive deed they perform must be an accident of circumstances (external), while their bad deeds are, of course, attributable to some flaw in their character (internal).

Let us look at a typical research project that has demonstrated the ultimate attribution error as an effect of intergroup relations. Hewstone and Ward (1985)—replicating an earlier study originally reported by Taylor and Jaggi (1974)—located the first of their two studies in Malaysia and compared the attributions made by Malays and Chinese to either positive or negative actions that had been performed by either a fellow in-group member or a member of the out-group. Subjects, all of whom were either Malay or Chinese university students, were presented with a set of stories in which a Chinese character or a Malay character engaged in either a positive action (e.g., helped when someone fell off their bicycle) or a negative action (e.g., failed to help this person). All subjects were told to imagine that they were the person toward whom the positive or negative action was directed. Their task was to select among either an internal explanation for the act (e.g., Chinese are very altruistic and helpful people) or an external attribution (e.g., since everyone was helping, this Chinese person had to as well).

Findings clearly indicated support for the ultimate attribution error among Malays, but not as clearly among Chinese subjects. That is, Malays attributed the positive actions of fellow Malays to something about their good character, while dismissing any negative actions as due to circumstances; on the other hand, the Malays saw positive Chinese acts as due to the situation the Chinese were in, while attributing their negative actions to their defective character. The Chinese, however, did not confirm this same effect, leading Hewstone and Ward both to wonder why and to move their second study to Singapore.

They reasoned that perhaps the Chinese were reluctant to express any hostility toward Malays or take any real pride in their own group because the Chinese lived in such a tenuous situation in Malaysia. In other words, perhaps the prejudice they experienced as Chinese in Malaysia led them to avoid making attributions that would put them at risk. By moving the same study to Singapore, which Hewstone and Ward assure us is much more comfortable with multiethnic diversity, perhaps they could get a sample of Chinese who were more willing to reveal the ultimate attribution error.

Repeating the same study in Singapore revealed a consistency among the Malay subjects, who once again repeated the same pattern they had shown in Malaysia: They made in-group serving attributions. The kind of out-group denigrating attributions that the Malays had made in Malaysia, however, were less striking in Singapore. This is to be expected, of course, if Singapore is truly more comfortable with diversity than Malaysia. In their turn, the Chinese were somewhat more willing to reveal signs of group pride in Singapore, but again without strong antagonism to Malays: The Chinese continued to attribute the positive actions of Malay characters to good qualities possessed by the Malays and were somewhat less likely to attribute negative actions of the Malays to poor qualities they may have possessed. The Chinese, however, did not confirm the expected attribution effects for their own in-group.

Taken all together, these findings suggest that the ultimate attribution error is not quite as neat as originally considered. In addition to an analysis of in-group and out-group relations, one must also be sensitive to the politics of the country in which the research is undertaken and to the kinds of status relationships that exist within that country. Minority or at-risk groups may avoid denigrating the out-group or taking especially great pride in their in-group, while majority groups may be somewhat more willing to reveal both out-group denigration and in-group pride. In this vein, a more recent study reported by Islam and Hewstone (1993), involving Muslims (majority) and Hindus (minority) in Bangladesh, replicated the ultimate attribution error noted in the preceding work; it also suggested support for the idea that the tenuous position of certain groups, in this case Hindus in Bangladeshi society, may minimize the likelihood of their making out-group denigrating attributions, even as they take pride in their in-group by making in-group serving attributions.

That the politics of a society are important to consider has also been demonstrated in the research reported by Jackson, Sullivan, and Hodge (1993). Although they replicated the attributional effects previously noted (e.g., the ultimate attribution error), they also demonstrated a reluctance on the part of white American college students to consider blacks in an unflattering manner. This reduced the expected relationship between group membership and derogating attributions for the out-group. Sounds a lot like the Judd research group's findings we previously considered.

Chapter Summary: Key Learning Points

1. Once people have been formed into groups, either for somewhat arbitrary reasons in the laboratory or for deeply significant reasons in the case of many naturally occurring groups, three major intergroup effects are typically observed:

   a. People tend to see greater variety or heterogeneity among members of their own groups and greater homogeneity among members of the out-groups.

   b. People tend to show a strong ethnocentrism, or favoritism toward members of their own groups, accompanied at times with derogation of the out-group and, as world events continue to demonstrate, at times with genocidal actions in the extreme.

   c. Certain attributional effects follow, in particular what has been called the ultimate attribution error: a tendency to explain the same behavior in positive ways when carried out by an in-group member and negatively when carried out by a member of the out-group.

2. Interpretations of some earlier work on intergroup attributions, when joined with several more recent investigations, suggest that making attributions (i.e., seeking to explain events) may not always follow the ultimate attribution error.

   a. Groups that occupy a precarious power position in a society may be less willing than powerful groups to make attributions that derogate their out-group, perhaps out of a fear of reprisals.

   b. On the other hand, we once again saw the tendency of the white groups within society to hesitate to make racially derogating attributions about African Americans, opting for a race-blindness strategy over a tendency to follow the ultimate attribution error.

Chapter 12

Theories of Intergroup Relations: Implications for Prejudice

Now that we have seen what is meant when we speak of intergroup relations (Chapter 10) and have examined some of the major effects (Chapter 11), it will be useful to consider several different theories that attempt to explain these effects. We will focus on four major theories: (1) social identity, (2) relative deprivation, (3) realistic conflict, and (4) psychoanalytic. Each theory emphasizes a somewhat different factor and directs us to the role that the factor plays in producing intergroup prejudice and discrimination:

> Our *identity* and our efforts to defend or enhance it are central to social identity theory.
>
> Achieving *justice and fairness* is the main focus of relative deprivation theory.
>
> Competition over *scarce resources* and protecting *group interests* are central to realistic conflict theory.
>
> The *unconscious processes* involved in group formation organize psychoanalytic theory's approach to intergroup relations.

Table 12.1 summarizes these several distinctions.

Social Identity Theory and Prejudice

Tajfel (1982; Tajfel & Turner, 1979) is a major figure associated with the social identity theory of intergroup relations. We have already encountered some of his ideas in previous chapters but now will pull them together into a few basic propositions.

Table 12.1

Four Theories of Intergroup Relations

Theory	Main Arguments
Social identity	Because people's social identity is invested in groups to which they belong, they enhance and protect their identity by ensuring that their in-group's standing is maintained or improved.
Relative deprivation	Judgments people make about their own lot in life are comparative. People feel a sense of injustice and unfairness if these comparisons place them or their group at a relative disadvantage. • Egoistic deprivation: when one's own situation compares unfavorably with others in the in-group • Fraternal deprivation: when one's own group's situation compares unfavorably with other groups
Realistic conflict	Group interests to maximize own group benefits—especially when resources are scarce—may lead members of one group to oppose members of other groups as they compete for these desired resources.
Psychoanalytic	Unconscious factors are involved in the manner by which groups form and become groups in the first place. The different unconscious ways of forming groups affect both intragroup and intergroup relations.

First, Tajfel assumes that a fundamental tendency of the human mind leads all people to sort or categorize the various objects in their world, including themselves and their fellow human beings. This produces the tendency to organize ourselves and others into in-groups and out-groups. Second, it is assumed that a significant part of our identity or sense of who we are is rooted in the groups to which we belong. This part is our social identity. Third, it is assumed that all people wish to belong to groups that are held in high esteem so that their social identity will be held in a positive light. Finally, it is assumed that people try to sustain their own positive identity by ensuring that their in-group is both highly valued and distinct from other groups.

Issues That Appear When Social Identity Is Satisfactory

Several consequences are said to follow from the preceding basic ideas. The first deals with the situation where people's in-groups compare favorably with various out-groups. Under this condition, people already have an adequate social identity and so work primarily to keep things as they are. Obviously, this would be the preferred strategy of people in socially dominant groups. These people should resist any changes that threaten their group's dominance and that thereby challenge the basis for their own sense of self-worth.

Many interpretations of the male backlash to the advances of women, for example (e.g., Faludi, 1991), have been framed in these terms. Feeling their social standing and thus their identities challenged by the growing demands for equality on the part of women, some men dig in their heels and refuse to concede any more points. They define male-female relationships using the metaphor of war. In war, there are winners and losers. Not surprisingly, these men do not wish to end up on the losing side.

A similar interpretation can be made of the dominant group's responses to other social movements that threaten to upset the balance of power and hence its self-esteem. Opponents of affirmative action, for example, are typically comprised of those who have benefited from a long history of advantage for their own group. Needless to say, they balk at any efforts that threaten their own advantage (e.g., see Skedsvold & Mann, 1996; Tougas, Crosby, Joly, & Pelchat, 1995).

Issues When Social Identity Is Unsatisfactory

How does social identity theory operate, however, under a different set of conditions? For example, what does it tell us about people whose in-group is not in a position of dominance? Under these conditions, the group does not provide the individual with a sense of positive self-worth, and thus its members do not wish for things to remain the same. These are the conditions that should promote change-oriented actions.

Two different forms of change-oriented actions have been identified: They may be *self-focused,* or they may be *collectivity-oriented.* Several authors refer to self-oriented or individual action as a *social mobility strategy,* while referring to the collectivity-oriented approaches as involving either *social creativity* or *social change* (e.g., Ellemers, Wilke, & van Knippenberg, 1993; Jackson, Sullivan, Harnish, & Hodge, 1996; Lalonde & Silverman, 1994; Tajfel & Turner, 1979; Wright, Taylor, & Moghaddam, 1990). Research has examined the conditions that lead to one or the other strategy of change among those in generally disadvantaged groups who thereby lack a satisfactory social identity. We will examine each strategy in turn.

Self-focused strategies of change   All self-focused strategies are designed to improve the individual's own identity without necessarily improving that of the denigrated in-group. There are several possible courses of action.

One approach that some people use to deal with the disadvantaged identity their in-group provides involves literally leaving the low-status group and seeking entry into a higher-status group. This approach obviously does not work if entry into the high-status group is not available—such as instances where women or African Americans are refused entry to an all-male or all-white private club.

If actual entry is denied, alternative strategies are used. For instance, people may *psychologically* leave their group. There are several different ways to accomplish this psychological departure:

People may try to decrease their identification with their in-group (e.g., when asked, they do not refer to themselves by using their group's label).

People may reduce their similarity with other in-group members (e.g., they try to distance themselves from their in-group by dressing and behaving differently from others in their group).

People may try to copy the behaviors and mannerisms of the higher-status group even though real entry remains closed to them (e.g., they put on airs and affected mannerisms and become one of those great pretenders of so many novels).

Collective strategies of change   In contrast to these individual strategies, all of the collective strategies of change involve attempts to improve the lot of the entire group and not simply oneself.

With a strategy of *social creativity,* people try to modify the undesirability of those very qualities that mark their group as different or distinct. For example, people may transform the stigma that casts their group in such negative terms into a mark of great pride. They co-opt the very terms of derision that have led them to feel so demeaned by making these the terms of a new group pride. We hear, for example, that black is beautiful, that older is wiser, that more weight brings more pleasure. In the realm of human sexuality, a more complex distinction has recently been made between homosexual theory and queer theory—the latter not only using the very term of approbation that had been applied to homosexuals, but also challenging the entire basis on which human sexuality is formed, heterosexual as well as homosexual (e.g., Boyarin, 1997; Halperin, 1995; Jagose, 1996; Minton, 1997). These efforts, of course, do not always produce the desired effects. Often, the dominant majority rejects the apparent extremity of these creative minority efforts, even as in-group members are not always prepared to embrace terms that they have known for so long as derisive references to them and their group.

A second and often related collective approach, referred to as a *social change strategy,* requires mobilizing in-group support to confront the social order and change the actual standing of the disparaged group in which one holds membership. The various social movements directed toward gaining equality for persons who had once been denied this equality are illustrative of this effort to change identity by changing the actual status of one's group.

Some relevant research   Most of the systematic research on these several possibilities has been concerned with determining the conditions that favor using an individual versus a collective strategy. Some investigators have suggested that people will first use an individual strategy and will turn to collective strategies only if the former fails to alter their own situation (e.g., Tajfel & Turner, 1979). Other researchers, however, have found support for the simultaneous operation of both individual and collective strategies (e.g., Jackson et al., 1996).

It has also been suggested, and at times found, that when actual mobility into a higher-status group is not possible, then collective strategies to produce a change in the low-status group's standing will be preferred over any individual approaches (e.g., Jackson et al., 1996). Not everyone, however, has found this effect. For example, it has been reported that even if the chances of individual mobility are minimal, people will continue using individual strategies in preference to collective approaches (e.g., Lalonde & Silverman, 1994; Wright et al., 1990).

The major contribution of social identity theory to our understanding of prejudice is its emphasis on the importance of issues of identity and self-esteem. How we relate to members of our own groups as well as to out-groups is significantly shaped by our concerns with maintaining or improving our sense of self-worth. In this view, therefore, a considerable advance to our understanding of the dynamics of prejudice can be gleaned from focusing on how people's identities are thoroughly wrapped up in their group memberships. Other groups are thereby not simply neutral items on our landscape, but stand always as potential rivals to challenge our self-esteem and sense of self-worth.

Relative Deprivation Theory

Several observations made about military personnel around the time of World War II led to the development of the theory of relative deprivation (e.g., Stouffer et al., 1949). This theory emerged from efforts to evaluate the conditions that made American soldiers feel either satisfied or dissatisfied about their situation. The key observation involved comparing personnel in the Air Force with Military Police. It was generally well known that there were greater opportunities for advancement to higher rank in the Air Force than in the Military Police. It was also known that members of the Air Force often felt dissatisfied, while members of the Military Police felt comparatively better about their situation. This was the puzzle that led to the theory of relative deprivation and its idea that the reality that counts most is very much in the eye of the beholder.

Consider the following two situations. In one, you belong to a branch of the service with good promotional opportunities and you are not promoted. In the other, you belong to a branch with few chances for promotion and you are not promoted. In both situations, therefore, your objective situation involves not being promoted. But in the one case this makes you feel bad, while in the other it is not a big deal.

This is where the idea of relative deprivation comes in. The idea is that people compare their own lot in life with others in a generally similar situation and use this comparison as a basis for determining if they are well off or not doing too well. If you are in a branch of service that has few promotional opportunities (e.g., the Military Police), your own failure to be promoted does not make you feel especially worse off than others in your group. On the other hand, if you are in a branch of service with many promotional opportunities (e.g., the Air Force), and you have not made your move, then you feel relatively deprived—that is, relative to those with whom you compare yourself, you feel deprived.

A similar finding was also observed in comparing the satisfaction of black soldiers in the South with black civilians. In this case, the black soldiers, comparing themselves with black civilians, felt relatively well off and so felt good about their lot in life.

Relative deprivation theory tells us that first, we make social comparisons with others in roughly similar circumstances, and second, on the basis of these comparisons, we judge whether we are relatively well off or relatively deprived. It did not take very long before this idea took hold in a variety of contexts outside the military. For example, when poor whites compared themselves with other whites, they felt relatively deprived. When they compared themselves with poor blacks on the other hand, they felt they were in relatively good shape. One consequence of this, however, was their need to keep poor blacks down so that that they, the poor whites, could continue to feel good about themselves. If this is beginning to sound a bit like social identity theory, it should. As we will soon see, there is a similarity between both theories once personal identity is at issue.

A similar argument from relative deprivation theory can be made concerning policies that lead one group to feel its own status is placed in jeopardy by the relative advances made by another group that formerly served as a comparison. Female career and financial gains, for example, may make many men concerned about their own relative worth. No longer can they compare themselves to women and find themselves relatively well off. In many of today's comparisons, men feel relatively deprived even if objectively they are still much better off than the average female worker (e.g., see Tougas et al., 1995).

For example, statistical summaries reported in 1993 (e.g., see *Higher Education & National Affairs,* March 8, 1993; *San Francisco Examiner & Chronicle,* March 28, 1993) show that women continue to lag behind men in pay at all levels of the workforce—from executive to laborer—while both African Americans and Latinos lag behind whites in their average monthly income at every level of educational attainment—from high school diplomas to graduate degrees (Fendel, Hurtado, Long, & Giraldo, 1996). Yet, in spite of these facts, as Tougas and colleagues (1995) report, many white males report feeling disadvantaged—a sure sign of relative deprivation and the key role that perceived injustices play in shaping intergroup relations.

Although identity is clearly at issue in most situations involving relative deprivation, the central focus of the theory is on people's perceptions of justice and fairness. These judgments are made on a comparative basis: I feel that my lot in life is fair, even if not filled with wonder, because in comparing my situation with many others, I feel that justice and fairness have been served. I would surely not feel so pleased about my own situation, however, if you and I are roughly in the same boat as far as our qualifications go, but you are luxuriating on your yacht while I am trying to maneuver around in a leaky canoe. No justice here.

Two Types of Relative Deprivation

In 1966, Runciman introduced a useful distinction to relative deprivation theory. He distinguished between two types of relative deprivation (also see Crosby, 1976). Runciman referred to one form as *egoistical deprivation* and described it as occurring when people feel relatively deprived because of their relative placement within their *own* group. A female worker who compares herself with other workers in her factory, for example, and finds that she earns less than the average others, might feel egoistically or personally deprived.

The other form of deprivation is *fraternal deprivation* and occurs when a person's group stands in a lesser position than other groups in society. Those same female workers in the preceding example might feel themselves fraternally deprived if they compare the wages of women as a group with those of men as a group and observe that their income is substantially lower even when they perform the same job.

It is obvious, then, that people can experience both forms of deprivation, one form, or neither. It is also apparent that both types of deprivation involve the issue of justice. With egoistical deprivation, people experience a personal injustice; with fraternal deprivation, they experience an injustice served on their group as a whole.

A valuable study examining the relationship between these two types of deprivation and prejudice gives us further insights into what may be operating here. In this study, Vanneman and Pettigrew (1972) interviewed various people in several major U.S. cities between 1968 and 1971. As part of these extensive interviews, they asked subjects to consider their own economic gains over the last 5 years as compared with other members of their own social class and race (e.g., blue-collar workers and other whites) as well as with members of the out-group class and race (e.g., white-collar workers and blacks). Vanneman and Pettigrew identified four major patterns of response to these several comparative judgments:

1. People feel *doubly gratified* because both their personal situation and their group's situation are in relatively good shape (e.g., not only am I doing relatively well in comparison to other whites, but whites as a group are doing well in comparison with other racial groups).
2. People feel *doubly deprived* because both their personal situation and their group's situation show that they are not relatively well off (e.g., not only am I personally doing less well than other whites, but whites in my community are doing relatively less well than other racial or ethnic groups).

3. People feel *egoistically but not fraternally deprived* because they are doing less well than other whites in their community, but whites overall are doing better than other racial groups.

4. People feel *fraternally but not egoistically deprived* because they are doing personally well in comparison with other whites, but whites as a group in their community do not fare as well as other racial groups.

Vanneman and Pettigrew next examined which of these four patterns was most related to racial prejudice as measured by a variety of survey-type interview questions (e.g., objecting to having a black person home for dinner; objecting if a black family moved into their neighborhood). The results were clear: Those who experienced the greatest anti-black prejudice were either *doubly deprived* (pattern 2 above) or *fraternally deprived* (pattern 4). But are these the results we would expect? A closer look reveals a few surprises.

In regard to pattern 1 above, it was not surprising to find that those who were doubly gratified were relatively less prejudiced, because they seem to have little to complain about. The relatively low prejudice among people with response pattern 3, however, was more unexpected. If we were to follow the ideas contained in the original frustration-aggression theory of prejudice (e.g., Dollard et al., 1939), we might expect that people who were egoistically deprived would feel frustration and anger, and that they would displace their anger onto groups unlikely to be able to retaliate, resulting in prejudiced attitudes and even actions (e.g., see Hovland & Sears, 1940, for a study relating economic downturns and lynchings of blacks). But Vanneman and Pettigrew did not find especially higher prejudice among the egoistically deprived, suggesting that at least this early form of frustration-aggression theory does not hold. Perhaps the revised form of the theory, as proposed by Brown (1986) and studied by Rabbie and Lodewijkx (1995), might prove more useful. The latter suggest that intergroup aggression emerges less from purely egoistic comparisons than from frustrations that involve violations of important concepts of fairness and justice occurring at the group level. (This is part of what occurs in response pattern 4.)

Now consider patterns 2 and 4. Of course we are not surprised that the doubly deprived were highly prejudiced. It makes sense that an injustice experienced both personally and as a member of a group might well trigger anger toward a relatively more benefited out-group. But what may strike us as surprising is the finding that people who were fraternally deprived were so highly prejudiced. Apparently it was not their personal situation but their group's situation that seemed to fuel their prejudice.

We commonly believe that if one group's *personal* situation is poor relative to another racial group, for example, that will trigger intergroup hostility and prejudice. But the Vanneman and Pettigrew findings suggest otherwise. It was not people's personal situation but their group's situation that was most related to prejudice. Similar connections between fraternal (but not egoistic) injustices and both prejudice and social activism have been reported by several other investigators as well (e.g., see Brown, 1995; Taylor & Moghaddam, 1987).

A Quick Comparison

Throughout this discussion, we have encountered a similarity between the ideas proposed by social identity theory and those that have emerged from relative deprivation theory. Both emphasize the importance of judging one's own situation comparatively; and both emphasize the importance of people's group memberships for determining out-group attitudes. Where they differ most is that social identity theory places its major bet on the importance of comparisons involving a person's sense of identity and self-worth, while relative deprivation theory invests most of its concerns around issues of justice and fairness. I am not arguing that identity and justice have no connection. My point, rather, is that these are two separable factors of great importance to all of us. We not only care about our self-worth but also care that decisions that may put us at a relative disadvantage are rendered fairly and with justice. Research on what has been referred to as *procedural justice* generally confirms this interpretation (e.g., Lind & Tyler, 1988; Tyler & Lind, 1992).

People may be more willing to accept disadvantages to their own group when they believe that the advantages and disadvantages have been fairly apportioned. It is when we see that my people always get the disadvantages, and your people reap the benefits, that injustice becomes important in much the same manner as we previously saw identity concerns to be important.

Realistic Conflict Theory

Social identity theory is primarily concerned with intergroup relations as they impact on people's identity and sense of self-worth; relative deprivation theory addresses how intergroup relations impact on people's sense of living in a just and fair world. Realistic conflict theory emphasizes groups that are placed into a competitive situation in which vital group interests are at stake. As we unfold the elements of this theory we will see that we have not really left the identity or justice issues behind, but simply placed an accent mark on a slightly different element in the overall story of intergroup relations and prejudice

Sherif and Sherif Return

The Sherif and Sherif study we first considered in Chapter 11 provides us with an excellent illustration of realistic conflict theory. Recall that the Sherifs set up various competitions between groups of summer campers in which there would be winners and losers. We might say that winning is a scarce resource: If one group accomplishes it, it is denied to all others. Each group thereby has a definite and real interest in winning. I have just described what is commonly referred to as a *zero-sum* situation (i.e., if one wins, the other must lose). Not all of life's situations are of this sort. The winner need not invariably take it all, leaving nothing for the others. But, as with most competitive games, zero-sum is an apt description.

Recall what happened in the Sherifs' summer camp: The zero-sum competition between the groups created rather strongly held intergroup hostilities. What we did not consider at that time, but will in this present context, is how the Sherifs used realistic conflict theory to reverse the damaging effects that the competition had created.

The Sherifs turned to realistic conflict theory because they felt that simply bringing together people who hold very different interests might only produce argumentation that would intensify their conflicts rather than reduce them (Deutsch & Krauss, 1960, make the same point). And so, rather than allowing communication between the warring groups or scheduling sensitivity sessions designed to sensitize the boys to their prejudices, the Sherifs felt that the best way to restore harmony in the camp would be to transform their competing interests into a commonly shared all-camp interest.

Without the boys' awareness, the Sherifs and their band of helpful "camp counselors" rigged the camp's water system so that it would not function. The warring groups now had a unifying interest in repairing the water supply. As the Sherifs are quick to note, calling on all groups to help deal with this problem did not immediately reduce the intergroup hostility that had built up. Groups continued fighting and name calling. Over time, however, these signs of intergroup hostility began to decrease and signs of cooperation and intergroup harmony took their place. As the Sherifs comment, at the end, the groups decided to treat each other to a shared campfire and even asked to be on the same bus for their ride back home!

Realistic conflict theory tells us that the many negative intergroup effects we encounter when people are members of different groups arise from a situation of real conflict over group interests and scarce resources. The way to address such conflicts and so reduce intergroup hostility and prejudice involves changing the scarcity that creates the competing interests in the first place. This can be achieved either by the technique recommended by the Sherifs— finding some *superordinate goal* that gives all the groups the same interests— or by transforming the nature of the scarcity or the manner by which the scarce resources are allocated.

There are no guarantees in any of this. For example, creating a superordinate goal as the Sherifs recommend may provide only temporary relief. After the problem has been solved, competing interests may reappear.

This suggests that dealing with the issue of resource scarcity might prove much better in the long run. Too often resources are scarce only because they have been designed as such in order to continue to benefit one group and to disadvantage another. To see how this operates, we need only think of how major international groups control the supply of oil in order to keep the prices at a given level. In this case, scarcity is designed to benefit oil producers by pushing up the costs to oil consumers. Under these conditions, realistic conflicts between producers and consumers can be settled only by addressing the production of the scarcity itself.

This is not intended to deny the importance of attempting to reduce realistic intergroup conflicts by employing the superordinate goal technique recommended by the Sherifs. It is rather to point out another feature of realistic conflict theory that may require addressing many other features of the intergroup situation. What the theory continues to remind us, however, is that some of the important reasons for intergroup prejudice reside in competing group interests.

I think that we have come along far enough together to be blunt: Men and women and whites and blacks may get into some of the prejudicial intergroup tangles they do because each group has competing interests and wants to win! Dominant white males, for instance, may be sensitive, open, and just plain wonderful human beings—and yet believe that their interests are best served if they, not women or blacks or other groups, get the lion's share of scarce resources (e.g., Tougas et al., 1995). Their prejudice toward others therefore involves a competitive interest in seeing that their own advantages are sustained.

If we now turn to the Sherifs' recommended resolution, we might agree with them that simply bringing everyone together into one sensitivity group might not work because sensitivity may have little effect when competing interests are at stake. Instead of calling on people's goodwill, moral spirit, or humane intentions when realistic interests are at issue, we must help people realize that it is indeed in *their* best interests to share, because unless they do, they may not have anything of value remaining even for themselves. Some advocates of environmentalism have taken this approach (albeit with only mixed success), reminding everyone that we live together on one fragile planet and that it is of interest to all of us to watch how we use its resources or else there will be no resources remaining for anyone.

Cooperation: Non-Zero-Sum Life

Not all situations in life involve the winner-take-all, win-lose arrangement of the competitive games that the Sherifs studied. Many situations involve the possibilities for a win-win approach, in which everyone stands to gain if they can cooperate.

One of the earliest and yet most enduring investigations of the benefits of moving from win-lose competition to win-win cooperation was proposed by Morton Deutsch (1953, 1969) in some very early research on group dynamics. Deutsch created two differently structured classrooms, one of which was based on win-lose competition: If one student got a top grade, this meant that grade was already taken and so would not be available to other students. The cooperative classroom, by contrast was of a win-win sort: One student's doing well meant that everyone else in the class would also do well. Notice how group interests differ in these two classrooms. In the competitive environment, my interest lies in getting the good grade for me. In the cooperative classroom, my interest lies more congruently with yours: If you do well, so do I; and if I do well, so do you.

Deutsch's findings are interesting to consider. For example, the level of tension and hostility within the competitive classroom was far greater than within the cooperative classroom. Competition set people at one another's throats, if not literally, then figuratively, as each sought to toot his or her own horn and drown out the other tooters. Not so in the cooperative classroom, in which all could cheer any one person's success because this meant success for all. And so people were less tense, more agreeable, and more pleased with one another under cooperative conditions.

We might extrapolate from these findings and suggest that the more one can create cooperative intergroup settings in which each group's positive movement forward means the positive movement of all other groups as well, we might undermine the negative and prejudicial consequences of intergroup competition. All easier said than done, but opening us to issues that bear further discussion.

Psychoanalytic Theory of Intergroup Relations

The major focus of all three theories we have considered thus far primarily involves conscious processes or at least processes about which people can usually be made consciously aware. People generally tend to be aware of those times in which their self-esteem is at risk, when injustices for them and their groups prevail, and when competition over resources and interests pits them against others. Are there things beyond our *conscious* awareness that also must be considered, however, if we hope to fully understand some of the hateful activities that groups inflict upon one another? Any interest in the unconscious side of life must necessarily turn to the ideas developed originally by Freud (1922) and amplified or modified by others (e.g., Bion, 1959; Klein, 1948; Redl, 1942).

We first encountered the role of the unconscious in our consideration of implicit stereotyping. With a few exceptions (e.g., Billig, 1976; Taylor & Moghaddam, 1987), however, social psychologists interested in intergroup relations have not emphasized unconscious processes in their work. We will correct that oversight.

Because a grand tour of the unconscious world would take us into some very complex territory, with side trips that would exhaust even the most hearty of tourists, I will simplify my account and emphasize two areas of group relations said to be significantly shaped by unconscious processes: (1) the formation of a group and thus the forces that bind members to one another, and (2) the implications of these processes of group formation for subsequent intragroup and intergroup relations.

Group Formation: The Ties That Bind

In his original study of groups, Freud was primarily concerned with those unconscious factors that operate to transform a collection of individuals into a group. Freud argued that people are bound together into a group through their common identifications with a central figure or leading idea. He used the church as one of his examples. It was through their sharing an identification with Jesus as the Christ, argued Freud, that individuals were bound together into their religious groups. In other words, the ties that bound members of a religious group to one another were to be found in the ties that connected each individual to the central figure, in this case Jesus.

The church was only illustrative of similar processes that he said operated in all groups. The basic model outlined by Freud involved two unconscious elements—the identification of each individual with a central figure, and the binding together that this shared identification allowed.

Freud was intrigued with the dramatic changes that individuals underwent when they became members of groups, citing some provocative accounts written by the French student of crowds, Le Bon (1895/1960), for whom people in groups had lost their unique individuality and descended to the lowest common denominator. Freud reasoned that these changes to individuals must have come about because of the very unconscious processes by which they formed into a group in the first place.

To be in a group, said Freud, meant to be bound in two ways. First, each individual was bound to the leader or central figure. Second, each individual was bound to others through having shared this common identification with the central figure. These two commitments meant that people would have less energy available to engage in the critical and thoughtful activities that marked them as individuals. To oversimplify, if in my state as an individual, I have 100 energy units available to use in my everyday dealing with others, when I form into a group, I may expend 25 of those units in my identification with the central figure and another 25 units in my identification with others who have similarly identified, leaving only 50 units remaining. It is this reduction, argued Freud, that transforms people in groups.

From this account it would seem clear that people in groups are less able to think critically and analytically and are more subject to the whims of their passions. They could, then, more readily be led astray and undertake activities of which they might think better in their more complete status as individuals. However, Freud did allow for a type of group whose organizational structure would permit people to be members and yet not lose their critical ability.

Generally, however, Freud remained suspicious of the possibility that individuals could retain their rationality while being members of a group.

Because the ties that bind people to their groups are, in this view, primarily unconscious identifications, people's loyalties to their groups are driven by forces of which they remain quite unaware. And since their loyalties remain largely beyond their awareness (e.g., I didn't know why I felt so strongly about my nation, my team, my family, until we were attacked), the intensity with which a group may seek to protect and defend itself may also lie well beyond any member's conscious awareness or ability to understand. Irrationality and passion more than critical thinking are likely to be at work in most intergroup contexts.

Social identity theory, as we have seen, is also concerned with identity and how in the name of protecting their own social identity people may act in ways that derogate other groups. Freud would not have disagreed with this formulation. But, he would have insisted that the identities about which we feel so strongly are unconsciously sustained. In addition, he would have emphasized how our own social identity is unconsciously bound in with the social identity of others, to provide a rather potent source of intergroup hostility (e.g., in questioning Jesus, you are attacking me; in burning the flag, you are destroying me).

Intragroup and Intergroup Relations

Freud's emphasis on the importance of the central person in the formation and maintenance of groups provided a direction that many subsequent psychoanalytically oriented theorists used in developing their own ideas. Fritz Redl (1942) was especially impressed by how these individual identifications with a central figure took various forms. Redl suggested that there were many different ways with which individuals could identify with a central person; in turn, each way of forming an identification created a very differently structured group with some very different implications for both intragroup and intergroup relations.

I will only illustrate a few elements of Redl's ideas in order to reveal the general directions of his thinking. Redl reminds us that groups may form around both positive identifications (e.g., feelings of love or admiration) as well as negative identifications (e.g., feelings of hate). One of Redl's illustrations is of a group that has formed around the kind of central person he refers to as the object of aggression or hate. Hate can bind people together as much as love. If you and I hate the same person or group, this hate that we share in common may serve to bind us together into a group, joined in this case by sharing our hates.

Nations under threat, for example, are often bound as one nation by virtue of having adopted the same enemy as their object of hate. Some of the hate groups we encountered in Chapter 6 (e.g., patriot militia, Christian Identity) are likewise bound together into their groups by sharing a common hatred of Jews, blacks, homosexuals, the federal government, and so forth. The problem with hate, however, as Redl suggests, is that the same hate that can bind people together can fade, either once the battle is over and peace is restored or when the hated object no longer serves that useful function. Without the binding force of shared hate, anarchy and confusion may result. In addition, the hate that was directed outward may now turn against members that had once been part of the common group (e.g., bickering and destructive conflict within the nation or within hate groups).

Perhaps what Redl has described is what we witnessed repeatedly during the latter part of the 20th century, as single nations that were held together by repressive regimes (e.g., the former Soviet Union, the former Yugoslavia) broke into destructively warring factions once the repressive leadership was overcome. In cases like these, the aggression directed toward the common repressive regime no longer serves to bind people to a single group when that regime is overcome. Aggression that was once directed toward the regime is now available to be directed toward others within the no longer unified nation.

Love and hate are not the only unconscious bases for group formation that Redl identified. Many other unconscious processes bind individuals into a group and define the very character of that group. It was Redl's contention that if we wish to understand how a group functions and in turn how it relates to other groups, we must go beyond conscious analyses and probe more deeply into the unconscious processes by which the group was formed in the first place. How it formed unconsciously will determine how it operates and relates to other groups.

Whatever one's feelings are about the psychoanalytic framework and its emphasis on these perhaps mysterious-sounding forces beyond our ability to grasp, there is a compelling sense about two ideas that this theory has brought to our attention. First is the idea that intergroup relations are significantly influenced by the manner in which the contending groups are themselves formed. Second is the notion that the full story of intergroup relations will never be understood unless we are willing to push our search into those deep and dark recesses of unconscious life. There are simply too many intense feelings that get aroused when groups come into contact not to suspect that cognitive categorization, competing interests, feelings of injustice, or even concerns about self-esteem are inadequate for telling the complete story.

Chapter Summary: Key Learning Points

1. This chapter has examined four different yet complementary theories of intergroup relations that are centrally implicated in prejudice and discrimination:

   a. Social identity theory focuses on the role that our group memberships play in our sense of self-esteem.

b. Relative deprivation theory emphasizes issues of justice and fairness as we compare our own lot in life with that of others.

c. Realistic conflict theory reminds us that an important source of intergroup tension and hostility involves competition over scarce resources and competing group interests.

d. Finally, psychoanalytic theory reminds us that what we see on the surface of intergroup relations is often not all of what there is—that hidden unconscious processes may shape how one group relates to another.

2. Social identity theory helps us understand how in the effort to maintain an already satisfactory social identity, one group may derogate and reveal strong prejudices toward other groups. It has also helped us to see the various change-oriented strategies, both individual and collective, that people employ when their current social identity is not satisfactory.

3. Relative deprivation can be divided into two different forms:

a. Egoistical deprivation occurs when people compare their own position with others in their group and find they are not getting their fair share relative to these others.

b. Fraternal deprivation occurs when people compare their group's position with other groups and find that their group is not receiving its fair share relative to other groups.

4. Research has demonstrated that fraternal rather than egoistic deprivation is more associated with prejudiced attitudes toward various out-groups.

5. Realistic conflict theory suggests that warring groups may be helped to move toward peace if a superordinate goal can be established that joins competing interests into one shared interest, or if scarce resources are allocated more fairly.

6. Psychoanalytic theory suggests how the unconscious forces that bind people together into a group can play a significant role in the kinds of hateful attitudes toward others that may appear and that may even be directed inwardly toward other members of one's own group once the "enemy group" no longer exists.

The Effects of Prejudice on Identity and Society

Few of us doubt that the costs of prejudice and discrimination fall heavily on their targets—dreams denied and futures foreclosed simply because of one's group membership. These costs involve losses of both material benefits as well as psychological well-being. The material costs—poorer nutrition, worse housing, dangerous neighborhoods, deficient health care, dead-end jobs, inadequate education—are too high a price to pay for having done nothing more than being classified as lesser and undesirable. The psychological effects are likewise extreme—nagging doubts about one's own worth and value, frustration and a raging inner anger, troubled relationships, rejection and isolation, and for some, the pain of having to watch one's children repeat the cycle and not being able to help.

In Chapter 13, we examine some of the major effects of prejudice on those targeted because of their differences in gender, in race and ethnicity, in ability status, in sexual orientation, in belief. We will be especially concerned with the psychological consequences, not because these are greater or more important than the material, but because they are especially relevant to those concerned with the social psychology of prejudice. As we conduct this examination, however, we must realize that we can never fully disentangle the psychological from the material effects of prejudice. Poverty that results from prejudice and discrimination, for example, is both material and psychological in its consequences. To go hungry because you cannot afford food for yourself or your family is not simply to go hungry; it is also to feel something deeply wrong about oneself as an individual.

There is another piece to this story about prejudice, however, that is often not considered. When a society is filled with various forms of prejudice, it not only affects those targeted for its sting, but also those who carry the prejudice and even those who simply stand by silently and watch. Thus, in Chapter 14, we examine some of the broader consequences, both for those who harbor prejudice as well as for the larger society.

It is not my intention to weigh these two chapters in order to determine who suffers most: targets or perpetrators. Both suffer. Our task, rather, is to understand how individuals and groups in a society, in which some have been targeted for prejudice while others are its active or silent carriers, are caught together like dancers on a tightrope strung over a chasm. The inevitable fall has severe consequences for everyone.

Chapter 13

Self-Worth, Double Consciousness, and Inequality: Some Consequences of Being the Target of Prejudice

What happens to individuals who are brought up in a society in which they and their people are the targets of prejudiced attitudes and discriminatory behavior? Focusing on race and particularly on African Americans, sociologist W. E. B. Du Bois, the first African American to receive a Ph.D. from Harvard University, penned the following words in 1903. They introduce us to the two ideas that will organize our understanding of how prejudice affects a person's identity:

> It is a peculiar sensation, this double-consciousness, this sense of always looking at one's self through the eyes of others, of measuring one's soul by the tape of a world that looks on in amused contempt and pity. (1903/1995, p.45)

Reading the quote carefully will reveal Du Bois's two-part answer to the question at the beginning of this chapter. The first part focuses on the effects of seeing and measuring oneself through the eyes of those who hold you in contempt or disdain: Surely, this must have an enormously damaging effect on the person's sense of identity and self-worth.

Also writing early in the 20th century, in 1921, Kurt Lewin (see Lewin, 1948), a psychologist and a Jew who escaped from Nazi-era Germany, lets us see that the first effect identified by Du Bois is not restricted to African Americans:

> The feeling of inferiority of the Jew is but an indication of the fact that he sees things Jewish with the eyes of the unfriendly majority. (p. 198) . . . It is

recognized in sociology that the members of the lower social strata tend to accept the fashions, values and ideals of the higher strata. In the case of the underprivileged group it means that their opinions about themselves are greatly influenced by the low esteem the majority has for them. (p. 194)

And so, both Du Bois and Lewin agree that one of the primary effects of being the target of prejudice is to see oneself and to measure one's self-worth through the disparaging eyes of the dominant majority. How difficult it must be to stand tall and feel good about who one is when the only mirror available sends back a distorted, negative picture.

The second part of Du Bois's answer, conveyed in the opening quote from his writings, introduces us to the idea of a *double consciousness* or a *twoness of identity* based on being split between two worlds. This leads us to ask questions about how people who are split in two manage their lives and with what consequence to their overall well-being.

Although Du Bois's ideas were particularly concerned with African Americans and Lewin's with Jews, the clues they offer have a far broader applicability. They can be usefully applied to all persons who are the targets of prejudice and who thereby have come to see themselves through the eyes of those who hold them in disdain. We will begin our examination in this chapter with the consequences to African Americans of seeing themselves and measuring their self-worth through the eyes of the dominant white majority. We will then move on to examine the impact on the identity and self-worth of other groups who are similarly seen and judged by disparaging eyes. At that point, we will be prepared to examine the second part of Du Bois's answer as it applies to all those—African Americans and others—whose lives are rent in two by virtue of their living between cultures, the double consciousness or twoness to which Du Bois refers.

Identity and Self-Worth

Groups targeted for prejudice cannot help but look at themselves through the eyes of the very people who hold them in contempt or disdain. Under such conditions, it is very difficult not to see oneself in an uncomplimentary light— as never quite white enough, Christian enough, heterosexual enough, young enough, slim enough, able enough to pass muster. We begin our examination with the group to which Du Bois focused his original attention, African Americans.

African Americans and the Question of Self-Worth

Shortly before the outbreak of World War II, Clark and Clark (1939/1952) reported a study of black children's awareness of their own ethnicity as well as their ethnic preferences. This study triggered a host of similar research as well as the usual assortment of critiques, either confirming or challenging their disturbing findings. Here is what they did and what they found in that original social psychological investigation.

Their subjects were 253 black children, ages 3 through 7, some from Arkansas, the rest from Massachusetts. All children were presented with four dolls—two were brown with black hair, and two were white with yellow hair. Each child was asked several questions: Some were designed to determine the child's preferences (e.g., "Give me the doll you like best"); some, their awareness of racial differences (e.g., "Give me the doll that looks like a white child"); and one, the child's sense of her or his own color (e.g., "Give me the doll that looks like you").

Clark and Clark found that the children could accurately identify the white doll (94% chose white in response to this question) and the brown doll (93% chose the brown doll in response to the question asking them to select the colored doll, and 72% chose the brown doll when the question asked them to select the Negro doll). In general, therefore, these little children were aware of skin color and presumably of ethnic identification as well. When asked to select the doll that looked like themselves, however, the Clarks report that only 66% of these young African Americans chose the brown doll, while 33% chose the white doll. These findings suggest less clarity among these black children about their own ethnic identification.

The truly disturbing results, however, involved the children's preferences: "It is clear . . . that the majority of these Negro children prefer the *white* doll and reject the colored doll" (p. 557). About 66% of the children said that they liked the white doll best or would prefer playing with the white doll; 59% said that the brown doll looked bad; only 38% felt that the brown doll was a nice color. If there is anything hopeful about these findings, it appeared in the age trends. Although these black children at all ages preferred the white doll over the brown one, with increasing age, this preference grew less.

Needless to say, this study (as well as several others that preceded it) caused a great stir. The data suggested that one of the effects on a person's identity of being the target of prejudice and discrimination—an effect observed very early in the person's life—was self-denigration and rejection (i.e., a preference for white over black and indeed a rejection of black). Given that those expressing preferences for white were themselves black, this appeared to be a striking rejection of the self.

Efforts were soon directed to replicate the study (e.g., Asher & Allen, 1969; Goodman, 1952; Morland, 1962), to challenge its findings or their interpretation (e.g., Banks, 1976; Brand, Ruiz, & Padilla, 1974; Epstein, Krupat, & Obudho, 1976; Nobles, 1973), or to provide an analysis of how changing historical circumstances have brought about changes in self-evaluations (e.g., Brand et al., 1976; Hraba & Grant, 1970).

The Asher and Allen (1969) replication is striking for its confirmation of the original Clark and Clark findings. A sample of 186 black and 155 white children, ages 3 to 8, were presented with puppets who were alike in all respects but skin and hair color. These children were asked the same set of questions used in the Clarks' original study. Asher and Allen report that both black and white children revealed clear preferences for the white puppet in response to questions about which was the nice puppet, which they would prefer to play with, which one has a nice color.

It was thought that perhaps changing historical circumstances would produce different results—that as black became beautiful and racial pride took hold, black children's preferences would shift from white to black, as indeed some research had observed (e.g., Hraba & Grant, 1970). Asher and Allen tested this possibility by comparing the original 1939 data obtained by the Clarks with their own data obtained in the late 1960s. They found no support for this argument; that is, black preferences for white dolls were as high in their study as in the original 1939 study. It should be pointed out, however, that others have found support for this historical shift (e.g., Brand et al., 1974; Hraba & Grant, 1970; Ward & Braun, 1972), reporting that black preferences for black dolls seem to coincide with movements of black pride.

Still others have argued that the preference effect is not linked with race but rather with cleanliness (e.g., Epstein et al., 1976). That is, when both race and cleanliness are examined, children's preferences are based more on cleanliness than race. Others (e.g., Banks, 1976) suggest that there is no significant preference effect at all—that there is no phenomenon here worth worrying about!

Banks examined 21 studies, including Clark and Clark's, Asher and Allen's, and 19 others that studied racial preferences. Consider his conclusions: "69% of the reviewed studies showed nonpreference, 25% were found to have demonstrated black preference, and only 6% demonstrated a pattern of white preference in black subjects" (p. 1184). In other words, as Banks concludes, there is not even a phenomenon here worth trying to explain.

Developmental stages and racial preferences   Before we throw up our hands in exasperation over yet another collection of contradictory findings, let us add another element to this mix: developmental stages. Because all of us acquire our identities over time, passing through various stages, is it possible that at some points in our developmental history we reject ourselves, while at later points we become more accepting? In other words, perhaps self-rejection or self-acceptance is affected by the person's particular developmental stage. Those who are still wrestling with issues of their identity may be more self-rejecting than those who have made developmental progress and achieved a more satisfactory sense of self. If this is in fact the case, it would not take away from either Du Bois's or Lewin's claims, but rather would give us a richer view of how societal rejection of a group (e.g., African Americans for Du Bois; Jews for Lewin) may make it more difficult for persons to progress to a stage in which a satisfactory sense of self can emerge.

Various theories have been proposed to address the question of ethnic development—that is, stages by which persons acquire a sense of their own ethnicity and begin to operate in its terms (e.g., Phinney, 1990, as well as Ponterotto & Pedersen, 1993, summarize several of these theories and provide an integrative model). The theorists who have examined ethnic development suggest that a person's eventual identity is an achievement and that people pass through various stages on their way to this achievement. Everyone of us—black, white; female, male; straight, gay—must carve out a sense of our identity and establish a sense of our self-worth. Thus, identity is an achievement for all persons. Those who must carve their identity in a setting in which their group is a disparaged minority, however, have an especially difficult task. Not only must they work to transcend the dominant group's view of their people, they must also accommodate to the double consciousness that is part of being caught between two often contradictory worlds.

While each of the various models of ethnic identity development differ in certain respects, the four-stage integrative model presented by Ponterotto and Pederson (1993) offers a useful summary view of the stages through which persons are said to pass on their way to an achieved ethnic identity. We summarize it here:

Stage 1 involves an identification with the dominant social group, which in the case of African Americans means identifying with the white majority. This is what Clark and Clark and others observed among many of the young black children they studied. The children's preference for the white over the black doll suggested an identification with the white group and a rejection of their own group. As Ponterotto and Pederson comment, when adolescents and adults remain stuck in this early stage, they are likely to experience some negative consequences to their mental health: lowered self-esteem, higher anxiety, social withdrawal.

Stage 2 involves a more active questioning of the Stage 1 self. Persons in Stage 2 begin to challenge their former white preferences and begin a search for something in themselves they can feel good about. During this search, as Ponterotto and Pederson comment, the person is likely to be filled with "feelings of confusion, anger, and even embarrassment" (p. 59). While searching for a more positive sense of self, people may feel confused, sometimes revealing their white side, sometimes their black side. They may also harbor a great deal of anger over having been placed in such an untenable situation, confronting what seems to be an impossible choice between two contradictory types of consciousness. Embarrassment over not quite having figured out just who one is also appears during this second stage of ethnic identity development.

Stage 3 involves making a commitment to one's minority identity and fully immersing oneself in the minority culture: "Stage 3 individuals are likely to completely endorse the norms/values and customs of their own group, while at the same time completely rejecting values or norms associated with the

White establishment" (p. 60). It is during this stage that we can expect the individual to embrace her or his own culture in dress, mannerisms, and beliefs, while actively rejecting all that the white culture represents.

Finally, in *Stage 4,* the individual has achieved an identity based on resolving what appears to be an impossible situation: achieving a truly bicultural identity that cherishes the black world without a wholesale rejection of the white world. Obviously the task for the minority individual is made enormously more difficult by the disdain in which their minority identity may be held by the dominant majority. To achieve this Stage 4 identity, the person must reject this aspect of the majority's view while not rejecting the entire majority culture at the same time. Stage 4 clearly involves the second issue that Du Bois identified, involving the double consciousness that minority groups face, balancing the twoness of their being both black and American.

As the preceding model of ethnic identity development suggests, black preferences for whites might mark one (but only one) stage of development. We would expect black rejection of white at another stage (Stage 3) and a more balanced judgment at still another stage (Stage 4). Therefore, contradictory findings from the previous studies that have not taken these developmental possibilities into account might be less contradictory than we first imagined: That is, the contradiction could be resolved if we knew more about the particular stage of identity development in which the persons studied were located.

The apparent neatness of this developmental scheme, however—its stepwise march from self-rejection to self-and-other acceptance—should not conceal the extreme difficulties confronted by the minority person that people from the dominant majority do not have to deal with. It is extremely difficult for a person from a disparaged social group to move easily through these stages or to reach that final stage of self-and-other acceptance.

Before we move forward to examine more closely the second element of Du Bois's analysis of the effects of prejudice on identity (the double consciousness that we have already seen make its appearance in Stage 4), it will be helpful to examine the effects on identity and self-esteem for another group that has been the target of prejudiced attitudes and actions: women.

Gender and Self-Worth

Women as a group have been the targets more of what some have termed *ambivalent sexism* (e.g., Glick & Fiske, 1996) than of purely hateful sexism. Ambivalent sexism describes two contrasting views held about women as a group. On the one hand, throughout history as we have seen, women have been the targets of rather negative, even extremely hostile attitudes. And yet, women are also frequently held in high esteem, receiving what Glick and Fiske term benevolent sexist attitudes: They are, for instance, considered to be nurturers and help-givers—positive stereotypes, but stereotypes nevertheless. Thus, although the mirrors through which women view themselves have not been as uniformly negative as has been true of some other target groups, there is nevertheless every reason to anticipate important consequences for women's identity and sense of self-worth from being mirrored in such a stereotypic manner.

As we reflect back on discussions from previous chapters, we can see that we have already touched upon some of the effects of prejudice on women's identity. For example, in Chapter 4 we encountered a puzzling discrepancy between men's and women's math test scores (men scoring higher than women). Several efforts to explain this discrepancy have turned to an examination of the cultural prejudice against women's talents in this area and the effects of that prejudice on women's fear of taking math classes. To be repeatedly told that because you are a woman you have no business taking certain advanced math courses or for that matter even seriously considering those careers that require such courses as part of one's education is to confront an inhospitable setting for study. No wonder that many women decline to pursue such courses or careers, having accepted the cultural prejudices about their "native talents."

Recall as well Steele's (1997) work on women, stereotype threat, and math achievement that we considered in Chapter 9. There we saw how women's fears of fulfilling the stereotype held about them created the very anxieties that interfered with their performing as well as they should have on math ability tests. This case teaches us of the consequences of being the target of prejudiced stereotypes on people's sense of self-worth and test-taking performance.

Also recall Goldberg's (1968) study, first encountered in Chapter 9, in which females rated the same essay to be of higher quality when presumably written by a man than when believed to be written by another female. This is an effect that others have also noted: Persons deprecate their own group's competence, considering its members to be less competent simply because they are held to be lesser within the framework of their society.

In his study of colonizer-colonized relations which we first considered in Chapter 3, Memmi (1967) noted how frequently the colonized disparage anything that their own people make while extolling the virtues of everything associated with the colonizers. Not so surprising, then, to find women judging work by another woman to be of lesser quality than work produced by a man.

Androgyny   A view of the effects on women's sense of well-being comes from the collection of studies on androgyny and its correlates. Androgyny was originally defined as a person's possessing both stereotypically masculine and stereotypically feminine qualities (e.g., Bem, 1974, 1975); for instance, androgynous persons (male *or* female) would describe themselves as both assertive *and* nurturing. It was assumed that because androgynous persons could perform well in situations requiring both masculine assertiveness and feminine nurturance, they would have better overall adjustment than the sex-typed, nonandrogynous person. However, reexaminations of this idea cast it in a very different light (e.g., Taylor & Hall, 1982). Rather than the possession of both masculine and feminine qualities being the key to health and well-being, this reanalysis discovered that it was masculinity that correlated with measures of good adjustment and health. Femininity correlated with poorer adjustment.

Let us be clear about what has just been said. Data suggest that the best adjustment comes from possessing masculine (but not feminine) qualities. Possessing feminine qualities leads not to well-being but to its opposite. Traits held in less esteem correspond with femininity, another clear sign of the disparagement in which those traits most commonly associated with women are held. The implication, of course, is that insofar as women are socialized to learn feminine traits, they are taught to acquire the very qualities that their culture holds in low esteem: Hardly a way to think well of oneself.

Evaluating stereotypic traits   The important study of Broverman and her colleagues (1972) will help us better see the operation of this process and the often impossible situation that women confront. Broverman and her coauthors first developed a scale to measure male and female sex-role stereotypes, uncovering the usual listing of qualities that most of us have learned: Men are aggressive, independent, unemotional, objective, dominant; women are not aggressive, but are dependent, emotional, subjective, submissive, and so on.

This listing of male and female stereotypes was then presented to a group of subjects, who were asked to rate each trait for its desirability. Here is what Broverman and her colleagues concluded from this analysis: "The masculine poles of the various items were more often considered to be socially desirable than the feminine poles" (p. 65). As they reflected on these findings, the authors concluded that the male stereotype emphasizes competence, the female stereotype projects warmth. This implies that to be a woman is not to be competent!

In a culture where competence is highly valued, to be considered incompetent is to be on the receiving end of some rather strongly held negative evaluations. And to grow up as a woman, seeing oneself through the eyes of those who assume that women are incompetent, is to be saddled with a potentially damaging sense of one's overall worth.

Several further analyses add to this clearly emerging and disconcerting picture. Perhaps the most memorable finding from the Broverman group's study involves the ratings given by male and female mental health professionals (e.g., psychiatrists, psychologists, social workers). These professionals were presented with the same list of trait terms, but were asked to use them in describing a healthy adult, a healthy male adult, and finally, a healthy female adult. Results indicated all too clearly that the healthy male and the healthy adult were described in similar ways. By contrast, the healthy female was described very differently: "The general standard of health (adult, sex-unspecified) is actually applied to men only, while healthy women are perceived as significantly *less* healthy by adult standards" (p. 71). In other words, to be female is not to be able to live up to the standards that these mental health professionals say describe the healthy human being. Only by rejecting feminine qualities could women be considered healthy. To the extent that a woman describes herself in feminine terms, she is aligning herself with a portrait that professionals consider to be symptomatic of immaturity and poor mental health.

Growing up female   At this point in our discussion we should be able to see rather clearly some of the negative consequences to women's sense of identity and self-worth that comes from being a target of prejudice and discrimination. We should be sensitive as well to the same kind of dual consciousness for women that Du Bois identified as characteristic of African Americans. The more a women incorporates female characteristics as part of her identity, the less positively she is likely to view herself and be viewed as well by others. But, can a woman who rejects female characteristics as part of her identity feel good about herself?

Carol Gilligan (1982; Gilligan, Lyons, & Hanmer, 1990) and several of her associates have long been interested in women's unique developmental dilemmas and paths to adult maturity. In some of her more recent work, she and her colleagues have conducted lengthy interviews with young girls. She reports a sufficiently disturbing trend reported by the *New York Times* (January 7, 1990) in an article titled "Confident at 11, Confused at 16."

Gilligan and her colleagues observed that something seems to happen to young girls as they move from preadolescence into their adolescent years and beyond into adulthood. That something involves a loss for the developing young girl, rather than a gain. Consider some of the words Gilligan used to describe this developmental trend: She describes girls coming up against the "wall of Western culture," a tradition so dominated by male-centered understandings that the developing young woman cannot readily become "at once an adult and a woman" (Gilligan et al., 1990, p. 328).

Where have we heard this before? The processes that Gilligan and her colleagues uncovered, plus the research findings reported by Broverman and associates as well as other investigators, converge around a common theme for women and for other disparaged groups. Groups who have been the target of prejudice confront a serious conflict in their identity. For women, as we have seen, coming up against what Gilligan refers to as the "wall of Western culture," the conflict is between being a woman or being successful. For African Americans, the conflict involves the twoness or double consciousness that Du Bois suggested is a special problem for racial and ethnic minorities.

Troubling Options: Further Dilemmas for Identity

Consider Du Bois's description of the twoness of identity that the African American confronts, being both African American and yet also American: "two souls, two thoughts, two unreconciled strivings; two warring ideals in one dark body" (1903/1995, p. 45). The issue defined by Du Bois in 1903 involved how to be American without "being cursed and spit upon by his fellows" (p. 45) for having rejected that part of his fundamental twoness that is African, or having the "doors of Opportunity closed roughly in his face" (p. 46) for trying to belong to a white culture that will not have him because he is also African.

Remember that while the terms are different, the conflict of twoness remains much the same for women: to be feminine, or to be a mature, successful adult. It seems very likely that similar dilemmas confront all those who have membership in minority or nondominant social groups while dwelling at the same time in a world defined by those in dominant positions.

A helpful approach to defining the various ways in which individuals have sought to manage the dilemma of twoness has been provided by La Fromboise, Coleman, and Gerton (1993). It will be useful to examine several patterns they identify and to connect each with its likelihood of working beneficially or destructively for persons who "choose" one or the other way of managing the duality they face because they are the targets of prejudice and discrimination. (See Figure 13.1.)

Figure 13.1

Some consequences of being the target of prejudice

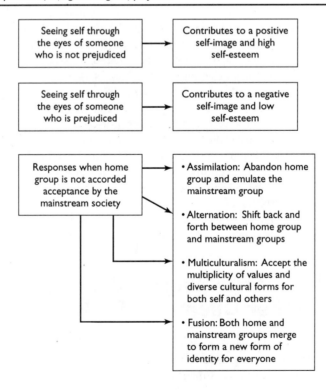

Assimilation

One manner of trying to resolve the twoness that comes from being both black and American, to continue with Du Bois's example, involves assimilation into the dominant culture along with rejection of the nondominant or disparaged culture. The concept of *racelessness* (e.g., Arroyo & Zigler, 1995; Fordham, 1988; Fordham & Ogbu, 1986) has been developed to describe one variation of this assimilative pathway. To be raceless is to deny that one is black while pursuing the ideals that the other part of one's twoness represents. To use gender as another example, assimilation on the part of women would produce a kind of genderlessness: affirming things that are masculine while rejecting things that are feminine.

It does not demand a great inferential leap to observe that assimilation, by which people reject one part of their identity and affirm another, may appear among almost any group that has been the target of prejudice. A male homosexual, thereby, may seek to affirm the part of his identity that permits access to the heterosexual world while denying the part of his identity that allows his homosexual desires to gain expression. He is closeted even to himself, suffering the isolation of belonging to neither the straight world nor the gay world.

What, however, are the effects of assimilation and the consequent racelessness that emerges when the twoness involves a double racial consciousness? Those who developed the concept of racelessness have argued that this option leads to many symptoms of strain and personal confusion. Fordham (1988) goes so far as to describe the choice between one's racial group and the American ideal as a *pyrrhic victory*—that is, a victory won at such a high cost that it could hardly be considered a real victory.

The well known journalist and author Carl Rowan (1996) offers a poignant example of just what this means. He describes the reading of the honor roll during an assembly at a predominantly black school in Washington, D.C. Many black honorees refused to stand when their name was read: "Bright black kids could not stand against the peer pressure that said those who had made the honor roll were nerds, geeks, and, worst of all—acting like Whitey" (pp. 267–268). In other words, if they accepted the honors they had earned, they would feel like traitors to their own group!

Systematic research has examined this dilemma among blacks who chose to become successful in school by rejecting their own community's views (see Fordham, 1988; Fordham & Ogbu, 1986; La Fromboise et al., 1993). Those who made this choice were found to suffer more stress than those who declined to assimilate to the dominant culture's educational ideals.

Not everyone, however, has fully supported this conclusion. Arroyo and Zigler (1995), for example, while finding some support both for the idea of racelessness and its negative consequences among black adolescents, also found a similar pattern among white adolescents: Choosing school over friends turned out to be one of those pyrrhic victories for white adolescents as well. Meanwhile Rogler, Cortes, and Malgady (1991) considered the case for Latinos and concluded that the issue hinges on the degree of disparity between the two cultures: That is, it may not always be necessary to reject one's own culture, disparaged as it might be, in order to assimilate to the new culture, because the two cultures may not be as opposed in every detail as we commonly think.

When it comes to school success, however, there often is a contradiction between the peer culture and one's home culture as well as the dominant culture's ideals. A study reported by Steinberg, Dornbusch, and Brown (1992), for example, found that among African American adolescents, in particular, there is substantial home support for doing well in school, but minimal peer support. As Rowan's example suggests, this makes it difficult for black youngsters to find a peer group that affirms their schooling desires, making it more likely, therefore, that only by rejecting the peer group and becoming in this sense raceless, can the person do well. Here we go again with that pyrrhic victory. The choice between rejecting one's peers and doing well in school or accepting one's peers and doing poorly is a nonwinning choice that, not surprisingly, leads to high levels of stress.

All things considered, I think it is fair to conclude that resolving one's twoness through assimilation is neither as easy as it may have initially appeared nor as satisfactory a resolution as we sometimes imagine. If in order to fit into the larger culture, persons must abandon their own culture or significant parts of it (e.g., peer group support), whatever they may gain through assimilation, they lose through rejecting their own people. I suspect that the case is much the same whether we focus on African Americans, other racial or ethnic groups, or for that matter on any other group that has been the target of prejudice.

Alternation

A second pattern for dealing with the twoness of identity that results from being the target of prejudice, identified by La Fromboise and her colleagues (1993), is familiar to most people who have found themselves caught in this contradiction. To alternate is to do precisely what the term suggests: switch back and forth between the two contrasting cultural identities. Let me illustrate through a personal experience.

The real estate agent that my wife and I used to purchase our home is a white woman who had been married to a black man. Now divorced, she has a son, Eric. I needed some assistance in getting things moved around our new house and so hired Eric to work with me for a few hours. Eric is about 23, clearly identifiable as black. As we drove around together and worked together, I found that we chatted easily and unexceptionably. On the way back to his home, I wanted to drop off some of the recyclable debris at the Berkeley recycling center. We drove up and were greeted by a young black man who was in charge of the center. On seeing him, Eric shouted out the window,

"Hey Bro!" using a vocal tone, accent, and vocabulary that was quite different from the manner in which he and I had just been chatting. Not a big deal at all, but an illustration of alternation.

Most sojourners between two contrasting cultures have learned how to move back and forth between the two, putting one on and then the other as the situation and audience demand. Homosexual males, for example, can camp it up at one moment and then appear to be super-butch the next, returning again moments later to their camp style, moving between the two contrasting cultures. The apparent benefits of alternation, as La Fromboise and her coauthors note, is that it does not demand that persons ever choose between the twoness they confront: They can be both. She and her colleagues report several studies involving Native Americans, for example, who have learned how to behave one way on the reservation and alternate this with a contrasting manner when visiting in town: Language changes, mannerisms change, their whole being takes on a different cast as they alternate between the two disparate and differently evaluated cultures.

Although alternation would seem workable in most situations, there is always a price to pay. Concerns over "leaking" the wrong identity, for example, loom large for many people caught between two cultures, attempting to negotiate the two by alternating in an appropriate manner. Pride of group membership is also missing for those persons who too easily portray both cultures and, although belonging to two, can never really claim pride in either one of them.

Multiculturalism

The very term *multiculturalism* or *biculturalism* nowadays either brings cheers or boos (see Taylor and Gutmann, 1994). The idea that we live in a world with equal but different cultural points of view, with no one better, wiser, or more correct than any other, sounds pleasing to those for whom pride in one's own group has become important, but displeasing to those who continue to believe that their way is the only way or the best way and the rest are poor imitations. The ideal of multiculturalism involves achieving a positive sense of self and self-worth in a person's own culture while not diminishing or denigrating any other cultural form. As La Fromboise and her coauthors describe this ideal, it involves pride in one's own culture along with tolerance, contact, and sharing with the other—in other words, a rather thoroughly unprejudiced option. We previously encountered much this same ideal in considering the final stage of identity development. Recall that in this final stage, persons achieve a genuinely bicultural identity: They do not reject their "home" culture, even while accepting the value of the other cultural views as well.

Whether or not such an ideal can ever be attained—or if achieved, sustained—remains as yet an open question. Multiculturalism too readily breaks down into either the return of one dominant culture or perhaps even fusion, to which we now turn our attention.

Fusion

Fusion turns out to be more myth than reality. To have a genuine melting pot—which is what fusion implies—involves both dominant and nondominant cultures transforming themselves in such a manner that an entirely new, fused culture is created. In the more usual case, as Du Bois's ideas of twoness and Gilligan's ideas of basic conflicts for women suggest, rather than a fused melting pot, the nondominant group may melt itself into the dominant mainstream, while that mainstream is maintained with minimal change. Genuine melting or fusion, however, would entail, for example, undoing the challenges posed by Du Bois and Gilligan by providing an identity that fused black and white, male and female. For this to be accomplished, of course, the dominant groups (e.g., male and white) must yield every bit as much as the nondominant groups. This is an occurrence not yet observed, though for some it remains an ideal.

Chapter Summary: Key Learning Points

1. It is difficult to establish or to maintain a positive and healthy image of oneself when brought up and living one's life in a society that has systematically devalued and denigrated one's social group—whether this group be African Americans, women, homosexuals, or others who have found themselves the targets of prejudiced attitudes and actions. Much of this difficulty is based on having to see oneself through disparaging eyes, mirrored by people who have negative views of one's own people.

2. These same conditions also make it difficult to establish or sustain a coherent sense of identity when one's consciousness of self is split in two, presenting conflicting loyalties: one's own group versus the dominant group in society.

3. We examined both of the preceding effects especially as they have appeared among African Americans and women:

   a. We saw how difficult it has been for African American youth to form a positive self-image as black without rejecting the dominant white culture within which they live.

   b. We saw the difficulties that women face as they seek to grow up feeling good about being a woman—even as they, to borrow a term from Carol Gilligan, come up against the "wall of Western culture" and its denigration of many qualities that women have sought to nurture in themselves.

4. We examined various strategies that people have developed for dealing with the complexities of being not quite a full-fledged member of society:

   a. Assimilation entails trying to join the dominant group's culture by abandoning one's home culture. This strategy, however, often results in a kind of racelessness, a victory with negative consequences for the individual.

   b. Alternation as a strategy allows an individual to move back and forth between two contrasting and often disparate identities— often, however, resulting in a commitment to neither.

   c. Multiculturalism, perhaps the best resolution (though difficult to achieve), involves a mature view of oneself as a member of one's own group, even while not rejecting the dominant culture's values (i.e., forming an ethic that values all forms of diversity).

   d. Fusion requires an idealized and not yet realized merging of the divergent cultural identities in which each yields and so produces an entirely new, fused social identity for all people.

Chapter 14

Whiteness, Maleness, and Heterosexuality: Some Effects of Prejudice on Identity and Society

Too often we think of prejudice as though it only affects its victims. And so we focus, as we did in Chapter 13 for example, on the effects of racism on African Americans or sexism on women, while ignoring other members of the cast. Let me illustrate what I mean.

Suppose you were asked to write a brief essay on how racism shapes people's lives. What groups would you write about? It is likely that your essay (like Chapter 13) would focus on African Americans, Latinos, and perhaps Native Americans. It is less likely that you would mention whites as a group whose lives have also been shaped by racism. Of course, your essay might mention whites as the perpetrators—but other than occupying that role in the story of racism, whites would probably play no other part in your essay. It would be as though racism affected only groups that we commonly think *have race*—and in our minds, that usually excludes whites.

In her analysis of this issue, Ruth Frankenberg (1993) offers us another example of this same point. Suppose you were conducting a study of workers at a nearby manufacturing firm. As Frankenberg states it, "a study of the workplace involving Chicana workers will probably address race and culture; a study of white women workers probably will not" (p. 18). In other words, the very term *race* has come to mean something other than white. White is presumed to be the category *without race*. Another way of stating this is to say that white is the norm, the standard, the invisible background against which "color" is marked as racial. Because white has come to mean the absence of color, it is unmarked (also see Dyer, 1997).

In a similar way, if we were to focus on sexism, women would be central, with men entering as those who *do* sexism to women, but not as people who are *in themselves* shaped by sexism. That is, we commonly think of sexism as something that shapes women's lives, not men's. And, if our essay were to focus on sexual orientation, it would be those with a homosexual, but not heterosexual, orientation that would be the center of our attention. In other words, we assume that heterosexuality is not at issue, not something important to study and to understand; only homosexuality comes under our microscope. As we will examine later, however, queer theory (see Chapter 12) has turned this focus around, making heterosexuality as much an issue as homosexuality currently is.

Because of this rather common way of thinking about prejudice, we will find little systematic research dealing with the neglected partners in prejudice—that is, with whiteness, maleness, and heterosexuality. What is missing, therefore, is a careful examination of the manner by which the privileged and advantaged identities of the unmarked groups (e.g., whites, males, heterosexuals) are built on a foundation of prejudice and discrimination. We come to think of prejudice and discrimination as something that happens to the marked groups and so fail to see their role in sustaining the privileged identity of the unmarked groups.

In addition to this dearth of research on the privileged and advantaged, we also find few systematic studies of the effect of prejudice on society more generally. It takes little imagination, however, to realize that racism, sexism, and anti-homosexual attitudes and actions are not simply problems for those on the receiving end but problems for everyone. Racism is not only a black problem, it is also a white problem with consequences for the entire society. Sexism is not only a women's problem, but a men's problem as well, with consequences for the entire society. Anti-homosexualism likewise is not simply a gay and lesbian problem, but a problem for the entire society. These frequently missing sides to the story of prejudice are explored in this chapter.

Although, as I have noted, systematic research is sparse, there are several leads we can follow. The first lead comes from a perspective that views each person's identity as a collaborative, mutual achievement. This means that who I am is influenced by who you are and vice versa. For our purposes, therefore, your disadvantages and my advantages are intimately joined. I could not have a privileged identity without your having a disadvantaged one, even as your disadvantage builds on my advantage. This is why prejudice and discrimination join us together and make it *our* problem, not simply yours. We open this chapter with this idea, intriguing though at times difficult to grasp.

The next set of leads directs us to examine the broader effects on society that occur when systems of inequality are sustained through prejudice and discrimination. We will look at the costs to Nazi Germany, for example, that occurred as they relentlessly pursued an eliminationist anti-Semitism and so invested time and resources in this endeavor rather than fighting the war. We will also consider the loss of qualified persons that occurs when a society structures itself along lines that are marked more by prejudice than by rational planning. Finally, we will consider the impact of prejudice and discrimination on the legitimacy of the social order, on its ability morally rather than coercively to bring people together.

Creating Mutual Identities

In order to understand how prejudice shapes everyone's lives and not simply the lives of those who are its typical targets, we need to consider just how our identities are shaped, and especially how you play a role in my identity even as I do in yours. Let us develop this point by using both race and gender as examples. Ruth Frankenberg (1993) applied this idea to her work on racism; if we examine her thoughts we will get a better sense of what it means to argue that racism is a problem for white identity and not simply for black identity (Thompson & Tyagi, 1996, have edited a valuable collection of personal essays that converge around this same theme; also see Anderson, 1995; Bingham, 1993; Dyer, 1997; McIntosh, 1993).

Frankenberg conducted a series of interviews with white women, asking them how racism constructed their lives—in other words, how their whiteness was affected by others' blackness. Not surprisingly, the initial response of many of the women she interviewed was puzzlement. After all, they were white, not black—and white, in their eyes, was "colorless." Racism meant talking about blacks and other minorities, not about whites. In time, however, her interviews discovered just how much each woman's whiteness was shaped by the existence of blackness and especially prejudice.

In particular, Frankenberg was interested to discover that far from whiteness being without color, it was rather filled with the colors of privilege and power. Whiteness meant privilege. Whiteness meant power. Being white was thereby to be very colorful indeed. Although many of the women she interviewed would hardly describe themselves as being privileged or powerful—after all, they too were struggling to get through each day in their lives—when measured against the lives of people who were not white, it became apparent that whiteness conveyed privilege and power in a society constructed along racial lines.

Whiteness, argues Frankenberg, places people in positions of advantage and of privilege. Nonwhiteness places people in positions of lesser standing. Given this, it is difficult to maintain, as some continue to insist, that racism is a problem confronted only by people of color. Whiteness is a color—in this case a color marking privilege and advantage—that shapes people's lives in a manner that they would not be shaped if they lived in a world without nonwhites to occupy positions of lesser standing. Racism, in other words, creates both black and white identity, not simply black identity.

We first encountered this idea in Chapter 2, especially in the writings of authors such as Cornell West (1993) and Toni Morrison (1992). Recall how

West stated this point: "Without the presence of black people in America, European-Americans would not be 'white' " (p. 156). In short, whiteness is built on blackness every bit as much as blackness is built on whiteness. The advantages of being white, then are built on the disadvantages of being a color other than white. All of this makes it difficult to maintain that racism has nothing to do with whites. Racism has everything to do with the very manner by which white privilege is constructed.

Peggy McIntosh's (1993) reflections on what she refers to as her own "invisible knapsack" of white privilege—a knapsack filled with ways in which being white has made a significant difference in her own life—gives us a concrete example of what all of this means. Here is a sampling of some items she discovered when she unpacked her own white privilege:

1. She can wear whatever kinds of clothing she wishes, including second-hand clothes from the nearby thrift store, without worrying that people will feel pity for her poverty. Her white privilege means that people will see her making a statement about her nonconcern with fashion, rather than being trapped by poverty into having to wear hand-me-downs.
2. She can complete a challenging activity without having to listen to people comment about how she is a credit to her race or her people.
3. Whenever she speaks, she is rarely heard as someone speaking for her race.
4. If she has a bad day, she never needs to look closely to see if this is because of her race.
5. She can wander in and out of stores and never worry that she is being followed or closely watched because of her race.

As McIntosh continued her reflections, she noted many other features of her everyday life in which her race and the privilege it confers are never at issue, because in being white, her racial markings are as invisible as the advantages and privileges that go along with her whiteness.

In speculating about why the invisibility of whiteness seems so firmly embedded in our culture, McIntosh comments that white invisibility is like male invisibility: By keeping these marks of privilege invisible, the myth of meritocracy, of individual personal achievement, is maintained. It would be difficult to maintain the notion that people's outcomes—their winning or losing the games of everyday life—are the result of their individual merits if it were as clear as it has become to McIntosh, Frankenberg, and others that many outcomes are not the result of merit, but of race, gender, and other marks of difference.

Much of this same point can be made about other groups who are the targets of prejudice. Pleck (1993), for example, examined the meaning of heterosexual masculinity as another unmarked category that gives its possessors special but invisible advantage (see also Boyarin, 1997; Minton, 1997; Richardson, 1996). This invisibility is based on the common assumption that only what is different needs to be explained. Therefore, in this standard view, it is homosexuality but not heterosexuality that must be explained, because heterosexuality is assumed not to be a special kind of sexual orientation. What we take for granted here as elsewhere (e.g., the invisibility of maleness and of whiteness) is said to require no further examination.

In the view adopted in this chapter, however, it is precisely what we take for granted (i.e., the invisible partner) that definitely needs to be examined. If we fail to examine what we take for granted about ourselves and others, we forget the ways in which who we are has been shaped by our views of others' differences. Perhaps we need to see our own whiteness, maleness, or heterosexuality as different so that we can explain them as well.

Pleck regards masculinity as an achievement that is always vulnerable to challenge (Gilmore, 1990, makes this same point). Pleck suggests that both women and homosexual men represent threats to this achievement. Women challenge men's power through their ability to deny men the heterosexual conquests by which they have come to define their very masculinity. And, if we accept Kitzinger's (1987) arguments, lesbian women provoke an even more serious challenge, as they appear not to need or to desire men at all. Meanwhile, homosexual men are a challenge to the entire system of masculine power insofar as they are men who do not define their power in terms of heterosexual conquest (see Boyarin, 1997, who explores this idea further).

Pleck argues that a line dividing "real men" from "homosexual male pretenders" is central to masculine self-definitions as powerful. That line symbolizes the very definition of masculinity. "Real men" are forever wary about crossing this line. It is not simply a division based on sexual orientation, but one defined through the power and privilege it gives to the heterosexual male. To cross the line, then, is to lose the very privilege that the line was created to sustain. Pleck's analysis helps us see how the identity of the heterosexual male—the power and privilege he has—is defined by sustaining prejudice toward both women and homosexual men and women.

Frankenberg's study of anti-miscegenation laws (forbidding interracial marriage) adds race to this picture. She argues that the very meaning of masculinity (and femininity) is also racially defined. The many laws that forbid marriage between whites and persons of color were designed to protect the purity of white women from what was said to be the bestial excesses of people of color, while simultaneously defining true masculinity in terms of the protection of white women's purity.

In 1661, Maryland was among the first states to enact laws forbidding intermarriage between whites and blacks or Native Americans. Over the next several hundred years, some 38 states followed suit, sometimes adding new groups to the forbidden list. It was only in 1948 that the California Supreme Court declared such laws unconstitutional in California, and in 1967 that the United States Supreme Court declared *all* such laws to be unconstitutional. Consider that date again: 1967! Until that time, it was still illegal in some states for a white person to marry a person of color, even as today a marriage is not legal if it involves persons of the same sex.

Frankenberg, however, is not interested in simply recounting some historical tidbits about prejudice; she hopes to teach us how the very definitions of masculinity (as the protector of women's purity) and femininity (as having such purity) are sustained by maintaining discriminatory practices toward other groups. White women are pure and genuinely feminine insofar as they maintain their distance from the dangerous sexuality of men of color. Meanwhile, white men are masculine insofar as they pass and enforce laws against intermarriage that will protect the virtue of white women.

In a nutshell, women's femininity and sexuality, argues Frankenberg, are built on a racist view of the world, even as men's masculinity and sexuality are similarity constructed. Without racism, then, women would not be women, nor men, men. And, if we add Pleck's argument, we would have to say that masculinity is also built on sexism and anti-homosexual bias.

It is very difficult to come away from considering these aspects of our own culture without finally realizing that prejudice and discrimination are every bit as relevant to the identities of persons who are white, male, and heterosexual as they are to those groups we usually consider to be the targets of prejudice. Racism, sexism, and heterosexism thereby are not just issues that "others" face. We should now be better able to see how one group's identity is not only built on others' but on sustaining prejudice toward those others. Prejudice does not only affect the usual targets, but also those who gain its invisible benefits.

Broader Societal Effects of Prejudice and Discrimination

As in so many cases, the headings that divide a chapter into seemingly neat units are never quite as neat as one might believe. In the preceding section we described the way prejudice impacts everyone's identity, not just those individuals and groups who are the targets of prejudice. This present section, in which we examine the societal consequences of prejudice and discrimination, thereby simply expands on this theme. Here, however, rather than focusing on people's identity, I would like us to consider the effects of prejudice on other features of society at large:

> First, we consider how qualified personnel are lost to society by virtue of their being defined as lesser beings. Here we will see how societal goals are thereby made more difficult to achieve.

> Second, we see how serious questions about the legitimacy of the entire society emerge as prejudice and discrimination cast a pall over the moral persuasiveness of the social order.

Figure 14.1 diagrams the effects discussed earlier in the chapter as well as those to be examined in this section.

Figure 14.1

Some general consequences of prejudice and discrimination on society

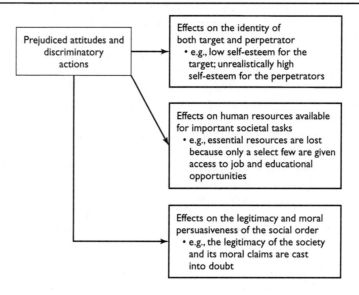

Societal Examples: From Nazi Germany to the United States

I sometimes believe that if the real Nazis had never existed to provide an exemplar of how not to function, we would have made up something like the Nazis in order to provide the kind of moral lesson we need. In this case, as numerous reports suggest (e.g., Goldhagen, 1996), the Nazi war effort was made a shambles by its virulent anti-Semitism. In the first place, some of the very brain power that prewar Germany had in place was drained away by eliminating all Jews from their positions of influence in the universities, in science, in medicine, and in law. We are all aware of some of the names of those who left Germany—Einstein and Freud, for example—whose continued presence in Germany might have substantially benefited that nation.

But, because all persons of Jewish descent had to be eliminated as part of the national policies of purity, this meant that many qualified personnel were denied access to influential positions. Unfortunately, we do not need to go as far away as Nazi Germany to see some of these same effects. In the early part of the 20th century in the United States, persons of Jewish background were not considered qualified to attend the nation's most select colleges and universities, nor were they permitted entry to careers in medicine, for example.

In recounting some of these early denials, Karen Sacks (1994) tells of the Protestant elite at the dominant eastern universities who rejected Jews because they were "unwashed, uncouth, unrefined, loud, and pushy" (p. 82). A president of Harvard University (President Lowell) as well as a president of Bryn

Mawr College (President Thomas) openly opposed the admission of various groups, including Jews and blacks. President Thomas also actively opposed the advancement of any Jewish faculty at Bryn Mawr. In 1918, at a meeting of the deans of New England's elite colleges and universities, fear that Jews might soon overrun the hallowed halls of ivy were openly expressed by many. In 1919, Columbia University developed procedures designed to cut down on the number of Jews who would be admitted. Apparently their procedures were so effective that other Ivy League institutions sought to copy them.

Jews are not the "problem" today as they were earlier in the United States—but in many highly prestigious colleges and universities, the new "problem" groups are of Asian background, and the issue is how to manage what would otherwise become an all-Asian entering class. As I said, we need not go to Nazi Germany to discover some of the same issues emerging, although Germany's way of eliminating "undesirables" continues to haunt all of us.

In addition to its active elimination of persons with Jewish background from all key positions in society, thereby denying its nation the knowledge and skills that such persons possessed, Germany's obsession with the elimination of Jews became so all-encompassing that *it,* rather than winning the war, took over wartime Germany. Goldhagen's (1996) analysis, for example, suggests how much of Germany's resources and personnel were required simply in order to maintain the numerous concentration camps and manage the Jews and other prisoners. Indeed, so many people and railway supplies were required that the ability of Germany to wage the war successfully was put in jeopardy.

Meanwhile, rather than effectively using its prisoners to conduct the work needed for their war effort, the Germans' views about the Jews was such that they often considered them poor workers, thus undercutting their ability to serve Germany's war machinery. Through beatings, starvation, crowded and disease-ridden living conditions—and of course methodical extermination—Jews whose labor might have been put to work on behalf of Germany's war effort were cast aside.

Again, we need not spend all of our time in Nazi Germany, with its obsession with the Jewish problem, to see how prejudice and discrimination weaken a society's ability to carry out essential functions. As we know from studying even the relatively recent past in the United States, many reputable academicians believed that women were not well designed to go to college; or if they went, they should only attend special women's colleges that would polish their artistic and homemaker skills, making them better wives for up-and-coming men. Thus, the entire society was denied the talents in the full range of professions that are now increasingly being opened up to women. And until very recently, systematic exclusion of blacks and other persons of color from access to higher education not only had disturbing consequences for the people involved, but also for the society that was denied the talents that these individuals could have provided.

In short, prejudice and discrimination deprive society of the benefits that many people could provide by denying such people access to the educational systems and employment opportunities that come from a nonprejudiced system.

Legitimacy and Moral Persuasion

Perhaps more difficult to measure than some of the other consequences of prejudice and discrimination that we have considered, yet arguably as important in the long run as any of the others, is the potential damage that prejudice causes to the delicate fabric of trust and legitimacy that holds together any but the most totalitarian society. No society can long endure without the willing agreement of its members to live peacefully within that society. And, no amount of force by itself can keep people in line for very long. People must believe that the social order is legitimate, fair, and just. Prejudice and discrimination undermine those beliefs.

The idea of legitimacy is often used to describe a relationship among persons who willingly agree to accept the authority of others because they consider that authority to be functioning in a fair-minded manner. Legitimacy conveys the meaning of willing acceptance rather than coercive force. When the social order is considered to be legitimate, brute force is not required to sustain everyday order. People agree to abide by rules because they see these rules to be legitimate: The rules were arrived at democratically, through fair procedures, and are not biased either to the advantage of some or to the disadvantage of others.

Let us go back to that fateful day in 1995 when literally millions of Americans were glued to their TV sets waiting for the jury to hand down its decision in the infamous murder case involving O. J. Simpson. The jury entered the courtroom and announced its verdict on each count against Simpson: "Not guilty." It is a reasonably safe bet that if you were white and observing this moment, you felt shocked, even disappointed: From your perspective, justice had not been served. Yet, if you were African American, you very likely applauded a decision that in your eyes finally brought justice to a black man, whatever else you might think of Simpson. Informal observations and polling results suggest a black-white split in reactions to this verdict: approval by blacks; disapproval by whites (e.g., Rowan, 1996). Examining the legitimacy of the criminal justice system helps us better understand these divergent reactions.

To be black in the United States today is to feel that many parts of the larger social system, but especially the criminal justice system, operate in a highly prejudicial and illegitimate manner. This illegitimacy involves what to many blacks is the justice system's tendency to unfairly disadvantage blacks and advantage whites in arrest, prosecution, and sentencing. Recent research findings lend credence to these perceptions.

For example, nearly 33% of African American males in their twenties are involved in some manner or another with the criminal justice system—in jail or prison; on probation or parole (e.g., see *Los Angeles Times,* October 5, 1995). African Americans and Latinos comprise approximately 90% of those offenders sentenced because of drug possession. Consider the following passage from the research report on which these figures were based, comparing the reactions to the O. J. Simpson trial with these statistics:

> Regardless of where one stands on his guilt or innocence, what is clear is that a wealthy and famous African American was able to assemble a very formidable defense. This is contrasted with the typical scene in almost every courthouse in cities across the country, where young African American and Hispanic males are daily processed through the justice system with very limited resources devoted to their cases. (from *Los Angeles Times,* October 5, 1995, p. A19)

Meanwhile, a recent study of sentencing in federal courts in the western United States during 1994 and 1995 reported a clear distinction based on race. For example, the average sentence for convicted whites was 38.5 months; the average for blacks was 61 months. The Latinos' average was even lower than for whites, however, at 36.5 months. The commission issuing the report suggested that it found no basis for racial bias in these sentencing figures. This conclusion, however, was refuted by others who felt that even if the disparities in sentencing were not biased, bias was rampant in the justice system's selection and prosecution of minorities. And so, when O. J. Simpson was found not guilty it meant that at long last some sense of justice had finally been achieved, in the eyes of many blacks and other minorities, in a system that has not had a very good track record for being fair.

Whites, on the other hand, have had difficulty in accepting this portrayal of the justice system as illegitimate. After all, in their view the justice system has been thoughtfully designed to operate in a fair and legitimate manner. Of course, we all recognize the occasions in which justice is not as blind as usually depicted but rather sees a bit too much. Yet for many whites, things in general seem to work fairly in most cases. For many whites, however, the O. J. Simpson case proved to be an exception to this otherwise fair and legitimate system: Justice seems to have bent over backward to let a guilty man off the hook for his crime.

I am not siding here with the actual guilt or innocence of O. J. Simpson. The point of this brief encounter with recent history is to indicate how one and the same system within the larger society may be perceived as legitimate by one group while illegitimate by another. Usually, when prejudice is at work, those who are its targets feel that they will not get a fair hearing: Things never work to their advantage. In their eyes, therefore, the system is illegitimate. To those who occupy more advantaged places on the social ladder, who tend to benefit from the way things currently function, legitimacy would be at issue only if *they* were unfairly accused and found guilty.

The preceding lessons tell us that one of the first casualties of prejudice and discrimination is the sense of the legitimacy of the society in which the disadvantaged live. When legitimacy is either not present or not a vibrant force in people's lives, the entire social order suffers. When people no longer believe the social order is legitimate because it is biased, the orderly operation of the entire society increasingly requires force to create an order that willing agreements cannot obtain.

Moral persuasiveness   Another facet of legitimacy involves a society's moral persuasiveness. Unless brute force is used to keep people in line, people usually abide by the rules because they are responsive to the moral persuasiveness of their society. With prejudice, however, there comes a withering away of the ability of the society to engage moral persuasion on behalf of maintaining the social order.

Suppose you are asked to play a game using rules that guarantee you will always come out on the losing side. Once this feature of the game becomes clear, only a fool would want to continue to play for very long. If the game is stacked against you, there is no way that anyone could convince you to keep on playing: Their words would be seen as hollow appeals without any support in reality. Once prejudice erodes legitimacy, too many of life's games take on this quality; moral appeals no longer are effective in convincing people to continue playing games in which they have come to believe they will only be losers.

Some have interpreted the African American situation in these terms. Well meaning folks tell the young black adolescents that completing high school and graduating from college will assure them of a great future. For too long, however, they have found themselves stuck in a game that seems not to deal them a winning hand, no matter what level of schooling they have achieved. Therefore, many find these to be hollow appeals. Many believe that playing by the rules when those rules do not apply to your people offer little hope for improvement. And so alternative means to achieve the American dream are sought, some of which are generally accepted, others of which lead into criminal activity.

Throughout this discussion, I have been using racism as the primary illustration of the consequences of prejudice for the legitimacy and moral persuasiveness of the social order. I have done this because racism continues to be one of the prime examples of how prejudice erodes the legitimacy of the social order.

The other "isms," however, are not exempt from the same type of analysis. For example, where sexism rules in a society, women confront much the same sense of illegitimacy as do persons of color: They come to believe that it is not their brains but their seductive bodies that count, and only as long as they can maintain those bodies. Unfair? Yes. And this very unfairness creates trouble for a society that permits sexism to remain viable.

Harm to women, definitely. But harm as well to the larger society, including men, whose momentary benefits are readily swept away by the undermining of the larger social order in which they too play a part. There is no one, then, who gets off scot-free when prejudice and discrimination run rampant throughout a society. We all suffer, even if we think otherwise.

Can all of this also be said about each and every other "ism" by which prejudice appears? What about prejudices based on a person's sexual orientation? What is the harm to the larger society if people genuinely find homosexuality unnatural and sinful and so harbor strong negative feelings toward homosexuals? Let me repeat what I have been saying all along in this chapter and indeed in this text: To exclude any group through prejudice and discrimination, homosexuals included, is to undermine the legitimacy of the social order by revealing its fundamental unfairness. If anyone is not free, then everyone is not free; if anyone is denied rights, then everyone is denied rights.

We have created a delicate enterprise here: our society. Its delicacy is such that prejudice and discrimination, however they may appear and however reasonably justified they seem to be (after all, Jews were genuine horrors to many Germans), can only rip apart this home, this only home for all of us.

Chapter Summary: Key Learning Points

1. Because our own identities are created in tandem with others, the fate that befalls those others also has an important impact on who we are. Where prejudice and discrimination permeate a society, their effects are not only felt on those targeted for their harsh sting (e.g., blacks, women, homosexuals), but on everyone else as well.

2. Whiteness, maleness, and heterosexuality are built on blackness, femaleness, and homosexuality. The advantages of the former are thereby created and maintained by the prejudice and discrimination that are directed toward the latter.

3. In addition to the consequences of prejudice and discrimination on people's identity, we explored other consequences of prejudice for society:

   a. Prejudiced attitudes and actions deprive a society of the full use of its valuable human resources, limiting the society's opportunities for growth and advancement.

   b. Prejudiced attitudes and actions undermine both the legitimacy of the social order and its moral persuasiveness—its ability to motivate people's willing acceptance to do what is needed in order to maintain their society without requiring the use of force or coercion.

S E C T I O N

Conclusions: Challenging Prejudice

We have been on a tour of the often ugly world of human relationships, a world in which some groups have been marked by others for disparaging attitudes and unequal treatment. We have seen the face of prejudice and sought to understand some of the reasons for its sure grip on humanity for so many thousands of years. We have seen the complexity of the problem and thus the variety of lenses we must use to fathom its character.

We first used the lens of history and saw how from the earliest recorded times groups have employed the terms that we now consider to be the signs of prejudice to explain their feelings, their views and their actions toward their fellow human beings who for various reasons they never considered to be quite as human or worthy as they were.

We turned next to a lens that focused on the prejudiced person. We examined the personalities and the values of those who have an especially strong tendency to hate and derogate *individuals and groups* who differ from them as well as the cognitive processes of categorizing and stereotyping that make us all liable to construct our world in prejudiced ways.

Finally, we employed the lens of intergroup relations. We saw the all too human tendency to classify the world of people into categories of inclusion (the in-group) and exclusion (the out-group). We examined how this way of organizing humanity produces some of the familiar effects of prejudice: favoring the in-group, derogating or at times eliminating the out-group.

We are now prepared to take a closer look at some of the ways in which prejudice can be challenged and undone. Chapter 15 begins our examination by reviewing and focusing more closely on the lessons we have learned from the three lenses used to frame our understanding of prejudice in the first place.

Chapter 16 continues with our efforts to challenge prejudice, but this time by considering the role that power and domination play in prejudice and, therefore, how the empowerment of those who have been denied a voice might serve to challenge prejudice.

Given its deep roots, long history, and ongoing support, the challenge we face is obviously difficult. Yet it is a challenge we must undertake. It is unlikely that prejudice will disappear within our own lifetimes. But we have obligations that extend well beyond our own brief moment in world history. We learn about how to challenge prejudice not because we believe we will succeed in our own time—*but rather,* we mount this challenge in the hopes that the long night of human history will not be repeated in the future.

Chapter 15

Undoing Prejudice, I: Lessons From the Three Lenses

Suppose you accepted the mission, impossible as it might sometimes appear, to recommend ways to reduce, or even eliminate, prejudice. How would you go about this admittedly difficult task? You have completed reading a book on prejudice that offered (to use Allport's imagery) three lenses through which we might look in order to *understand* the nature of intolerance and discrimination. These lenses also provide a good starting point for visualizing ways to *challenge* prejudice: Each lens not only informs us about some of the reasons why prejudice has had such a firm grip on humanity but also recommends ways we might employ to be rid of it. Our task, then, involves returning to each lens to see what it can tell us about challenging prejudice. (See Table 15.1.)

Recall the three lenses we used: The first asked us to examine qualities of the targeted groups; the second focused on the prejudiced person; and the third looked at intergroup relations. We will examine each of these in turn for clues to challenging and undoing prejudice.

The First Lens: Questionable Legitimations

For some thousands of years, prejudice was considered to be a reasonable response to negative characteristics of selected target groups: That is, because *they* are dirty, aggressive, and dangerous, even the offspring of Satan, it is only reasonable to dislike them and to try to isolate or destroy them so that they will not pollute the good people of the world. What clues does this lens provide for challenging prejudice?

Table 15.1

Challenging Prejudice

	Focus	**Recommendation**
Lens #1	Target characteristics	Education about the complex causes of human differences; skepticism about overly simplistic analyses explaining differences in terms of group characteristics
Lens #2	Prejudiced persons	Challenging the four attitude functions prejudice may serve: • Ego-defensive • Social-adjustive • Value-expressive • Cognitive
Lens #3	Intergroup relations	Evaluating three strategies for re-framing group relations: • Decategorization • Recategorization • Subcategorization

The answer is deceptively simple and yet often difficult to implement. Our task involves questioning the validity of each and every claim that is made about a given target group's fundamental characteristics. As we have already seen, each time an article or book is published that captures the public's attention because it "definitely" establishes the special traits of this group or that, a dedicated cadre of scientists refutes its arguments by uncovering fundamental flaws in reasoning, data, or interpretation. For every *Bell Curve,* we have found a challenger; for every story about the qualities that women, blacks, or homosexuals possess, we have found a challenger that questions the validity of these accounts.

For example, a recent newspaper article (Davidson, 1996) reported on the formation of a group calling itself the California Biotech Action Coalition, comprised of various scientists dedicated to challenging what they refer to as "genetic hucksterism": the excessive claims made on behalf of genetic and other forms of biological determinism too often used, as we have seen, not to enlighten us about differences but rather to strengthen the hold of prejudice on a populace unfortunately all too ready to believe the worst about others and to seek ways to justify these negative beliefs.

Using this first lens to understand prejudice, we see that our task is to support critical scholarship and critical education that questions these claims to have discovered a basic truth about the characteristics of selected target groups. This lens teaches us that to challenge prejudice we must remain wary of all those who employ religion, mythology, folklore, and even science to support prejudiced views of certain groups, however subtle these claims might be. Our task is to remain vigilant and to question those who offer easy legitimations that help support prejudice and discrimination.

The Second Lens: Challenging the Prejudiced Person

We have several avenues open to us once we decide to challenge prejudice by dealing with the prejudiced person. A useful way of organizing our plan of attack derives from some theoretical ideas about the functions that prejudiced attitudes serve in the life of an individual (based on the work of Katz, 1960; also Katz & Stotland, 1959). Four specific functions have been identified: (1) ego-defensive; (2) social-adjustive; (3) value-expressive; and (4) cognitive.

Ego-Defensive Functions

What do we mean when we say that prejudiced attitudes play an ego-defensive function in people's lives? The authoritarian personality comes quickly to mind (see Chapter 6). These are people for whom prejudice toward nearly all out-groups plays a central role in defending themselves from an awareness of their own forbidden desires and impulses. Recall that authoritarians manage the seething turmoil of aggression and forbidden sexuality that lives inside them by projecting such desires onto others, who then become feared and hated objects. *Ego-defensive* therefore refers to the idea that prejudiced attitudes help protect people from themselves, from their own impulses.

The problem with trying to change prejudices that serve ego-defensive functions stems from their usually being both unconscious and irrational. That is, people are generally unaware that they are projecting unwanted parts of themselves onto others and thus that there is anything irrational about their perceptions of other people. Given these qualities, it makes little or no sense to use arguments based on logic or facts to appeal to a person whose hateful attitudes toward various groups serve an ego-defensive function. Trying to help them understand, for example, that homosexuals, whom they hate intensely, are just people with a different lifestyle, who deserve the same rights as everyone else, simply does not ring true. Their hateful views of homosexuals help hold these people together; without that hate, they would have to contend with their own inner turmoil.

Two leads: Bullies and Nazis   But, if education and rational argumentation will not work, then what might we do? There are two possible directions that we might take. One leads into the sometimes fuzzy world of individual psychotherapy. But psychotherapy on such a large scale is much too costly to be practical. Furthermore, it is highly unlikely that the persons for whom prejudice serves this ego-defensive function would even consider psychotherapy: After all, such people are quite unaware of being prejudiced and so would scoff at their needing psychotherapy. Furthermore, since one of the qualities of authoritarians is their refusal to be introspective, to look inward to examine their own motivations, they would assume that psychotherapy is a treatment modality that runs directly counter to everything they feel comfortable doing. Given these constraints, this first route seems to hold little hope of being effective other than in a few selected cases.

The second possibility is suggested by some work on what might at first seem like a tangential issue, but which I think offers a helpful alternative for addressing prejudice that is based on ego-defensiveness. This involves some work on bullying recently reported by Dan Olweus (1995).

One of the first things to observe about bullying is how common it is around the world. In his work in Scandinavia, for example, Olweus reports that approximately 15% of students in grades 1 through 9 were involved either as bully or victim; he suggests that similarly high percentages are found in other nations as well. Olweus has been interested in determining both the types of people who are most likely to bully others and the kinds of intervention that might prevent bullying from occurring.

According to Olweus, the typical bully has a distinct set of personality traits. For example, bullies tend to be aggressive toward everyone, both children and adults; they are impulsive and have a strong desire to dominate; they show little empathy toward others. Opposing the usual belief that bullies are really frightened and insecure people, Olweus reports that bullies tend to be minimally anxious or insecure individuals when compared with their nonbullying peers.

Armed with this portrait of the bully's personality, what kind of interventions would you think of using to reduce bullying? Olweus adopts a position in this case that is consistent with the same kind of argument we would apply to the authoritarian personality: It does little good to argue that because their personality disposed them to be mean to others our task is to place bullies in some treatment program designed to cure them of their personality disorder. Olweus suggests that trying to change personality is a less reasonable way to proceed than to intervene at the level of the school itself. Consider his conclusion:

> It is thus important to try to create a school . . . environment characterized by warmth, positive interest, and involvement from adults, on the one hand, and firm limits to unacceptable behavior, on the other. (p. 199)

In other words, the way to cut down the high incidence of bullying is not to try to cure bullies of their personality defects, but rather to alter the school environment, making the expression of aggressive behavior inappropriate, subject to careful monitoring and stern sanctions whenever it occurs.

Consider what has just been said about bullying. Yes, bullies do have a particular set of personality characteristics. And yes, their aggressive behavior may very well serve ego-defensive functions. But no, undoing bullying does not involve taking bullies aside and trying to change their personality. We challenge bullying best by addressing the school environment, so that this behavior is not accepted there. In short, changing the social environment's receptivity and openness is the pathway to challenge bullying.

Another approach that focuses on the troubled individual's environment is the model or paradigm we first encountered in Chapter 4, described as the bidirectional scientific paradigm (e.g., Azar, 1997; Bronfenbrenner & Ceci, 1994; Fausto-Sterling, 1992; Gallagher, 1994; Gladwell, 1997; Rutter, 1997). Although this view was concerned with genetic-environment interactions (nature versus nurture), its message is relevant to our present concern with addressing individually rooted prejudices. That a person may be a "bad seed" because of some genetic issue or for some other reason (e.g., an abusive early environment) is no reason to throw up our hands in despair. Bad seeds make the importance of good environmental management (e.g., good parenting and good schooling) even more important. In other words, even if we discover that some forms of prejudiced attitudes are like bullying or antisocial behavior, based on some very early and deeply rooted personality problems, this does not demand that we recommend individual psychotherapy, but rather may direct us toward restructuring the environment so that the attitudes do not gain the upper hand. We make the environment unreceptive to harmful attitudes and actions rather than trying to heal the roots of the person's problems.

Let me illustrate this point with another example, this time one that clearly involves prejudice during the Nazi era in Germany. Reports (e.g., Plant, 1986) suggest that the personality of Nazi Germany's second most powerful leader— the architect of the Holocaust, Heinrich Himmler—was reminiscent of the authoritarian personality we studied in Chapter 6.

Here are some of the qualities said to describe Himmler: He had a very stern and autocratic father against whom he would never dare to raise a hand let alone a protest; he was highly submissive to authority even while being unusually cruel in his treatment of those beneath him (the bicyclist's pattern); he is said to have been obsessive about order and purity, applying this obsession to both his passion for detailed record keeping as well as to the purification of the German "race." I could go on, but I think this is a sufficient amount of information to suggest that we have in Himmler a man who comes very close to fitting the classic authoritarian personality.

But, if our task would have been to challenge the kinds of prejudice toward Jews, gypsies, homosexuals, and political radicals that led Himmler to create concentration camps and to engage in some of the cruelest acts ever know to humanity, would we have tried to take him aside and attempt to use psychotherapy to heal his wounded personality? The work of Olweus and others suggests that the world may be abundant with people whose personalities dispose them to act in destructive ways toward others. We are unlikely to be able to heal those personalities through some massive program of individual psychotherapy. What we can do, however, is to *contain* these personalities so that the expression of their tendencies toward harm-doing is not socially approved. The implication, then, is that it was not Himmler's personality that was the problem, but rather the surrounding society that welcomed this kind of destructive personality and that provided him with the explicit means of acting on his impulses with social approval.

It is not the madman's or the bigot's impulses that are at issue; it is the receptivity of the larger society to those impulses. Himmler would have received hardly a nod of approval had he lived in another society or in Germany at another time. His rantings, ravings, and recommendations for purifying the world would have been received as the appeals of someone marginal to the society— a madman, perhaps a fool, but not someone put into a position of power who could live out in reality the torment he felt within. It is the world, then, the very fabric of society itself, that holds the key whenever we wish to challenge prejudices that stem from ego-defensiveness.

I am not saying that we should entirely ignore treatment designed to heal warped personalities. But of even greater importance is to address larger structures and institutions within which such personalities carry out their lives. There can be no doubt that Himmler's authoritarianism would have passed unnoticed by anyone perhaps other than some psychiatrists or close acquaintances and would surely have had only minimal social impact, had he not lived where he did and when he did.

The lesson, then, is to challenge prejudice that serves ego-defensive functions by making its expression unwelcome. And this means, perhaps paradoxically, that we accept a world filled with diverse people with diverse personalities, including personalities prone to think and act in highly prejudicial, even destructive ways; but that rather than courting them, we remain unreceptive to their expressions.

Social-Adjustive Functions

Our prejudiced attitudes, however, are not simply residents of our deep unconscious, propping us up and serving those hard-to-transform ego-defensive functions. Many of our prejudices simply help us better fit into the various social groups we inhabit. Take the following illustration, a slightly fictional version of what might actually have once taken place.

Jane is a new student at her exclusive eastern school, rather pleased to have been admitted and eager to do well, but especially eager to be accepted by her peers. She comes from a rather open and liberal family in which few if any serious prejudicial attitudes are expressed, let alone felt. In fact, although it may sound patronizing to say so, while growing up, some of Jane's best friends came from a wide variety of racial and ethnic groups. This new school, however, had an important social clique comprised of some rather snooty types—and no one, literally, could ever quite measure up to their standards. They considered themselves superior to others and they let everyone know of these feelings. (I know that this sounds like the plot of an old B-movie, but bear with me just a little longer!)

Jane soon learned that acceptance by this elite group would mean acceptance in the entire school. The price of belonging, however, was to adopt the group's discriminatory viewpoint and express negative attitudes toward the very people about whom she never had previously felt any prejudices. It is likely that in order to fit in and gain acceptance, Jane did not change her privately held attitudes, but rather changed what she publicly stated. This describes the social-adjustive function of prejudiced attitudes.

We might think poorly of Jane, wishing her to have a bit more backbone and perhaps even better taste in choosing friends, but most of us at one time or another find ourselves in situations—among friends, in a work setting, in a community—in which belonging and acceptance place demands on us to publicly express views that are not fully consistent with our private beliefs. The social-adjustive function of attitudes, then, refers to the role that our attitudes play in helping us fit into and belong to various social groups.

Attitudes and circumstances   A typical observation in social psychology is that what people say on one occasion may not be consistent with what they say on another: Attitudes, in other words, may change to fit the circumstances. This is what we have seen with Jane. When she returns home to visit her family during school vacations, she reverts to the less prejudiced views that make her welcome in that setting; but when the vacation is over and she goes back to school and that elite group of her friends, she again expresses the prejudiced attitudes that are welcome in that environment. I am not saying that all attitudes function in this manner, but rather those attitudes that serve primarily social-adjustive functions shift as circumstances change.

There is a rather extensive research literature in social psychology that has examined this phenomenon. Let us look at a few examples that will help clarify the issue. The classic study in this genre was conducted in the 1930s by La Piere (1934). This was a time of much anti-Chinese prejudice in the United States. And so, when he traveled around the country with a Chinese couple, entering restaurants and seeking hotel accommodations, La Piere anticipated encountering a great deal of resistance based on the prevailing prejudices. Nevertheless, after thousands of miles of travel and literally hundreds of occasions when they might have been refused service, La Piere reported only one instance of actual refusal. But there is more to his story. About 2 months after this trip, La Piere contacted all of the establishments that had been visited and asked them if they would accommodate some Chinese guests. He was repeatedly told "no." In other words, places that had in fact accepted the Chinese couple later claimed that they would not accept them!

Before addressing La Piere's findings, let us consider two related examples from the 1950s. Minard (1952) found an absence of anti-black prejudice among coal miners when they worked together down in the mines, but noted prejudiced attitudes when the miners returned to their homes aboveground. Before they entered a large department store, Saenger and Gilbert (1950) asked customers if they would permit a Negro salesperson to wait on them, observing them later in the store when a Negro actually waited on them. Findings suggested a discrepancy between what they declared before entering the store ("No, I definitely would not") and what occurred once inside the store.

In all three cases, then, we have a prejudiced attitude expressed on one occasion in one set of circumstances, and its absence on another occasion in a different set of circumstances. Does this not begin to sound like Jane's situation? That is, prejudiced attitudes in all of these cases may be serving social-adjustive functions, leading people to embrace prejudiced attitudes that help them fit into one set of conditions while rejecting such attitudes in another.

These several examples help us see that social-adjustive functions do not simply refer to attitudes necessary to fit into a given group (e.g., Jane's example), but more generally involve the attitudes we adopt in order to fit into a given social situation. The implication is that *some prejudices are highly situation specific.* This helps us see how to reduce those prejudices that are rooted in social-adjustment.

If some prejudiced attitudes are rooted in specific social situations, then by addressing ourselves to those situations we may effectively reduce prejudice. There are three possibilities: First, establish and enforce laws that make discriminatory actions illegal. Second, take personal actions that make others' expression of their prejudices unwelcome. Third, encourage people in key public positions to voice their disapproval of the expression of prejudiced attitudes.

Laws that make discriminatory behavior illegal may not directly alter a person's feelings about various groups, but they do have the effect of making it apparent that legally sanctioned social norms are not on the side of those who wish to maintain prejudice. For example, when it became illegal to refuse service to someone in a public accommodation (e.g., a hotel or restaurant) because of that person's racial background, social norms about the expression of prejudices were changed: Regardless of what people may have privately thought, they were obliged to provide service to everyone. In order to fit into their community, they could not act on whatever privately held prejudiced attitudes they had.

In a similar manner, if each of us takes it upon ourselves to refuse to accept any expression of prejudice that crops up in our own social groups, whether in the form of jokes, racial slurs, or any other form, we create an environment that says "no" to those who believe they will gain acceptance by being prejudiced. By rejecting these comments, we help to create an environment hostile to the expression of prejudice and so change the publicly stated views of people for whom prejudice serves social-adjustive functions. Our rejection of the expression of prejudiced views means that such people will have to keep their negative views to themselves if they want to associate with us.

Finally, of course, public officials can play an important role in creating a climate that discourages the expression of prejudices. When these officials, however, play what has been called "the race card"—for example, by using a semi-coded message designed to encourage divisiveness and prejudice—they effectively put out the welcome mat to all those who feel they can now fit in and gain acceptance by expressing their own prejudiced beliefs.

To summarize: When our prejudices are less a case of deeply held, hateful views of others than they are devices to help us better fit into our various social worlds (i.e., the social-adjustive function), then by changing the climate governing those situations we can effectively make the expression of prejudiced views unwelcome. In this, we all have a role to play.

Value-Expressive Functions

I can be relatively brief here. Chapter 7 already introduced us to the role that values play in prejudice. When I now refer to prejudice as serving a value-expressive function, I am emphasizing the arguments presented in Chapter 7: Specific prejudiced attitudes are seen as the expression of a person's underlying values. For example, a person who has accepted the Protestant Ethic's individualistic values—and so believes that all it takes to succeed in life is individual motivation and effort—is likely to harbor negative views (i.e., prejudices) toward those who have not succeeded. The underlying value tells them that people who are at the bottom of society's ladder of success undoubtedly belong there because they have never tried hard enough to make it.

If prejudice serves to express a person's underlying values, then the point of attack to challenge prejudice, as we saw in Chapter 7, would involve transforming those underlying values. For example, we might employ the value-confrontation technique recommended by Rokeach that we encountered in that chapter. Recall that the technique leads people to confront their conflicting value priorities, helping them to see, for example, that in ranking freedom higher than equality, they are actually undoing the chance for achieving equality. The argument is that this realization will induce people to change their underlying values, which in turn will effect the prejudiced attitudes that such values serve.

Another possibility that uses the value-expressive function of prejudiced attitudes involves helping people understand that a specific prejudice they have conflicts with other values they also hold. I have a colleague, for example, who at one time found himself feeling angry and put out whenever a student with a disability asked for what my colleague considered to be special arrangements for course examinations. That is, although other students would take exams during regularly scheduled class time in the regular classroom, some students with disabilities might request extra time to complete the exam or perhaps special reading and reporting technology in order to write out answers. While complying with university policy, he nevertheless complained rather loudly with his negative views of people who require such "special" arrangements.

This same professor, however, had long been a supporter of civil rights for all people, donating both time and money to help provide benefits for those who have been denied. In other words, one of his deeply held values involved a firm belief in equality for everyone. Thus, his prejudice toward students with disabilities was challenged by helping him see how his valuing of equality could be better achieved by accepting the 1990 Americans With Disabilities Act that was designed to give people with disabilities a chance to compete with all others. When he was made aware of this 1990 legislation and learned that its rationale was consistent with his own deeply held valuing of equality, he was able to work on his negative attitudes and in time even go out of his way to make essential accommodations so that all students in his classes would have a fair shake.

Cognitive dissonance and prejudice reduction   While we are considering my colleague's initial resistance and eventual change in prejudiced attitudes once he saw that his attitudes were inconsistent with important underlying values he also held, we should briefly consider a theoretical view in social psychology that has had a great deal to say about the role that such inconsistencies play in changing our attitudes. This is the theory of *cognitive dissonance* (e.g., Aronson, 1969; Festinger, 1957).

In a nutshell, the theory argues that when people encounter inconsistencies (or dissonance) between specific attitudes they hold, or between attitudes and values, or between attitudes and actions they undertake, they experience tension that they seek to reduce. One manner of reducing this tension is to change one's attitudes from inconsistency to consistency.

Although there have been many debates over how this theory actually works, there is an interesting use of its major ideas to reduce prejudice reported by Leippe and Eisenstadt (1994). They built their study around one of the central ideas of dissonance theory: If a person believes in X, but can be encouraged to publicly advocate an opposite belief (i.e., not-X), the inconsistency between "what I believe about X" and "what I just stated publicly about X" creates a tension that motivates the person to change his or her attitude about X. Since people cannot take back what they say as easily as they can change their attitudes to be consistent with what they say, it is the attitude that should show the greatest change.

For this to work as presented, however, people must feel that they voluntarily made the public statement that was inconsistent with their attitudes. Both dissonance theory and our common sense tell us that if people are compelled by force or strong inducements (e.g., offers of lots of money) to engage in a public action taking a position with which they disagree, they will experience little dissonance: "I did it because I had to; a gun was held to my head." On the other hand, if a person can more or less voluntarily take a public stance that opposes what they believe, they experience the kind of dissonance that demands they do something to reduce it. And, what can they do other than change their attitudes to fit their actions!

Leippe and Eisenstadt used these ideas from dissonance theory to reduce people's prejudiced attitudes. They asked a sample of white students to prepare an essay that endorsed a substantial increase in scholarship funds to be made available for black students, even though this increase would reduce the funding available for white students' scholarships. Leippe and Eisenstadt systematically varied the amount of pressure they used to get the white students to write this essay. Some were effectively in a free choice situation, while others were given this writing task as an assignment about which they had little or no choice.

The prediction from dissonance theory is that students under the free choice condition would experience dissonance and would reduce that dissonance by changing their attitudes to be consistent with the pro-black essay they had just written (i.e., they would record positive attitudes toward blacks). Students who were given no choice, by contrast, would not experience dissonance and so would not show a comparable change in their attitudes toward blacks.

Leippe and Eisenstadt's findings were consistent with these predictions. In other words, students who wrote the essay with minimal pressure reported stronger pro-black attitudes than students who were compelled to write the essay without much free choice in the matter. Can this approach be used more generally to affect prejudiced attitudes? Just consider how laws against discrimination might get people to change their attitudes to be consistent with the behaviors the law requires of them. To be sure, the very term "requirement" suggests more coercion than free choice; but over time, people will find themselves behaving in ways that do not quite fit consistently with their prior beliefs. And, since their behavior has already changed, then perhaps in time so too will their attitudes in order to be consistent with their actions.

Our brief focus on the theory of cognitive dissonance has moved us into the familiar territory of cognition. We have just seen how cognitive restructuring to reduce dissonance may produce attitude changes from prejudiced to unprejudiced. This, then, is one illustration of the fourth function that attitudes serve: the cognitive functions.

Cognitive Functions

It is apparent from our discussion in Chapters 8 and 9 that one of the central roles that attitudes play in all of our lives, including prejudiced attitudes based on stereotypes, involves providing us with a structured, organized, and meaningful world. For example, we saw the role that stereotypes play in categorizing the social world and in shaping our social interactions with others. Recall that stereotypes give us shorthand ways of categorizing and behaving with minimal individuating information about others; that is, we treat people in terms of their category membership rather than in terms of their personal qualities as individuals.

The cognitive functions that attitudes play direct us to reducing prejudices by dealing with the ways we categorize things in our world. In this case, changing prejudices involves changing *how* we think rather than *what* we think. No mean feat, as we have already seen. Let us recall a few attempts that we first visited in Chapters 8 and 9.

Subgrouping   Our well known tendency to confirm rather than test stereotypes suggests that it is difficult to change them. Yet, we did encounter one hopeful educational possibility involving the process identified as subgrouping. If we can learn to see the great diversity that exists among members of groups that we otherwise stereotype (i.e., subgrouping), we can be helped to reduce the ease with which we are likely to be guided by the stereotypes we hold. Rather than dismissing specific cases as exceptions, with subgrouping we come to see the diversity that resides among every human group, making any one group stereotype necessarily incorrect. This affects our stereotypes by undermining their vise-like grip over our understanding of other people.

Saying no   A second illustration involves inhibiting the operation of the stereotypes we all hold rather than trying to eliminate them altogether. By becoming aware of our tendency to employ stereotypes, we can use this awareness to refuse to act on their terms. For example, Jim's knowledge of his tendency to stereotype people of color who enter his store—Jim views them as potential shoplifters and so watches them with extra caution—can lead Jim to withhold being guided by that stereotype and so not relate to every person of color in its terms.

There is a paradoxical possibility here, however, that we first saw in Chapter 9. We may find that too much thought about a group stereotype might rebound, making it _more_ rather than less difficult to say "no" to the stereotype. That is, thinking about the stereotypes we hold may have an even greater effect on our behavior than not thinking about the stereotype.

Dealing with implicit stereotyping processes   Recall from Chapter 9 that Banaji and Greenwald emphasized three ways to minimize the impact of stereotypes that operate unconsciously: (1) blinding, (2) affirmative action, and (3) consciousness raising. If we hope to avoid the unconscious effects of stereotypes, we need to minimize the conditions under which their effects can operate. If we are in a position to make hiring decisions, for example, being blind to the categories of race and sex (e.g., hiring without awareness of the group membership of the candidates) helps to minimize the unconscious potential of stereotypes to affect our decisions. Symphony orchestras that select new members by holding auditions in which the candidates remain hidden behind a screen illustrate this approach.

On the other hand, the second approach—through affirmative action—demands that we _see_ the very differences that blinding seeks to conceal. In order to be sure that certain underrepresented categories of people have a fair chance at employment, for example, we cannot hire blind to the specific memberships of the potential job candidates. We need to be fully aware that candidate X is female and black, while candidate Y is male and white. In theory, affirmative action is intended to create a more diverse living and working environment for all of us (e.g., see Skedsvold & Mann, 1996, for a good analysis). In turn, this diversity can undermine group stereotypes by giving us a reality about others that we simply cannot ignore.

The third approach, consciousness raising, has become a familiar feature of many current attempts to help people become better aware of themselves, including becoming more sensitive to the prejudices they hold and the ways in which those prejudices affect their everyday encounters with other people. The goal of consciousness raising is to help people better understand just how often they use stereotypes. The assumption is that knowledge of one's own biases will help reduce their influence over judgments.

Consciousness raising, however, has another side to it that we will examine further in Chapter 16, involving the notion of *conscientizacion,* a concept that has been especially used in Latin American contexts.

But in addition to the three options just discussed, there is still another possibility for attacking the unconscious hold of stereotypes. Recall that one of the major methods for assessing implicit or unconscious stereotyping employed a technique known as *priming:* A stimulus that triggers commonly shared stereotypic associations affects later judgments. And so a person who unscrambles mixed-up sentences in which racial or gender stereotypes are embedded, when later asked to evaluate a hypothetical person's behavior, will unconsciously employ racial or gender stereotypes in these evaluations.

But, what if there are no stereotypic associations generally available in a given community? This is precisely the point raised by one of my more astute students. She asked about a hypothetical child who was brought up in a relatively stereotype-free community. "If the argument made by those studying implicit cognition is that various stimuli in our world trigger stereotypic thoughts unconsciously," this student asked, "then someone not having those associations in the first place would be unlikely to suffer from any unconscious biasing." The student was right!

After all, it would be very difficult to have unconscious stereotypes triggered if there were no basis in the first place! Utopian? Definitely! Likely within our lifetimes? No! A reasonable direction for our future efforts? Definitely!

The Third Lens: Intergroup Contact

Looking at prejudice with the third lens suggests the importance of addressing prejudice by dealing directly with intergroup relations. Based on some of Allport's (1954) original ideas, it has been suggested that one of the best ways to undo prejudice involves bringing people from diverse groups into contact with one another so that they can learn about one another. This idea has come to be known as *the contact hypothesis:*

> That contact between people—the mere fact of their interacting—is likely to change their beliefs and feelings toward each other. . . . If only one had the opportunity to communicate with the others and to appreciate their way of life, understanding and consequently a reduction of prejudice would follow. (Amir, 1969, pp. 319–320)

Major desegregation decisions (e.g., the well known 1954 *Brown* v. *Board of Education* decision of the U.S. Supreme Court) have been based in part on the idea that intergroup contact is essential for reducing prejudice. In this case, intergroup contact (i.e., interracial contact) would not only create an equal environment for blacks and whites, but also an environment in which by being together, former intergroup hostilities would presumably wane and be replaced by positive social relationships. As the subsequent history of black-white relations after 1954 suggest, however, things have proved not to be quite that easy. And, as we now know, contact may also serve to heighten intergroup tensions and solidify prejudice more than to reduce them.

Allport's Conditions for Successful Intergroup Contact

But, before we give up on the contact hypothesis, we need to turn again to Allport's analysis. He suggested several conditions needed if intergroup contact is to reduce rather than exacerbate prejudice. We will consider three: (1) equality of status, (2) institutional support, and (3) sense of common interests and common humanity.

Equal status   It was clear to Allport that if contact between two groups preserves their former status differences, this will not bode well if the goal is to reduce the prejudices and tensions that formerly described their relationship. For example, if a white woman's only contact with an African American involves interacting with her black maid, this contact is unlikely to have a significant effect in changing her view of blacks. In fact, seeing the maid in a subservient position might actually reinforce the stereotype she holds about people of color. Therefore, reasoned Allport, only contact between people whose status is equal can undermine the hold of prejudice.

This is one reason why affirmative action policies have been so strongly touted by their advocates. By increasing the diversity of the workforce, people are likely to come into the very kind of equal status contact with coworkers that can effectively reduce prejudices based on ignorance and misinformation (e.g., Skedsvold & Mann, 1996).

A question has been raised, however, about which type of status equality is required. Does equality refer to statuses *within* the contact situation itself, or must it involve equality outside the specific situation as well? For example, all of the students in a desegregated school have a kind of equality of status within the school situation (e.g., in class, in the gym, in the library, the study hall, the cafeteria). And yet, outside the school situation, the disparity of their statuses might undermine the school-based equality. That is, when they return home to their segregated neighborhoods, it is clear who has the most and who has the least standing in the larger community. While this issue remains unresolved, it seems reasonable to suggest that one of the first steps required if contact is to be effective in reducing prejudices is build on a firm base of equality of status *within* the contact situation (e.g., within the school).

Institutional support   The second condition necessary if contact is to reduce prejudices between groups involves the degree to which there is general support for the contact. This support can take several different forms—including, for example, formal laws such as the 1954 Supreme Court decision that legislated school integration, as well as informal customs and values within a given community that support equality for everyone.

When in response to the 1954 Supreme Court decision many school districts, with the full backing of their school boards, administrators, teachers, and parents, balked at integrating blacks and whites, the needed institutional support was effectively undermined. The likelihood that intergroup contacts would reduce tensions and prejudices was thereby also undermined. Contact without institutional support may even be worse than no contact at all.

Common interests and common humanity   A third condition necessary if intergroup contact is to work effectively to reduce prejudice includes two related ideas. First, the contact must occur within a generally cooperative rather than a competitive setting so that people can become aware of their commonly shared interests—much like the *superordinate goals* we considered in Chapters 11 and 12 involving the Sherif and Sherif summer camp study.

Second, the contact must give people a sense of their shared humanity. Unfortunately, most school environments seem to foster more competition than cooperation and thereby may undermine the possibility that intergroup contact will reduce prejudice. For example, most classrooms remain competitively organized, pitting each individual against every other individual for grades and for positive teacher attention—hardly an environment conducive to forming a sense either of common interests or of shared humanity.

Creating Cooperative Classrooms

One of the most extensive uses of the contact hypothesis has been directed toward the classroom environment. Would a classroom that was intentionally structured to encourage the three conditions of contact we just considered decrease intergroup prejudice? That is, would the kids in these specially structured classrooms, when compared with kids in regular classrooms, show more tolerance toward others, making more intergroup than intragroup friendship choices, for example? This focus on the classroom is especially important given that many studies have suggested that school desegregation in itself does not appear to produce the hoped-for reduction in prejudice and may even reinforce racial stereotypes as each group sticks to its own "kind" (e.g., Slavin, 1985). But perhaps if classrooms could be restructured so as to emphasize cooperative learning, this unfortunate situation could be changed.

Several different types of cooperative classroom arrangements have been explored (Slavin, 1985, e.g., summarizes seven approaches). Although each approach offers its unique view of how best to restructure the classroom, all share an interest in creating some form of cooperative or collaborative problem solving. We will explore one typical approach, called the *jigsaw classroom*, employed by Aronson and his colleagues in 10 fifth grade classrooms in seven elementary schools in Austin, Texas (e.g., Aronson & Bridgeman, 1979; Aronson et al., 1978). The kids met in what was called the jigsaw format for 45 minutes each day, 3 days each week, for a total of 6 weeks. But what is a jigsaw classroom?

First, the class is divided into groups of mixed racial and ethnic composition. Each group contains six students. For any given day's lesson, each student is given one part of the material necessary to deal with a question posed by the teacher. In order to get the correct answer, the individual pieces of the puzzle have to be put together. Since each piece of information is held by a different student, all must work together in order to solve the puzzle. It should now be apparent why this is called a jigsaw classroom. In order to work effectively, each student must not only learn her or his own particular part, but become an expert who can teach it to the other students so that it can all be joined together to reveal the answer to the puzzle. As Aronson and Bridgeman (1979) note, this process helps the children become aware of one another as valuable resources for problem solving.

The researchers measured the success of this arrangement by comparing these jigsaw classrooms with control classrooms, in which this specific procedure was absent. They were interested not only in how intergroup relations were changed, but also in how learning was affected. On both counts, the results were impressive. For example, Aronson reported greater feelings of attraction toward and more positive evaluations of students from other racial and ethnic groups as well as high levels of academic success among the jigsaw classrooms when compared with the more traditional classrooms. An added bonus is the increased sense of self-esteem that comes from the students' having achieved successfully. In the judgment of Aronson and his colleagues, the effectiveness of the jigsaw format lies in the new level of empathy it produces: Students learn to take another's perspective, to walk in someone else's shoes, so to speak. Increased empathy seems to undo the intergroup tensions and prejudices that would otherwise appear.

These effects are not restricted to the jigsaw format. Other approaches designed to create a cooperative learning environment report similar results (e.g., Slavin, 1985). Cooperatively structured classrooms increase cross-racial friendships: Students who have been through a cooperative classroom experience are more likely to have friends outside their own racial group when compared with students from more traditional classrooms, in which intergroup contact is present but without the other conditions necessary to transform mere contact into an effective means of reducing intergroup prejudices. To be sure, all is not perfection, nor are we yet out of the woods of intergroup disharmony and prejudice. But at least the cooperative classroom provides an approach that can be used effectively at an early age to begin to hack away at some of the foundations of troubled intergroup relations.

Review of Intergroup Approaches to Prejudice Reduction

It will prove helpful to wind down our consideration of how intergroup approaches can be effective in reducing prejudices to consider the summary analysis suggested by Brewer and Miller (1996). They distinguish between three major approaches: (1) decategorization, (2) recategorization, and (3) subcategorization.

Decategorization and prejudice reduction   The key to the decategorization approach to challenging prejudice is its emphasis on individuating and personalizing intergroup contacts and relationships. This approach asks us to minimize our focus on people's social identity and to maximize our focus on people's personal identity (this distinction is introduced in Chapter 10). Here is the conclusion from a research study reported by Miller, Brewer, and Edwards (1985) involving this approach: "Our results . . . suggest that whenever a classroom activity requires the formation of teams, it behooves teachers to avoid explicit or implicit use of racial or ethnic identity as a basis for team assignment" (p. 76). In other words, their findings lead them to recommend that people be encouraged to relate to one another as individuals rather than as members of social categories. This illustrates decategorization.

Recategorization and prejudice reduction   If the aim of the decategorization approach is to separate individual identities from group identities so that people can relate more as individuals, the effort of recategorization seeks to challenge the distinction between in-groups and out-groups by encouraging the development of a superordinate goal that will transform people from "us versus them" to "we." We saw this approach used in the Sherifs' summer camp study when the warring factions had to come together to confront a common problem (see Chapters 11 and 12). The common problem or superordinate goal compels people to recategorize their own and others' identity; no longer do they see the world in terms of competing groups, but rather in terms of one larger and more inclusive group in which everyone has membership.

Subcategorization and prejudice reduction   The third approach recognizes the importance of retaining one's own in-group identity even as we all learn to work cooperatively with others from different groups. It seeks to establish a context within which encounters will be pleasant or at least will be moderated by prior agreements (e.g., Hewstone & Brown, 1986; Kelman, 1997). An approach of this sort has become increasingly important in today's highly diverse world. Asking people to abandon their social identity may very well backfire, especially among groups for whom that identity is the source of their pride and political power. The task with subcategorization is not to have people give up their social identity, but rather to learn to adopt a cooperative working relationship with others.

For instance, Kelman (1997) has spent many years attempting to perfect an approach very much like the recommendations of subcategorization. He establishes problem solving workshops that bring together Israelis and Palestinians, including some important representatives of both groups. The workshops adopt a kind of therapeutic set of rules: The focus is on dealing analytically with problems, not argumentatively. People agree to keep everything said in the workshop private and confidential, without attribution to any specific individual or side. Facilitators are on hand to ensure that interactions stay focused, that people listen to one another, and that discussions—although often heated—always seek to examine and solve difficulties, not pile up further problems.

Kelman has noticed that this special kind of workshop interaction—he refers to it as following a kind of therapeutic model—works best only when each person feels comfortable maintaining his or her own social identity and does not feel that the price paid for working with the opposition involves abandoning that identity. As Kelman comments, the workshop will fail if people become too identified with the opposition, and thus lose sight of their own group's interests and their own social identity in that group.

Kelman reports that his workshop approach, which I have likened to the subcategorization technique, has worked rather effectively. Admittedly, open hostility between Israelis and Palestinians has not yet disappeared from the world scene. But, some of the proposals generated at these workshops, Kelman tells us, have found their way into the various peace accords that, while not yet totally resolving the conflict, have nevertheless given everyone hope that a resolution will someday be found.

Before we jump fully onto the subcategorization bandwagon, however, we must heed Brewer and Miller's (1996) warnings. They remind us that no one of these approaches by itself holds the key to successful prejudice reduction. Each has some successes as well as some glaring problems: Decategorization can undermine important social identities. Recategorization's superordinate goal may be successful only in the short term. Subcategorization without the kinds of controls imposed by Kelman, for example, may deteriorate to name-calling and an increased rather than decreased intergroup hostility. The best advice, then, is to come armed with a variety of options to be tested out as circumstances warrant.

Chapter Summary: Key Learning Points

1. The three lenses that guided our efforts to understand prejudice can also be usefully applied to its reduction.

2. The lens that focuses on characteristics of the targets of prejudice teaches us to remain ever vigilant and wary of those, from whatever source, who claim to have found a simple answer to why people are different and why therefore, many of our attitudes toward their differences may be justified.

3. The lens that focuses on the prejudiced person offers a variety of insights into prejudice reduction. Each of the four functions that prejudiced attitudes serve provides a different view of how to go about challenging prejudice:

   a. Prejudice that is rooted in ego-defensiveness may not invariably require personality change in order to heal the "disturbed" person; rather, changing the social environment may prove to be a more effective strategy of intervention.

   b. Prejudice that is rooted in social-adjustive functions that help people fit into their social groups can likewise be addressed by altering the social norms and public acceptability for expressing and acting on prejudiced beliefs.

   c. Prejudice that serves value-expressive functions may be challenged by using value-confrontation techniques or approaches based on a theory of cognitive dissonance.

   d. Prejudice that serves cognitive functions directs us to restructure the ways that people categorize the persons and objects of their world.

4. The lens that focuses on intergroup relations has introduced us to the importance of intergroup contact for reducing prejudice. That contact seems to work best, however, when the following circumstances exist:

   a. It involves people whose status at least within the contact situation is equal.

   b. The contact has generally widespread institutional support.

   c. The contact calls on people's sense of their common interests and common humanity.

5. The intergroup lens also introduced us to three major approaches that have been employed for challenging prejudice:

   a. Decategorization involves minimizing people's social identities and maximizing the relevance of their personal identities.

   b. Recategorization involves finding a superordinate goal that redefines relations from "us versus them" to "we."

   c. Subcategorization involves establishing ground rules for social interaction that preserves people's social identities while they work together in a cooperative, problem solving mode.

Chapter 16

Undoing Prejudice, II: Empowerment

What is the role that power plays in helping to create or sustain prejudice? Answering this question will give us some useful ideas about how to challenge prejudice. For example, if being powerless contributes to being targeted for prejudice, then empowerment—gaining power—may help break the hold of prejudice.

While power has been a theme that has appeared at various places throughout this text, just what is power? Although a variety of different forms of power have been identified (e.g., French & Raven, 1959; Lukes, 1986), our purposes will be served best if we consider two major types: (1) external forms of power based on a variety of mechanisms including the ability to control resources that people need; and (2) internal power based on the formation of those identities by which people know themselves and others.

Butler (1997) recently emphasized this distinction:

> We are used to thinking of power as what presses on the subject from the outside, as what subordinates.... But, if . . . we understand power as *forming* the subject as well as providing the very conditions of its existence . . . then power is not simply what we oppose but also . . . what we depend on for our existence. (p. 2)

Although her terms are different from the external and internal types I introduced, the ideas are much the same. The distinction is between those forms of power that come from outside of us and that constrain or subordinate us through the use of resources or other means that outside agents control and to which we respond—such as power that involves threats of punishment if we do not comply with the agent's demands—and those forms of power that form us by defining who we are as human beings and how we understand ourselves and others—such as power that sorts people into categories according to their sexual orientation and adopts one orientation (e.g., the heterosexual) as the standard against which others (e.g., the homosexual) are evaluated.

244

Figure 16.1

Power and prejudice

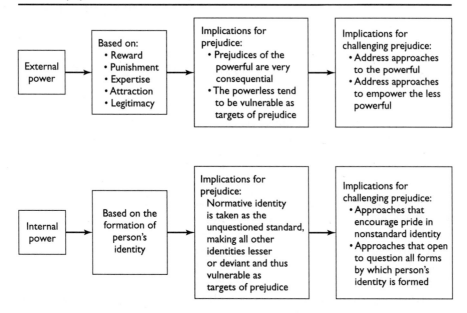

Each of these two types of power has a somewhat different implication both for understanding and for challenging prejudice. While these points are developed more fully throughout this chapter, a brief preview of where we are going will be helpful at this point. (Also see Figure 16.1, which illustrates the relationship between external power, internal power, and prejudice.)

There are two consequences for prejudice when power is understood as external to us and yet controlling us. First, the prejudiced beliefs and discriminatory actions of the powerful have more consequences for people's life chances than the prejudices of the less powerful. For example, the prejudices of the most powerful people in an organization can affect whether others get or keep a job. Second, there is a general tendency to harbor prejudiced attitudes toward the powerless, seeing their lack of power as caused by some deficiencies in their character. Remember, this is only a preview of coming attractions; these points will shortly be developed more fully.

There are also two consequences for prejudice when power is understood as internal, defining who people are. First, people are deprived of their own opportunities to define themselves; they are known by terms set for them by others. Second, and of equal importance, when those definitions become the standard by which normalcy is measured, the group that fits the standard is considered normal while others become "deviant" or lesser beings merely by accepting the categories of identity prevalent in their society. For example, when being heterosexual is defined as the only proper form of human sexuality, then no matter how much pride people may take in being gay and no matter how much tolerance others may direct toward them, they still remain trapped by understandings that create them as something other than the normative pattern of human sexuality.

External Power: Resources and Positions

In their theory of power, French and Raven (1959) described five *bases* by which one person or group can exercise power over others: reward, punishment, expertise, attraction, and legitimacy. Reward and punishment as bases of power are rather obvious to all of us: Someone who can either reward us or punish us has power over us, because that person controls the kinds of resources to which most people readily respond. For example, professors have both reward and punishment power over their students: The professor controls giving grades, rewarding excellent performance with a high grade and punishing poor performance with a low grade.

The remaining bases that French and Raven outline are also generally familiar; all involve some form of power that is external to us.

Experts have power, for example, because of the sheer weight of their knowledge. For example, the professor with expertise in her subject area may impress her students with that expertise; they willingly comply with her requests based on their having accepted her expertise.

To have power based on attraction is to gain compliance based on people's wishing to please a person they find appealing and likable and with whom they may even identify. A professor, for example, who has become a kind of role model for her students may gain their compliance based on their hoping both to please her and to be like her.

Finally, to have power based on legitimacy is to gain compliance from others because one's social position carries with it certain expectations that give its occupant the right to expect compliance, while others feel an obligation to comply. The professor's position in the hierarchy of the university gives her requests a legitimacy in that context that students recognize and generally accept.

External Power and Prejudice

There are two ways in which external power—whatever its basis—is linked with prejudice. First, the prejudices of those in powerful positions are more consequential than the prejudices of those without power. Second, there is a well known tendency, sometimes called "blaming the victim" (e.g., Ryan, 1971), to assume that people are responsible for their own outcomes in life and so deserve what they get (also see Caplan & Nelson, 1973; Lerner, 1980; Lerner & Miller, 1978; Ross, 1977; Ross & Nisbett, 1990). In other words, many harbor prejudice toward those in lower power positions, blaming them for the problems that being powerless brings upon them.

Prejudice and the Powerful

The prejudiced attitudes and actions of the powerful are generally more important than the prejudices we find among those of lesser power because the prejudices of the former are more consequential than those of the latter. Lukes (1986) illustrates this idea, as follows.

Each of us has a range within which we feel powerful enough to exercise control over our lives. For example, most of us can decide what we will have for breakfast or even if we will have breakfast at all. We can decide whether we will drive to work by turning left and taking the freeway or by turning right and moving along surface streets. This gives each of us an arena within which we may rightly consider ourselves to be powerful. And yet, when push comes to shove, there are people in our world who have really significant power over us and others—for example, our boss who can hire, promote, and fire people. Sure, we can choose our breakfast cereal. But our boss can affect whether we will even have enough money next week to buy any cereal at all!

The preceding teaches that although prejudice is something that can capture almost everyone within a society, from those on top to those lower down, prejudice on the part of those who occupy powerful social positions is more consequential for more lives than prejudice on the part of those in low-power positions.

Let us consider a large business corporation. It would not surprise us to hear prejudiced attitudes expressed within the mail room among the Latino and African American mail room clerks that work there: stereotypic images of their white bosses, perhaps even prejudiced attitudes about their coworkers. In other words, although both Latinos and African Americans are themselves often the targets of prejudice, as we commented in Chapter 1, this does not mean that, as a group, they are themselves without prejudice.

The point of introducing power into our equation for understanding prejudice, however, is to make the simple observation that prejudice heard among members of the corporate board room is more consequential than the prejudice of those mail room clerks. Suppose we could eavesdrop on the meetings of some of the corporate executives, perhaps even tape-record their discussions. Not only might we hear the familiar sounds of prejudiced beliefs being routinely expressed, but we would also suspect that the consequences of their prejudice will reverberate throughout the entire corporation, affecting who gets hired, who gets promoted, who gets fired.

The scandal hit the national news in late 1996 (e.g., see the *New York Times,* November 10, 1996). Someone had tape-recorded a meeting of several key executives of the Texaco Corporation. The tape was leaked to the public so that it could be used in an anti-discrimination lawsuit brought by several

Texaco employees against Texaco, for what they felt were discriminatory actions based on the employees' racial and ethnic backgrounds.

From a statistical standpoint alone, Texaco did not appear to be overly generous in its hiring or promotion of certain people. For example, although African Americans make up some 12% of the U.S. population, only 0.7% of the 873 top executives at Texaco are African Americans. As reported in the *New York Times* and elsewhere, analyses of the length of time it took for various groups to move upward in the corporation showed a similar pattern: Persons of color took much longer to be promoted than other workers.

It was the tape, however, that gave the kind of meaning to prejudice that these statistics could not, clinching the case and leading to some major reforms in the Texaco Corporation. Executives were caught on tape using some rather sharp racial slurs—referring to African American employees, for example, as "black jelly beans" and, of course, that old standby slur, "niggers." Further probing indicated just how extensively throughout the corporate structure—from near the top, down through middle managers and division heads—prejudicial beliefs were not only common but readily transformed into discriminatory practices of hiring, retention, and promotion.

The point of the preceding example is not simply to condemn Texaco Corporation; that has already occurred. The point rather is to indicate just how the prejudices of the powerful prove to be more potent than the prejudices of the less powerful. Again, this does not deny that prejudiced attitudes can and often do run rampant throughout all segments of society. The targeted groups can hardly claim high moral ground here (e.g., homosexuals who are firmly anti-heterosexual; women who are male bashers; blacks who hold stereotypes about whites that are as striking as the reverse). Yes, the targets also are prejudiced. But when we consider who holds the power to shape the lives of many people in society, the prejudice of the powerful is more consequential and hence more worrisome than that of the clerks chatting in the mail room.

The preceding example also rather strongly suggests that if we wonder just whose prejudices we need to challenge, we see that we might have the greatest overall effects by challenging prejudices held by the most powerful—not because others are without prejudice, but, as we have seen, because the prejudice of the former is more consequential for more people than the prejudices of the latter.

Prejudice Toward the Powerless

A body of theory and research from a variety of perspectives leads to the conclusion that people who lack power tend to become the targets of prejudice directed toward them simply because they are powerless. The research demonstrates that the reason why the powerless are such vulnerable targets of prejudice is that most people assume that one's fate in life is generally deserved. The fate of the powerless is thereby thought to be due to their own failures; we rarely admire people who we believe have personal deficiencies that account for their lowly position in society (e.g., see Caplan & Nelson, 1973; Lerner, 1980; Lerner & Miller, l978; Ross, 1977; Ross & Nisbett, 1990).

Ryan (1971) referred to this tendency to reject or feel negatively toward certain people who encounter difficulties in their lives as "blaming the victim": holding someone who has been the victim of a crime, for example, responsible for what happened. We learn that even if people were powerless to prevent the crime, the tendency to consider them somewhat blameworthy is strong. Consider, for instance, an innocent rape victim who is questioned about what *she* did to cause the rape (e.g., Howard, 1984; Brekke & Borgida, 1988).

Lerner (1980) has written about what he aptly terms the "just world hypothesis": the idea that people prefer to live in a world that is just, one in which good people deserve good outcomes, while bad people deserve bad outcomes. Justice is thereby served when the bad outcomes that the powerless experience are felt to be deserved simply because they are bad people.

As we noted in Chapter 8, Ross has referred to much this same tendency as the fundamental attribution error: People tend to discount situational causes for others' behaviors, settling more on dispositional explanations that involve some defects in people's character or motivation (see Ross, 1977; Ross & Nisbett, 1990). This leads people to view the powerless as having caused their situation; other plausible reasons for their lack of power, such as being the victims of prejudice or discrimination, are discounted.

Caplan and Nelson (1973) use the same ideas to suggest how people's belief that others deserve what they get in life helps to bolster the powerful's self-evaluation as good people who, of course, deserve to be on top!

All of these sources agree that for many people, the powerless—simply because they lack power—deserve to be held in low esteem. As much as many feel compassion toward the homeless, for example, it is not that unusual to hear people proclaim, "If they really wanted to work, they would find a job; they are just lazy, good-for-nothings who enjoy living off our own hard work."

External Power: Some Implications for Challenging Prejudice

Implications for challenging prejudice follow rather straightforwardly from an understanding of the role that external power plays in prejudice. As previously noted, because the prejudices of the powerful are more consequential than those of the less powerful, our efforts to challenge prejudice should invest more in the former than the latter. Recall that the argument is not that the powerless are without prejudice; rather, the point is that the powerful can determine outcomes that affect many people. It is their prejudices then that are worrisome and need to be challenged, calling on the techniques we considered in Chapter 15.

There are also some clear directions for challenging prejudice that come from our recognition that being powerless is in itself a condition that invites prejudice from others. If prejudiced attitudes toward the powerless occur because others consider their lack of power to be a personal deficiency, then perhaps if they can gain power, the prejudice directed toward them will be reduced, and even they will come to think better of themselves.

I am reminded here of a situation described recently in a book by Carolyn Heller (1997). Heller worked with a group of down-and-out women in the heart of San Francisco's Tenderloin area. She set up a women's writing group. Any woman could come into the storefront center and join in Heller's writing workshop. Initially, the women entered very tentatively, having no sense either of the skills required to write or that they had anything important enough to write about. After all, they were women without power: They didn't count in this world; they had no role, no importance, no purpose; who would ever want to read anything they wrote!

By working with these women over several months, Heller not only helped them learn some of the skills required to write well, but of even greater importance, she helped them see that they did have a story to tell and that their story was worthwhile. In other words, the writing workshop Heller developed helped boost these women's self-esteem—and along with that, gave them a renewed sense of power. They now mattered in a way that they had never previously considered.

Because Heller's work was not set up to carry out any extensive follow-up investigation nor to evaluate changes in the public's responses to these women, we cannot say with certainty that the initial prejudices toward them that they undoubtedly had experienced were reduced through the empowerment developed during their workshop participation. Given the research literature we previously considered that suggests that the powerless are vulnerable as targets of prejudice, it would nevertheless be reasonable to suggest that as these women gained in self-esteem and confidence in their own importance, they sowed the seeds for others having less prejudiced attitudes toward them.

Internal Power: The Forming of Identity

The second main form by which power operates is especially significant in modern society. This form of power has not replaced external power, but rather operates along with it, though in an often more subtle manner. Internal power involves the creation of the very meanings by which individuals and groups in a society come to know themselves and others; it is the power to form people's identities, and to do so in such a way that prejudiced attitudes are built into that very formation (e.g., see Butler, 1990, 1997; Foucault, 1978, 1979, 1985, 1986).

It is commonly thought that one of the worst fates that people can experience is to go through life and never be recognized. For instance, one of the founders of American psychology, William James (1910), suggested that this lack of recognition was perhaps the most painful thing that could ever happen to an individual; the well known African American writer, Ralph Ellison (1952), entitled one of his major works *Invisible Man*—in which he eloquently captured this feeling of spending one's entire life unrecognized. However, what this second form of power tells us is that however disturbing it may be to be lost, invisible, and unrecognized—with no name, no tag saying just who one is—nevertheless, an even more disturbing consequence stems from being defined by society. This internal power is insidious: People do have a name and a tag identifying just who they are—and it is that very name tag that forms their prison. In being named and recognized, internal power takes its hold over all of us.

Unlike external power, which tends to be concentrated in a few people or groups in society, internal power—the power to be identified and named—is not concentrated in any one person or group, nor located in any one place in society. Internal power is spread throughout much of the society—in the way experts in various domains (e.g., medicine, psychology) develop the categories by which people are sorted into "sick" and "healthy"; in the way educators develop and teach those ideas to their students; in the way the media represent various groups in society. Because internal power is not neatly concentrated in one or two locations in a society, it is much more difficult to get hold of and to challenge as compared with external power. When prejudiced views are contained in the very categories by which people come to know themselves and others, it becomes difficult to mount the very kinds of challenge that are needed to undo the hold of prejudice.

An example should help us better grasp this second form of power as well as its relation to prejudice. Nancy Scheper-Hughes (1992) spent some 25 years living among the poor sugarcane workers in Brazil. She found people living under miserable conditions of extreme poverty. But most striking to her was the fact that these people were starving: They were deprived of the very nutriments required for basic survival. Many of them, especially infants and young children, did not survive. But even those who made it past infancy entered a world of hunger where they were forever worn and fatigued.

"Nanci," as she was fondly known to the villagers, wandered through their shanties, interviewing them about their lives and the problems they confronted. She would frequently examine their crude kitchen cupboards only to discover shelves that were empty of food but plentifully supplied with bottles of tranquilizers provided by local physicians. When she asked the people what was bothering them and why they had so many bottles of tranquilizers but no food on their shelves, the people replied that they needed the medicines to treat the condition from which they suffered. And what was that condition? *Nervoso* they stated unhesitantly: a disease of the nerves that kept them so tired and always ill.

No villager talked about starvation, only the disease of *nervoso*. In short, they framed their condition as an illness that they had somehow contracted and from which they suffered, an illness that the local physicians could treat with a constant supply of tranquilizers. What had happened to poverty and starvation in their account?

As she further considered this situation, it became clear to Scheper-Hughes that the large plantation owners, sitting high in the hills in their splendid homes plentiful with food, believed that in providing tranquilizers to their poor workers they were doing their best to help an unfortunate condition that the poor often seemed to "catch." Low wages and abject poverty had little or nothing to do with the situation. But who helped to develop this understanding?

The physicians played a key role in defining what was a normal state of health and what was an illness and how to treat the illness. These understandings, however, were not simply concentrated in the owners or physicians but ranged widely throughout the region, entering into nearly every conversation held about the difficulties that the people faced and how they might best deal with their illness. In other words, while the physicians played a crucial role in defining health and illness, they were by no means alone: Everyone joined in affirming *nervoso* as the problem that affected the poor workers.

This example helps us see how internal power operates by entering into the very ways by which people in a society come to know and understand themselves and others. Not only the poor and starving workers, but the owners, the physicians, and others all viewed the workers as suffering from a disease they called *nervoso*. All parties agreed with this way of knowing the workers. The diagnosis, *nervoso,* shaped almost every feature of *everyone's* life: Workers knew they were ill and needed medical treatment; owners knew that their workforce suffered from a disease and so deserved less pay since they could not work up to the usual standards; physicians knew that they had a difficult battle in combating this peculiar ailment from which the workers seemed uniquely to suffer. Everyone's attitudes were shaped by the ways in which workers' identities as "ill" had been formed.

Because the ideas involved in this second form of power—the internal power to form person's identities—are complex and often difficult to understand, it will be useful to consider another example: homosexuality. The case of homosexuality will not only provide a good example of how internal power operates to form people's identities, but is also important for three other lessons it will teach us.

First, homosexuality has recently come under careful examination in precisely the terms of power that we are examining; that is, current scholarship argues that homosexuality and heterosexuality are names fully saturated with the operation of internal power and not natural conditions of human sexuality.

Second, homosexuality remains a vivid illustration of public prejudices, sometimes openly expressed without embarrassment, in a way that is no longer as clearly noted in other cases of prejudice. For example, in 1997 a large U.S. religious group urged its members to boycott Disney products because a major TV network owned by the Disney Corporation permitted a prime time program, "Ellen," to be put on the air, showing the main character "come out" as a lesbian.

Third, analyses of how internal power operates to secure ongoing prejudices toward homosexuals has suggested two different though related ways to challenge this prejudice: (1) group pride, versus (2) resistance to any and all forms by which one's singular identity is formed. Although we will examine these two ways as they have focused on challenging prejudice toward homosexuals, the lessons we learn from this examination are relevant to all those who have been the targets of prejudice based on the operation of internal power.

The Case of Homosexuality

The first idea we must learn about homosexuality—an idea relevant to considerations about gender and race as well—is that it has a history to it, but not in the way that we usually think of history. We usually think of history as telling us about how something that exists in our current world came to be there. This approach to homosexuality would lead us to look backward in time in order to see how people who were homosexuals were thought of in ancient times, during the Middle Ages, and now. The assumption that guides this approach is that there is a "thing" in the world (in this case, the homosexual) that has existed throughout the ages; in studying history, we simply note how that "thing" has been differently evaluated in different historical periods. What this understanding does not tell us, however, is that history actually creates different objects ("things"), not the same "thing" in different times. That is, the homosexual of the ancient world is not the homosexual of today. Let me illustrate, using Table 16.1 as a summary.

Table 16.1
The History of Homosexuality and Its Relation to Prejudice

Early Greek and early Christian views:

  Certain activities are either accepted and generally tolerated or are considered wrong and sinful (e.g., same-sex sexual acts occur and are either ignored or declared immoral and sinful)

Late 18th–mid-19th century view:

  A group of people become defined in terms of the sexual acts in which they engage as a specific type of human being; another type is then defined in terms of their *not* engaging in those same sexual activities (e.g., the homosexual as a type of person is defined; shortly thereafter, the heterosexual becomes defined as a specific type of person)

Late 19th–early 20th century view:

  Some members of this newly defined type accept their membership as shamefully different from the normal and work to gain more social acceptance and toleration (e.g., seeking public acceptance of the homosexual deviant)

Mid-20th century view:

  Events both within the larger society (e.g., the civil rights movement) plus events within the identified group (e.g., the Stonewall Inn riots) press for a change from shameful acceptance to prideful affirmation (e.g., Gay Pride and Gay Affirmation)

Late 20th century view:

  A slowly emerging awareness within the identified group joins with changed understandings within academic scholarship (e.g., postmodernism) to begin to question all forms by which human identities are formed and made an agency more of social control than human freedom (e.g., queer theory's challenge of all forms of identity)

It is now generally agreed that "homosexuality" as a defined identity is a very modern phenomenon, having entered our world a little over 100 years ago, some say about 1869 or 1870 (e.g., see Connell, 1987; Foucault, 1979, 1985, 1986; Jagose, 1996). Before then, people knew of intimate acts between members of the same sex but did not suggest that these acts were the basis for defining a certain type of human being with a specific identity: the homosexual. This makes homosexuality a modern form of human sexuality, not a form that has always existed throughout human history. Riley (1988; also see Laqueur, 1990) makes a similar case for the study of the identity of women; and likewise, as we have previously seen in Chapters 4 and 5, racial identity is a modern concept, not one whose form has been the same throughout human history.

Prior to about 1870, same-sex acts may have been accepted or condemned, but they were not generally used to sort people according to something basic or essential about their character. It was only when these acts became signs of personal identity that it became important for some segments in society to try to study and understand these "different types" of people. In other words, as long as same-sex activities were not a characteristic defining the essential nature of a person, there was no need to examine the people who engaged in such acts. It was only when the acts were used to define a definite type of person (the homosexual) who differed from another type of person (the heterosexual) that efforts directed toward understanding just who this deviant person was became important. It soon became the province of experts, medical and psychological, to study this "inverted type" of person.

Both the experts and those now identified as homosexuals entered this rather new game: The experts took charge of defining the causes of the homosexual condition while homosexuals and their supporters sought to create tolerance for this newly identified species of human being. We learn, for example, of the German scientist Magnus Hirschfeld, who tried to make conditions for homosexuals safe by defining homosexuality as a kind of third sex, neither male or female, caused by an innate biological disposition that would warrant compassionate rather than prejudiced attitudes and treatment (see Jagose, 1996).

The emerging new laws against homosexuality, however, were not significantly changed by such appeals. Even the medical and psychological experts were not convinced. For example, it was only in 1974 that the American Psychiatric Association and in 1975 that the American Psychological Association agreed, under much pressure, to remove homosexuality from among the list of pathologies used to diagnosis all forms of mental illness (e.g., Minton, 1997).

While definitions of homosexuality began to shift in the late 1960s from a pathological to a nonpathological view, this liberalization among professionals did not basically transform the underlying framework for understanding or defining human sexuality. Heterosexuality was named as the normal pattern of human sexuality against which homosexuality, while perhaps to be tolerated, remained a nonnormative, inverted form.

Challenging Prejudice: Homosexuality's Two Approaches

Two contrasting trends have emerged within the homosexual community to combat prejudice. By examining these approaches as they are used in the gay community, we can draw some lessons that are relevant to other contexts in which the power to form identities has been a central element in the prejudice directed toward others. The first approach adopted the general terms of the majority culture and so defined homosexuality as a nonpathological alternative to the accepted heterosexual norm, appealing for a combination of pride among members of the homosexual community (e.g., the Gay Pride movement) and tolerance and nondiscrimination laws on the part of the rest of society. The second approach exchanged the term *gay* for the term *queer* and pressed its case for challenging all attempts to divide the world's sexualities into a normative heterosexual and a nonnormative homosexual form.

Gay pride and identity politics   Gay Pride took hold in a society already prepared by the other civil rights movements of the 1960s involving women and blacks to hear the sometimes noisy voices demanding group recognition, pride, and equal rights. Some mark the key moment in gay history as the police attack on a gay bar in New York's Greenwich Village, the Stonewall Inn, in June 1965—when rather than going quietly with the police, the gay community fought back in outrage with several days of street demonstrations and riots (see Deitcher, 1995; Jagose, 1996). This date and these events are commonly taken as a sign of gay empowerment rather than resignation; and with empowerment came a changed view of homosexuality. The term *gay* became less a pejorative term of reference than a sign of pride. People came out of their closets into the public eye, declaring themselves gay and proud of it. This sense of pride rather than shameful resignation inaugurated an era of what has been termed identity politics.

The term *identity politics* is a relatively recent concept that refers to the efforts of various groups—usually defined by race, ethnicity, gender, and now sexual orientation—to gain a voice in setting the terms for their own group's identity and in determining just how they will be represented in the public's eye. African Americans, for example, resisted the earlier film representations of the shuffling, slow speaking, and dim-witted black servant and sought to take collective control over the ways in which blacks would be represented on the big screen. Women likewise sought to transform the representations of the little girl dressed in frilly lace and unable to take an active part in the rough and tumble of everyday life with an image more in keeping with pride in women's ability to achieve and accomplish just as well as men. And, homosexuals entered as well, seeking to ensure that the lisping, limp wristed, and effeminate male stereotype would be replaced with gay images that had been developed by the gay community itself and not foisted upon it by others in society. In short, each group not only took pride in its own identity but sought to have a significant voice in defining the characteristics of their own people and how those characteristics would be represented to the public.

The politics of identity and group pride therefore has become one way that the gay community has followed the lead of other communities (e.g., the feminist and black civil rights movements). Efforts in each case are designed to overturn prejudice by (1) increasing the power of the once-demeaned group, (2) using this power to control the very terms by which the group is known, (3) getting nondiscriminatory laws enacted, and (4) helping group members take a prideful rather than a shameful self-deprecating view of themselves.

Where black becomes beautiful, where women succeed in once-privileged male domains (e.g., sports, the military, business), where declaring oneself to be gay and proud replaces being gay and shameful, and where ethnic pride makes more and more citizens of the United States affirm their own unique culture—here we see identity politics at work, making less and less room available for prejudice and discrimination.

Queer theory: beyond identity politics   In several previous places throughout this text I made reference to queer theory to describe the rapidly emerging step beyond identity politics among some gay and lesbian theorists (e.g., Boyarin, 1997; Butler, 1990, 1993, 1997; Halperin, 1995; Jagose, 1996; Minton, 1997; Sedgwick, 1990). It will be useful for us briefly to consider queer theory as it teaches us more about how deeply internal power operates and about how far people must go to resist its vise-like grip.

Queer theory argues that identity politics, which is based on a group's embracing its unique identity, buys into the very system that continues to define and oppress the group. Therefore, something beyond identity politics is essential if a group is, if not to be free, then at least to engage in a more informed and effective resistance against prejudice and discrimination. What does it mean, however, to speak of the homosexual community's having bought into prejudice while expressing pride in being gay? Remember as we try to answer this question, that although our focus here is on homosexuality, the arguments are said to be similar for all other people who have come under the grip of internal power's self-forming approach.

The argument at the center of queer theory is that human sexuality cannot be neatly divided into homosexual and heterosexual; that, in fact, this dualistic splitting is itself the basis of continuing prejudice. Queer theory argues that human sexuality cannot be organized around two categories, one of which (the heterosexual) has become the norm, making the other (the homosexual) necessarily deviant. Queer theory argues that to combat this way of thinking, people must come to realize that all categories of human sexual identity are fluid and changeable; that no neat boundaries separate any one from any other.

These ideas by themselves do no good in challenging prejudice until they become part of people's consciousness. One way to accomplish this is to use an approach developed in the Latin American context of worker and peasant oppression and referred to by the term *conscientización* (e.g., Friere, 1970;

Martín-Baró, 1994). The term describes a process of critical consciousness raising: Members of an oppressed group, who are often unaware of the scope and depth of the prejudice directed against them (i.e., prejudice dwells in their very character and identity) must first see, know, and experience this depth. Over an extended period of time, in small group discussions, people learn how the identity by which they know themselves and perhaps now even take some pride carries many of the seeds of their oppression and prejudice. In time, they come to see how to combat prejudice: They must redefine themselves, but in this case not by redefining only who they are, but rather the entire system by which people are sorted and defined in the first place.

Concientización in the case of homosexuality would therefore require a growing awareness of the degree to which heterosexuality has taken charge of all human sexuality and how this norm of human sexuality must be questioned even more than one must take pride in being labeled gay. The issue, then, becomes not just who are homosexuals, but who are heterosexuals as well. In other words, human sexuality itself is questioned, not just homosexuality.

The idea behind queer theory is not simply to seek a voice for the gay community—a voice that must speak in terms that already destine it for secondary standing. Rather, the idea is to challenge the entire idea of a gay community or a straight community. Queer theorists see the dualistic division into gay and straight as a trap that continues to imprison them as different from the supposedly healthy social norm of heterosexuality. By challenging that norm, space is opened up to move about more freely with whatever forms of sexuality people may employ.

Empowerment and Challenging Prejudice: A Lesson to Be Learned

Although we have been examining the different ways that power is linked with prejudice and how these differences suggest somewhat different approaches to challenging prejudice, I think it reasonable to suggest that they all boil down to one key idea: empowerment. Even the distinctions between the politics of identity and the politics of queer theory require that people who have been the targets of prejudice collectively take an active role in setting the terms of their own lives—in other words, empowerment is central.

While empowerment in the case of pride in group identity would lead to a different set of actions than would empowerment in the case of queer theory, both begin with empowerment. To have pride in being black, gay, ethnic, female, elderly, or whatever, and to work collectively to ensure that one's own group will be represented as the group wishes, first demands empowerment: becoming aware that only through collective action can a group take charge of how it will be known. And, even as queer theory may challenge these approaches through group pride—advocating ongoing resistance to any and all attempts to append labels that define the norm of sexuality, gender, culture, age, race, and so forth—its first step also requires empowerment.

The central lesson, therefore, is that where prejudice is constructed by power—as it usually is—to challenge prejudice requires, if I may borrow a metaphor, fighting power with power.

Chapter Summary: Key Learning Points

1. Power is intimately involved in both creating and sustaining prejudice, and thereby dealing with power must be part of any challenge to prejudice.

2. We considered two major types of power and their role in prejudice:

   a. External power focuses on resources that people have by which they can control others' behavior. Prejudice is involved in two different ways: First, the prejudices of those in positions of power are more consequential for more people than are the prejudices of those in positions of lesser power, making it even more important to challenge the prejudice of the powerful. Second, there is a well known tendency—which goes by various names (e.g., blaming the victim; belief in a just world; fundamental attribution error)—to express prejudice toward people who are powerless simply because their lack of power suggests some defect on their part, as though they deserve the consequences that their low power provides.

   b. Internal power involves the creation of the very meanings by which people come to know who they are. This process usually involves an implicit comparison in which one group becomes the normative standard against which all others not fitting this norm are presumed to be deviant. Prejudice toward a given group thereby tends to be built into the very systems by which people are sorted and identified as a particular type of person.

3. We used homosexuality as a major example of the operation of internal power, examining both how the power to form identities carries within it the seeds of prejudice as well as how one might challenge this form of power and the prejudice it carries. We considered two approaches:

   a. The first approach accepts the standard definitional system by which heterosexuality is the norm and homosexuality is presumed to be deviant, while still proclaiming pride in group membership. The pursuit of group pride not only characterizes many homosexual efforts to challenge prejudice but also describes the efforts of many other social groups who have experienced both oppression and prejudice—including, for example, women and people of color.

   b. The second approach challenges the very systems by which human sexuality is identified and ordered, calling for as thorough an examination of heterosexuality as has heretofore been implicated in the study of homosexuality. In this approach, no one form of sexuality takes privilege over any other; no one form of human identity is attached on a permanent basis to any individual. All human identities are seen to be fluid and ever shifting. While this challenge has taken shape within homosexuality's pursuit of what is called queer theory, a similar challenge has appeared with respect to several other groups, including challenging the very meaning of "woman" as well as the very meaning of "race."

4. The chapter concluded by arguing that whatever the form that power takes and whatever the suggested avenue to its challenge, all approaches converge around the single idea of empowerment—fighting the power that oppresses with the power that resists.

References

Adorno, T. W., Frenkel-Brunswik, E., Levinson, D. J., & Sanford, R. N. (1964/1950). *The authoritarian personality.* New York: Wiley Science Editions.

Alba, R. (1985). *Italian Americans: Into the twilight of ethnicity.* Englewood Cliffs, NJ: Prentice-Hall.

Allport, G. W. (1950). Prejudice: A problem in psychological and social causation. *Journal of Social Issues, Supplement Series, Number 4.*

Allport, G. W. (1954). *The nature of prejudice.* Cambridge, MA: Addison-Wesley.

Allport, G. W., & Kramer, B. (1946). Some roots of prejudice. *Journal of Psychology, 22,* 9–30.

Allport, G. W., & Postman, L. J. (1952/1945). The basic psychology of rumor. In G. E. Swanson, T. M. Newcomb, & E. L. Hartley (Eds.), *Readings in social psychology* (pp. 160–171). New York: Holt.

Altemeyer, B. (1981). *Right-wing authoritarianism.* Winnipeg: University of Manitoba Press.

Altemeyer, B. (1988). *Enemies of freedom: Understanding right-wing authoritarianism.* San Francisco: Jossey-Bass.

Altemeyer, B. (1994). Reducing prejudice in right-wing authoritarians. In M. P. Zanna & J. M. Olson (Eds.), *The psychology of prejudice: The Ontario Symposium, Volume 7* (pp. 131–148). Hillsdale, NJ: Erlbaum.

Amir, Y. (1969). Contact hypothesis of ethnic relations. *Psychological Bulletin, 71,* 319–343.

Anderson, V. (1995). *Beyond ontological blackness: An essay on African-American religious and cultural criticism.* New York: Continuum.

Aronson, E. (1969). The theory of cognitive dissonance: A current perspective. In L. Berkowitz (Ed.), *Advances in experimental social psychology: Vol. 4* (pp. 1–34). San Diego: Academic Press.

Aronson, E., & Bridgeman, D. (1979). Jigsaw groups and the desegrated classroom: In pursuit of common goals. *Personality and Social Psychology Bulletin, 5,* 438–466.

Aronson, E., Stephen, C., Sikes, J., Blaney, N., & Snapp, M. (1978). *The jigsaw classroom.* Beverly Hills: Sage.

Arroyo, C. G., & Zigler, E. (1995). Racial identity, academic achievement and the psychological well-being of economically disadvantaged adolescents. *Journal of Personality and Social Psychology, 69,* 903–914.

Asher, S. R., & Allen, V. L. (1969). Racial preferences and social comparison processes. *Journal of Social Issues, 25,* 157–166.

Azar, B. (1997, April). Environment is key to serotonin levels. *APA Monitor, 26,* 29.

Banaji, M. R., & Greenwald, A. G. (1994). Implicit stereotyping and prejudice. In M. P. Zanna & J. M. Olson (Eds.), *The psychology of prejudice: The Ontario Symposium, Volume 7* (pp. 55–76). Hillsdale, NJ: Erlbaum.

Banaji, M. R., Hardin, C., & Rothman, A. J. (1993). Implicit stereotyping in person judgment. *Journal of Personality and Social Psychology, 65,* 272–281.

Banks, W. C. (1976). White preference in blacks: A paradigm in search of a phenomenon. *Psychological Bulletin, 83,* 1179–1186.

Barkun, M. (1994). *Religion and the racist right: The origins of the Christian Identity movement.* Chapel Hill: University of North Carolina Press.

Batson, C. D., & Burris, C. T. (1994). Personal religion: Depressant or stimulant of prejudice and discrimination? In M. P. Zanna & J. M. Olson (Eds.), *The psychology of prejudice: The Ontario Symposium, Volume 7* (pp. 149–169). Hillsdale, NJ: Erlbaum.

Batson, C. D., Flink, C. H., Schoenrade, P. A., Fultz, J., & Pych, V. (1986). Religious orientation and overt versus covert racial prejudice. *Journal of Personality and Social Psychology, 50,* 175–181.

Batson, C. D., & Schoenrade, P. A. (1991a). Measuring religion as quest: 1. Validity concerns. *Journal for the Scientific Study of Religion, 30,* 416–429.

Batson, C. D., & Schoenrade, P. A. (1991b). Measuring religion as quest: 2. Reliability concerns. *Journal for the Scientific Study of Religion, 30,* 430-447.

Bay, C. (1967). Political and apolitical students: Facts in search of theory. *Journal of Social Issues, 23,* 76-91.

Benokraitis, N. V., & Gilbert, M. K. (1989). Women in federal government employment. In F. A. Blanchard & F. J. Crosby (Eds.). *Affirmative action in perspective.* (pp. 65-80). New York: Springer-Verlag.

Billig, M. (1976). *Social psychology and intergroup relations.* London: Academic Press.

Bingham, S. (1993). The truth about growing up rich. In V. Cyrus (Ed.), *Experiencing race, class and gender in the United States* (pp. 111-115). Mountain View, CA: Mayfield.

Bion, W. R. (1959). *Experiences in groups.* New York: Basic Books.

Bodenhausen, G. V. (1990). Stereotypes as judgmental heuristics: Evidence of circadian variations in discrimination. *Psychological Science, 1,* 319-322.

Bourhis, R. Y., Sachdev, I., & Gagnon, A. (1994). Intergroup research with the Tajfel matrices: Methodological notes. In M. P. Zanna & J. M. Olson (Eds.), *The psychology of prejudice: The Ontario Symposium, Volume 7* (pp. 209-232). Hillsdale, NJ: Erlbaum.

Bowles, S., & Gintis, H. (1972, November-December & 1973, January-February). IQ in the U.S. class structure. Reprint from *Social Policy, 3* (4-5), 1-27.

Boyarin, D. (1994). *A radical Jew: Paul and the politics of identity.* Berkeley: University of California Press.

Boyarin, D. (1997). *Unheroic conduct: The rise of heterosexuality and the invention of the Jewish man.* Berkeley: University of California Press.

Brand, E. S., Ruiz, R. A., & Padilla, A. M. (1974). Ethnic identification and preference: A review. *Psychological Bulletin, 81,* 860-890.

Brekke, N., & Borgida, E. (1988). Expert psychological testimony in rape trials: A social-cognitive analysis. *Journal of Personality and Social Psychology, 55,* 372-386.

Brewer, M. B. (1979). Ingroup bias in the minimal intergroup situation: A cognitive-motivational analysis. *Psychological Bulletin, 86,* 307-324.

Brewer, M. B., & Gardner, W. (1996). Who is this "we"? Levels of collective identity and self representations. *Journal of Personality and Social Psychology, 71,* 83-93.

Brewer, M. B., Manzi, J. M., & Shaw, J. S. (1993). In-group identification as a function of depersonalization, distinctiveness, and status. *Psychological Science, 4,* 88-92.

Brewer, M. B., & Miller, N. (1996). *Intergroup relations.* Pacific Grove, CA: Brooks/Cole.

Bronfenbrenner, U., & Ceci, S. J. (1994). Nature-nurture reconceptualized in developmental perspective: A bioecological model. *Psychological Review, 101,* 568-586.

Broverman, I. K., Vogel, S. R., Broverman, D. M., Clarkson, F. E., & Rosenkrantz, P. S. (1972). Sex-role stereotypes: A current appraisal. *Journal of Social Issues, 28,* 59-78.

Brown, P. (1988). *The body and society: Men, women and sexual renunciation in early Christianity.* New York: Columbia University Press.

Brown, R. (1995). *Prejudice: Its social psychology.* Oxford: Blackwell.

Brown, R. J., & Turner, J. C. (1981). Interpersonal and intergroup behaviour. In J. C. Turner & H. Giles (Eds.), *Intergroup behavior* (pp. 33-65). Oxford: Blackwell.

Brown, R. (1986). *Social psychology* (2nd ed.). New York: Free Press.

Bruner, J. (1990). *Acts of meaning.* Cambridge: Harvard University Press.

Buss, D. M. (1994). *The evolution of desire.* New York: Basic Books.

Buss, D. M. (1995). Psychological sex differences: Origins through sexual selection. *American Psychologist, 50,* 164-168.

Buss, D. M., & Schmitt, D. P. (1993). Sexual strategies theory: An evolutionary perspective on human mating. *Psychological Review, 100,* 204-232.

Butler, J. (1990). *Gender trouble: Feminism and the subversion of identity.* New York: Routledge.

Butler, J. (1993). *Bodies that matter: On the discursive limits of "sex."* New York: Routledge.

Butler, J. (1997). *The psychic life of power: Theories of subjection.* Stanford: Stanford University Press.

Cadinu, M. R., & Rothbart, M. (1996). Self-anchoring and differentiation processes in the minimal group setting. *Journal of Personality and Social Psychology, 70,* 661-677.

Caplan, N., & Nelson, S. D. (1973). On being useful: The nature and consequences of psychological research on social problems. *American Psychologist, 28,* 199-211.

Caporael, L. R., & Brewer, M. B. (Eds.). (1991). Issues in evolutionary psychology [Whole issue]. *Journal of Social Issues, 47(3).*

Ceci, S. J., & Williams, W. M. (1997). Schooling, intelligence, and income. *American Psychologist, 52,* 1051-1058.

Chalk, F., & Jonassohn, K. (1990). *The history and sociology of genocide: Analyses and case studies.* New Haven: Yale University Press.

Christie, R., & Jahoda, M. (1954). *Studies in the scope and method of "the authoritarian personality."* Glencoe, IL: Free Press.

Clark, K. B., & Clark, M. P. (1939/1952). Racial identification and preference in Negro children. In G. E. Swanson, T. M. Newcomb, & E. L. Hartley (Eds.), *Readings in social psychology* (pp. 551-560). New York: Holt.

Connell, R. W. (1987). *Gender and power.* Stanford: Stanford University Press.

Crocker, J. (1981). Judgment of covariation by social perceivers. *Psychological Bulletin, 90,* 272-292.

Crosby, F. (1976). A model of egoistical relative deprivation. *Psychological Review, 83,* 85-113.

Darley, J. M., & Gross, P. H. (1983). A hypothesis-confirming bias in labeling effects. *Journal of Personality and Social Psychology, 44,* 20-33.

Davidson, K. (1996, September 22). Genes don't fit the hype, say DNA skeptics. *San Francisco Examiner,* pp. 1A, 8A.

Deitcher, D. (Ed.). (1995). *The question of equality.* New York: Scribner's.

De Mott, B. (1995). *The trouble with friendship: Why Americans can't think straight about race.* New York: Atlantic Monthly Press.

Deutsch, M. (1953). The effects of cooperation and competition upon group processes. In D. Cartwright & A. Zander (Eds.), *Group dynamics: Research and theory.* Evanston, IL: Row Peterson.

Deutsch, M. (1969). Conflicts: Productive and destructive. *Journal of Social Issues, 25,* 7-41.

Deutsch, M., & Krauss, R. M. (1960). The effect of threat upon interpersonal bargaining. *Journal of Abnormal and Social Psychology, 61,* 181-189.

Devine, P. G. (1989). Stereotypes and prejudice: Their automatic and controlled components. *Journal of Personality and Social Psychology, 56,* 5-18.

Dion, K., Berscheid, E., & Walster, E. (1972). What is beautiful is good. *Journal of Personality and Social Psychology, 24,* 207-213.

Dollard, J., Doob, L., Miller, N., Mowrer, O. H., & Sears, R. R. (1939). *Frustration and aggression.* New Haven: Yale University Press.

Dover, K. J. (1978). *Greek homosexuality.* Cambridge: Harvard University Press.

Dovidio, J. F., & Gaertner, S. L. (1996). Affirmative action, unintentional racial biases and intergroup relations. *Journal of Social Issues, 52,* 51-75.

Dovidio, J. F., Mann, J., & Gaertner, S. L. (1989). Resistance to affirmative action: The implications of aversive racism. In F. A. Blanchard & F. J. Crosby (Eds.), *Affirmative action in perspective* (pp. 83-102). New York: Springer-Verlag.

Du Bois, W. E. B. (1903/1995). *The souls of black folk.* New York: Signet.

Duckitt, J. (1994). *The social psychology of prejudice.* Westport, CT: Praeger.

Duncan. B. L. (1976). Differential social perception and attribution of intergroup violence: Testing the lower limits of stereotyping of blacks. *Journal of Personality and Social Psychology, 34,* 590-598.

Eagly, A. H. (1987). *Sex differences in social behavior: A social-role interpretation.* Hillsdale, NJ: Erlbaum.

Eagly, A. H. (1995). The science and politics of comparing women and men. *American Psychologist, 50,* 145-158.

Eagly, A. H., Karau, S. J., & Makhijani, M. G. (1995). Gender and the effectiveness of leaders: A meta-analysis. *Psychological Bulletin, 117,* 125-145.

Eagly, A. H., & Steffen, V. J. (1984). Gender stereotypes stem from the distribution of women and men into social roles. *Journal of Personality and Social Psychology, 46,* 735-754.

Efron, J. M. (1994). *Defenders of the race: Jewish doctors and race science in fin-de-siecle Europe*. New Haven: Yale University Press.

Ellemers, N., van Knippenberg, A., de Vries, N. K., & Wilke, H. (1988). Social identification and permeability of group boundaries. *European Journal of Social Psychology, 18*, 497-513.

Ellemers, N., Wilke, H., & van Knippenberg, A. (1993). Effects of the legitimacy of low group or individual status on individual and collective status-enhancement strategies. *Journal of Personality and Social Psychology, 64*, 766-778.

Ellison, R. (1952). *Invisible man*. New York: Random House.

Epstein, Y. J., Krupat, E., & Obudho, C. (1976). Clean is beautiful: Identification and preference as a function of race and cleanliness. *Journal of Social Issues, 32*, 109-118.

Ezekiel, R. S. (1995). *The racist mind: Portraits of American neo-Nazis and klansmen*. New York: Viking.

Fairchild, H. H. (1991). Scientific racism: The cloak of objectivity. *Journal of Social Issues, 47*, 101-115.

Faludi, S. (1991). *Backlash: The undeclared war against American women*. New York: Crown.

Fausto-Sterling, A. (1992). *Myths of gender: Biological theories about women and men*. New York: Basic Books.

Fausto-Sterling, A. (1997). Beyond difference: A biologist's perspective. *Journal of Social Issues, 53*, 233-258.

Fendel, N., Hurtado, S., Long, J., & Giraldo, Z. (1996, Spring). Affirmative action: Who does it help? Who does it hurt? *CFA Professor, 28*(2), 13-17.

Festinger, L. (1957). *A theory of cognitive dissonance*. Stanford: Stanford University Press.

Fiorenza, E. S. (1989). *In memory of her: A feminist theological reconstruction of Christian origins*. New York: Crossroad.

Fischer, C. S., Hout, M., Jankowski, J. S., Lucas, S. R., Swidler, A., & Voss, K. (1996). *Inequality by design: Cracking the Bell Curve myth*. Princeton: Princeton University Press.

Fish, J. M. (1995). Why psychologists should learn some anthropology. *American Psychologist, 50*, 44-45.

Fordham, S. (1988). Racelessness as a factor in black students' school success: Pragmatic strategy or pyrrhic victory? *Harvard Educational Review, 58*, 54-84.

Fordham, S., & Ogbu, J. U. (1986). Black students' school success: "Coping with the burden of acting white." *Urban Review, 18*, 176-206.

Foucault, M. (1978). *The history of sexuality: Volume I. An introduction*. New York: Vintage.

Foucault, M. (1979). *Discipline and punish: The birth of the prison*. New York: Random House.

Foucault, M. (1985). *The use of pleasure*. New York: Vintage.

Foucault, M. (1986). *The care of the self*. New York: Pantheon.

Frankenberg, R. (1993). *White women, race matters: The social construction of whiteness*. Minneapolis: University of Minnesota Press.

Fraser, S. (Ed.). (1995). *The Bell Curve wars: Race, intelligence, and the future of America*. New York: Basic Books.

Freire, P. (1970). *Pedagogy of the oppressed*. New York: Continuum.

French, J. R. P., Jr., & Raven, B. H. (1959). The bases of social power. In D. Cartwright (Ed.), *Studies in social power* (pp. 150-167). Ann Arbor: Research Center for Group Dynamics/Institute for Social Research.

Freud, S. (1922). *Group psychology and the analysis of the ego* (J. Strachey, Trans.). New York: Boni and Liveright.

Gaines, S. O., Jr., & Reed, E. S. (1995). Prejudice: From Allport to Du Bois. *American Psychologist, 50*, 96-103.

Gallagher, W. (1994, September). How we become what we are. *Atlantic Monthly*, pp. 39-55.

Gardner, R. C. (1994). Stereotypes as consensual beliefs. In M. P. Zanna & J. M. Olson (Eds.), *The psychology of prejudice: The Ontario Symposium, Vol. 7* (pp. 1-31). Hillsdale, NJ: Erlbaum.

Gilbert, D. T., & Hixon, J. G. (1991). The trouble of thinking: Activation and application of stereotypic beliefs. *Journal of Personality and Social Psychology, 60*, 509-517.

Gilbert, D. T., & Malone, P. S. (1995). The correspondence bias. *Psychological Bulletin, 117*, 21-38.

Gilbert, G. M. (1951). Stereotype persistence and change among college students. *Journal of Abnormal and Social Psychology, 46,* 245-254.

Gilmore, D. D. (1990). *Manhood in the making: Cultural concepts of masculinity.* New Haven: Yale University Press.

Gladue, B. A. (1994). The biopsychology of sexual orientation. *Current Directions in Psychological Science, 3,* 150-154.

Gladwell, M. (1997, February 24/March 3). Crime and science: Damaged. *The New Yorker,* pp. 132-147.

Glick, P., & Fiske, S. T. (1996). The ambivalent sexism inventory: Differentiating hostile and benevolent sexism. *Journal of Personality and Social Psychology, 70,* 491-512.

Goldberg, P. (1968). Are women prejudiced against women? *Transaction, 5,* 28-30.

Goldhagen, D. J. (1996). *Hitler's willing executioners: Ordinary Germans and the Holocaust.* New York: Knopf.

Gordon, L. (1990). Family violence, feminism and social control. In L. Gordon (Ed.), *Women, the state and welfare.* Madison: University of Wisconsin Press.

Gordon, L. (1994). *Pitied but not entitled: Single mothers and the history of welfare.* Glencoe, IL: Free Press.

Green, B. G. (1992). Expose or smear? The Burt affair. *Psychological Science, 3,* 328-331.

Greenwald, A. G., & Banaji, M. R. (1995). Implicit social cognition: Attitudes, self-esteem and stereotypes. *Psychological Review, 102,* 4-27.

Grube, J. W., Mayton, D. M. II, & Ball-Rokeach, S. J. (1994). Inducing change in values, attitudes, and behaviors: Belief system theory and the method of value self-confrontration. *Journal of Social Issues, 50,* 153-173.

Halperin, D. M. (1990). *One hundred years of homosexuality and essays on Greek love.* New York: Routledge.

Halperin, D. M. (1995). *Saint Foucault: Towards a gay hagiography.* New York: Oxford University Press.

Halpern, D. F. (1997). Sex differences in intelligence: Implications for education. *American Psychologist, 52,* 1091-1102.

Hamilton, D. L., Sherman, S. J., & Ruvolo, C. M. (1990). Stereotype-based expectancies: Effects on information processing and social behavior. *Journal of Social Issues, 46,* 35-60.

Harding, J., Proshansky, H., Kutner, B., & Chein, I. (1969). Prejudice and ethnic relations. In G. Lindzey & E. Aronson (Eds.), *Handbook of social psychology: Vol. 5* (pp. 1-76). Reading, MA: Addison-Wesley.

Heath, S. B. (1989). Oral and literate traditions among black Americans living in poverty. *American Psychologist, 44,* 367-373.

Heller, C. E. (1997). *Until we are strong together: Women writers in the Tenderloin.* New York: Columbia University Teacher's College Press.

Herdt, G. H. (1984). *Ritualized homosexuality in Melanesia.* Berkeley: University of California Press.

Herrnstein, R. J., & Murray, C. (1994). *The bell curve.* New York: Free Press.

Hewstone, M., & Brown, R. J. (1986). Contact is not enough: An intergroup perspective on the "contact" hypothesis. In M. Hewstone & R. J. Brown (Eds.), *Contact and conflict in intergroup encounters* (pp. 1-44). Oxford: Basil Blackwell.

Hewstone, M., & Ward, C. (1985). Ethnocentrism and causal attribution in Southeast Asia. *Journal of Personality and Social Psychology, 48,* 614-623.

Hirsch, J. (1981, May). To "unfrock the charlatans" [Whole issue]. *Sage Race Relations Abstracts, 6*(2).

Hirschfeld, L. A. (1996). *Race in the making: Cognition, culture, and the child's construction of human kinds.* Cambridge: MIT Press.

Ho, D. Y. F. (1995). Selfhood and identity in Confucianism, Taoism, Buddhism, and Hinduism: Contrasts with the West. *Journal for the Theory of Social Behavior, 25,* 115-139.

Hofstede, G. (1980). *Culture's consequences: International differences in work-related values.* Beverly Hills: Sage.

Hofstede, G. (1991). *Culture and organizations.* London: McGraw-Hill.

Hogg, M. A., & Turner, J. C. (1987). Intergroup behaviour, self-stereotyping and the salience of social categories. *British Journal of Social Psychology, 26,* 325-340.

Hovland, C., & Sears, R. R. (1940). Minor studies in aggression, VI: Correlation of lynchings with economic indices. *Journal of Psychology, 9,* 301-310.

Howard, J. A. (1984). Societal influences on attribution: Blaming some victims more than others. *Journal of Personality and Social Psychology, 47,* 494-505.

Hraba, J., & Grant, G. (1970). Black is beautiful: A reexamination of racial preference and identity. *Journal of Personality and Social Psychology, 16,* 398-402.

Hunsberger, B. (1995). Religion and prejudice: The role of religious fundamentalism, quest, and right-wing authoritarianism. *Journal of Social Issues, 51,* 113-129.

Huo, Y. J., Smith., H. J., Tyler, T. R., & Lind, E. A. (1996). Superordinate identification, subgroup identification, and justice concerns: Is separatism the problem; is assimilation the answer? *Psychological Science, 7,* 40-45.

Hyde, J. S., Fennema, E., & Lamon, S. J. (1990). Gender differences in mathematics performance: A meta-analysis. *Psychological Bulletin, 107,* 139-155.

Islam, M. R., & Hewstone, M. (1993). Intergroup attributions and affective consequences in majority and minority groups. *Journal of Personality and Social Psychology, 64,* 936-950.

Jackson, L. A., Sullivan, L. A., Harnish, R., & Hodge, C. N. (1996). Achieving positive social identity: Social mobility, social creativity and permeability of group boundaries. *Journal of Personality and Social Psychology, 70,* 241-254.

Jackson, L. A., Sullivan, L. A., & Hodge, C. N. (1993). Stereotype effects on attributions, predictions, and evaluations: No two social judgments are quite alike. *Journal of Personality and Social Psychology, 65,* 69-84.

Jagose, A. (1996). *Queer theory: An introduction.* New York: New York University Press.

James, W. (1910). *Psychology: The brief course.* New York: Holt.

Jensen, A. R. (1969). How much can we boost IQ and scholastic achievement? *Harvard Educational Review, 39,* 1-123.

Jensen, A. R. (1995). Psychological research on race differences. *American Psychologist, 50,* 41-42.

Jensen, A. R., & Johnson, F. E. (1994). Race and sex differences in head size and IQ. *Intelligence, 18,* 309-333.

Jones, E. E. (1990). *Interpersonal perception.* New York: Freeman.

Jones, J. M. (1997). *Prejudice and racism.* New York: McGraw-Hill.

Jordon, W. D. (1968). *White over black: American attitudes toward the Negro 1550-1812.* Chapel Hill: University of North Carolina Press.

Judd, C. M., & Park, B. (1988). Out-group homogeneity: Judgments of variability at the individual and group levels. *Journal of Personality and Social Psychology, 54,* 778-788.

Judd, C. M., & Park, B. (1993). Definition and assessment of accuracy in social stereotypes. *Psychological Review, 100,* 109-128.

Judd, C. M., Park, B., Ryan, C. S., Brauer, M., & Kraus, S. (1995). Stereotypes and ethnocentrism: Diverging interethnic perceptions of African American and white American youth. *Journal of Personality and Social Psychology, 69,* 460-481.

Judd, C. M., Ryan, C. S., & Park, B. (1991). Accuracy in the judgment of in-group and out-group variability. *Journal of Personality and Social Psychology, 61,* 366-379.

Kanter, R. (1977). *Men and women in the corporation.* New York: Basic Books.

Karlins, M., Coffman, T. L., & Walters, G. (1969). On the fading of social stereotypes: Studies in three generations of college students. *Journal of Personality and Social Psychology, 13,* 1-16.

Katz, D. (1960). The functional approach to the study of attitudes. *Public Opinion Quarterly, 24,* 163-204.

Katz, D., & Braly, K. W. (1952/1933). Verbal stereotypes and racial prejudice. In G. W. Swanson, T. M. Newcomb, & E. L. Hartley (Eds.), *Readings in social psychology* (pp. 67-73). New York: Holt.

Katz, D., & Stotland, E. (1959). A preliminary statement to a theory of attitude structure and change. In S. Koch (Ed.), *Psychology: A study of a science: Vol. 3* (pp. 423-475). New York: McGraw-Hill.

Katz, I., & Hass, R. G. (1988). Racial ambivalence and American value conflict: Correlational and priming studies of dual cognitive structures. *Journal of Personality and Social Psychology, 55,* 893-905.

Kelley, H. H. (1973). The process of causal attribution. *American Psychologist, 28,* 107-128.

Kelman, H. C. (1997). Group processes in the resolution of international conflicts: Experiences from the Israeli-Palestinian case. *American Psychologist, 52,* 212-220.

Kelman, H. & Pettigrew, T. (1959). How to understand prejudice. *28,* 436-441.

Kimball, M. M. (1989). A new perspective on women's math achievement. *Psychological Bulletin, 105,* 198-214.

Kinder, D. R., & Sears, D. O. (1981). Symbolic racism versus racial threats to the good life. *Journal of Personality and Social Psychology, 40,* 414-431.

Kitzinger, C. (1987). *The social construction of lesbianism.* London: Sage.

Klanwatch Intelligence Report. (1996, August). No. 83. Montgomery, AL: Southern Poverty Law Center.

Klein, M. (1948). *Contributions to psychoanalysis: 1921-1945.* London: Hogarth.

La Fromboise, T., Coleman, H. L. K., & Gerton, J. (1993). Psychological impact of biculturalism: Evidence and theory. *Psychological Bulletin, 114,* 395-412.

Lakoff, G. (1987). *Women, fire and dangerous things: What categories reveal about the mind.* Chicago: University of Chicago Press.

Lalonde, R. N., & Cameron, J. E. (1994). Behavioral responses to discrimination: A focus on action. In M. P. Zanna & J. M. Olson (Eds.), *The psychology of prejudice: The Ontario Symposium, Vol. 7* (pp. 257-288). Hillsdale, NJ: Erlbaum.

Lalonde, R. N., & Silverman, R. A. (1994). Behavioral preferences in response to social injustice: The effects of group permeability and social identity salience. *Journal of Personality and Social Psychology, 66,* 78-85.

La Piere, R. T. (1934). Attitudes vs. actions. *Social Forces, 13,* 230-237.

Laqueur, T. (1990). *Making sex: Body and gender from the Greeks to Freud.* Cambridge: Harvard University Press.

Le Bon, G. (1895/1960). *The crowd.* New York: Viking.

Leippe, M. R., & Eisenstadt, D. (1994). Generalization of dissonance reduction: Decreasing prejudice through induced compliance. *Journal of Personality and Social Psychology, 67,* 395-413.

Lerner, M. J. (1980). *The belief in a just world: A fundamental delusion.* New York: Plenum.

Lerner, M. J., & Miller, D. T. (1978). Just world research and the attribution process: Looking back and ahead. *Psychological Bulletin, 85,* 1030-1051.

Le Vay, S. (1991). A difference in hypothalamic structure between heterosexual and homosexual men. *Science, 253,* 1034-1037.

Lewin, K. (1948). *Resolving social conflicts: Selected papers on group dynamics.* New York: Harper.

Lewontin, R. C. (1991). *Biology as ideology: The doctrine of DNA.* New York: HarperCollins.

Lind, E. A., & Tyler, T. R. (1988). *The social psychology of procedural justice.* New York: Plenum.

Lippmann, W. (1922). *Public opinion.* New York: Harcourt Brace.

Loftus, E. F. (1979). *Eyewitness testimony.* Cambridge: Harvard University Press.

Loftus, E. F. (1992). When a lie becomes memory's truth: Memory distortion after exposure to misinformation. *Current Directions in Psychological Science, 1,* 121-123.

Loftus, E. F. (1993). The reality of repressed memories. *American Psychologist, 48,* 518-537.

Loftus, E. F., & Hoffman, H. G. (1989). Misinformation and memory: The creation of new memories. *Journal of Experimental Psychology: General, 118,* 100-104.

Lukes, S. (Ed.). (1986). *Power.* New York: New York University Press.

Luria, A. R. (1976). *Cognitive development: Its cultural and social foundations.* Cambridge: Harvard University Press.

MacKinnon, C. A. (1989). *Toward a feminist theory of the state.* Cambridge: Harvard University Press.

Macrae, C. N., Bodenhausen, G. V., Milne, A. B., & Jetten, J. (1994). Out of mind but back in sight: Stereotypes on the rebound. *Journal of Personality and Social Psychology 67,* 808-817.

Macrae, C. N., Milne, A. B., & Bodenhausen, G. V. (1994). Stereotypes as energy-saving devices: A peek inside the cognitive toolbox. *Journal of Personality and Social Psychology, 66,* 37-47.

Markus, H., & Kitayama, S. (1991). Culture and the self: Implications for cognition, emotion, and motivation. *Psychological Review, 98,* 224-253.

Martín-Baró, I. (1994). *Writings for a libera-tion psychology.* Cambridge: Harvard University Press.

Maurer, K. L., Park, B., & Rothbart, M. (1995). Subtyping versus subgrouping processes in stereotype representation. *Journal of Personality and Social Psychology, 69,* 812-824.

Mayton, D. M. II, Ball-Rokeach, S. J., & Loges, W. E. (1994). Human values and social issues: An introduction. *Journal of Social Issues, 50,* 1-8.

McConahay, J. B. (1986). Modern racism, ambivalence, and the modern racism scale. In J. F. Dovidio & S. L. Gaertner (Eds.), *Prejudice, discrimination and racism* (pp. 91-125). Orlando: Academic Press.

McConahay, J. B., & Hough, J. C., Jr. (1976). Symbolic racism. *Journal of Social Issues, 32,* 23-45.

McGrane, B. (1989). *Beyond anthropology: Society and the other.* New York: Columbia University Press.

McGuire, W. J., McGuire, C. V., Child, P., & Fujoka, T. (1978). Salience of ethnicity in the spontaneous self-concept as a function of one's ethnic distinctiveness in the social environment. *Journal of Personality and Social Psychology, 36,* 511-520.

McGuire, W. J., & Padawer-Singer, A. (1976). Trait salience in the spontaneous self-concept. *Journal of Personality and Social Psychology, 33,* 743-754.

McIntosh, P. (1993). White privilege: Unpacking the invisible knapsack. In V. Cyrus (Ed.), *Experiencing race, class and gender in the United States* (pp. 209-213). Mountain View, CA: Mayfield.

McNeil, D. G., Jr. (1997, February 9). Black, yet white: A hated color in Zimbabwe. *New York Times,* pp. 1, 6.

Meloen, J. D., Hagendoorn, L, Raaijmakers, Q., & Visser, L. (1988). Authoritarianism and the revival of political racism: Reassessments in the Netherlands of the reliability and validity of the concept of authoritarianism. *Political Psychology, 9,* 413-429.

Memmi, A. (1967). *The colonizer and the colonized.* Boston: Beacon.

Minard, R. D. (1952). Race relations in the Pochontas coal field. *Journal of Social Issues, 8,* 29-44.

Minton, H. L. (1997). Queer theory: Historical roots and implications for psychology. *Theory & Psychology, 7,* 337-353.

Monteith, M. J. (1993). Self-regulation of prejudiced responses: Implications for progress in prejudice-reduction efforts. *Journal of Personality and Social Psychology, 65,* 469-485.

Morrison, T. (1992). *Playing in the dark: Whiteness and the literary imagination.* Cambridge: Harvard University Press.

Mullen, B., & Hu, L. (1989). Perceptions of ingroup and out-group variability: A meta-analytic integration. *Basic and Applied Social Psychology, 10,* 233-252.

Murray, C., & Herrnstein, R. J. (1994, October 31). Race, genes and I.Q.—An apologia. *New Republic,* 27-37.

Neisser, U., Boodoo, G., Bouchard, T. J., Jr., Boykin, A. W., Brody, N., Ceci, S. J., Halpern, D. F., Loehlin, J. C., Perloff, R., Sternberg, R. J., & Urbina, S. (1996). Intelligence: Knowns and unknowns. *American Psychologist, 51,* 77-101.

Nelson, L. J., & Miller, D. T. (1995). The distinctiveness effect in social categorization: You are what makes you unusual. *Psychological Science, 6,* 246-249.

Nobles, W. W. (1973). Psychological research and the black self-concept: A critical review. *Journal of Social Issues, 29,* 11-31.

Norris, W. L., & Reardon, M. (1989). Employment screening, qualifications, and gender discrimination: A case study of the New York City firefighters. In F. A. Blanchard & F. J. Crosby (Eds.), *Affirmative action in perspective* (pp. 51-63). New York: Springer-Verlag.

Ogbu, J. U. (1978). *Minority education and caste: The American system in cross-cultural perspective.* New York: Academic Press.

Olweus, D. (1995). Bullying or peer abuse at school: Facts and intervention. *Current Directions in Psychological Science, 4,* 196-200.

Ostrom, T. M., & Sedikides, C. (1992). Outgroup homogeneity effects in natural and minimal groups. *Psychological Bulletin, 112,* 536-552.

Pagels, E. (1988). *Adam, Eve and the serpent.* New York: Vintage.

Pagels, E. (1995). *The origin of Satan.* New York: Random House.

Pardes, I. (1992). *Countertraditions in the Bible: A feminist approach.* Cambridge: Harvard University Press.

Park, B., & Hastie, R. (1987). Perception of variability in category development: Instance- versus abstraction-based stereotypes. *Journal of Personality and Social Psychology, 53,* 621-635.

Peters, M. (1995). Race differences in brain size. *American Psychologist, 50,* 947-948.

Peters, R. S. (1958). *The concept of motivation.* New York: Humanities Press.

Peterson, C., Seligman, M. E. P., & Vaillant, G. (1988). Pessimistic explanatory style is a risk factor for physical illness: A thirty-five year longitudinal study. *Journal of Personality and Social Psychology, 55,* 23-27.

Pettigrew, T. F. (1979). The ultimate attribution error: Extending Allport's cognitive analysis of prejudice. *Personality and Social Psychology Bulletin, 5,* 461-476.

Phinney, J. S. (1990). Ethnic identity in adolescents and adults: Review of research. *Psychological Bulletin, 108,* 499-514.

Plant, R. (1986). *The pink triangle: The Nazi war against homosexuals.* New York: Holt.

Pleck, J. H. (1993). Men's power with women, other men and society. In V. Cyrus (Ed.), *Experiencing race, class and gender in the United States* (pp. 221-225). Mountain View, CA: Mayfield.

Plomin, R., & Petrill, S. A. (1997). Genetics and intelligence: What's new? *Intelligence, 24,* 53-77.

Ponterotto, J. G., & Pedersen, P. B. (1993). *Preventing prejudice: A guide for counselors and educators.* Newbury Park, CA: Sage.

Rabbie, J. M., & Lodewijkx, H. F. M. (1995). Aggressive reactions to social injustice by individuals and groups as a function of social norms, gender, and anonymity. *Social Justice Research, 8,* 7-40.

Redl, F. (1942). Group emotions and leadership. *Psychiatry, 5,* 573-596.

Richardson, D. (Ed.). (1996). *Theorising heterosexuality: Telling it straight.* Buckingham, England: Open University Press.

Riger, S. (1997). From snapshots to videotape: New directions in research on gender differences. *Journal of Social Issues, 53,* 395-408.

Riley, D. (1988). *"Am I that name?" Feminism and the category of "women" in history.* Minneapolis: University of Minnesota Press.

Robinson, R. J., Keltner, D., Ward, A., & Ross, L. (1995). Actual versus assumed differences in construal: "Naive realism" in intergroup perception and conflict. *Journal of Personality and Social Psychology, 68,* 404-417.

Roediger, D. (1991). *The wages of whiteness: Race and the making of the American working class.* London: Verso.

Roediger, D. (1994). *Towards the abolition of whiteness: Essays on race, politics and working class history.* London: Verso.

Rogler, L. H., Cortes, D. E., & Malgady, R. G. (1991). Acculturation and mental status among Hispanics: Convergence and new directions for research. *American Psychologist, 46,* 585-597.

Rojas, A. (1996, July 18). State's tolerant image tarnished. *San Francisco Chronicle,* pp. 1A, 15A.

Rokeach, M. (1960). *The open and closed mind.* New York: Basic Books.

Rokeach, M. (1973). *The nature of human values.* New York: Free Press.

Rokeach, M. (Ed.). (1979). *Understanding human values.* New York: Free Press.

Rokeach, M., & Ball-Rokeach, S. (1989). Stability and change in American value priorities, 1968-1981. *American Psychologist, 44,* 775-784.

Rosch, E., & Lloyd, B. B. (Eds.). (1978). *Cognition and categorization.* Hillsdale, NJ: Erlbaum.

Rose, P. L. (1990). *German question/Jewish question: Revolutionary antisemitism from Kant to Wagner.* Princeton: Princeton University Press.

Rosenthal, R. (1994). Interpersonal expectancy effects: A 30-year perspective. *Current Directions in Psychological Science, 3,* 176-179.

Rosenthal, R. (1995). Critiquing Pygmalion: A 25-year perspective. *Current Directions in Psychological Science, 4,* 171-172.

Rosenthal, R., & Jacobson, L. (1968). *Pygmalion in the classroom.* New York: Holt, Rinehart and Winston.

Ross, L. (1977). The intuitive psychologist and his shortcomings: Distortions in the attribution process. In L. Berkowitz (Ed.), *Advances in experimental social psychology: Vol. 10.* New York: Academic Press.

Ross, L., Amabile, T. M., & Steinmetz, J. L. (1977). Social roles, social control and biases in social-perception processes. *Journal of Personality and Social Psychology, 35,* 485-494.

Ross, L., & Nisbett, R. E. (1990). *The person and the situation*. New York: McGraw-Hill.

Rowan, C. T. (1996). *The coming race war in America*. New York: Little, Brown.

Ruggiero, K. M., & Taylor, D. M. (1995). Coping with discrimination: How disadvantaged group members perceive the discrimination that confronts them. *Journal of Personality and Social Psychology, 68*, 826–838.

Runciman, W. G. (1966). *Relative deprivation and social justice: A study of attitudes to social inequality in twentieth-century England*. Berkeley: University of California Press.

Rushton, J. P. (1995). Construct validity, censorship and the genetics of race. *American Psychologist, 50*, 40–42.

Rushton, J. P. (1996). Race differences in brain size. *American Psychologist, 51*, 556.

Rutter, M. L. (1997). Nature-nurture integration: The example of antisocial behavior. *American Psychologist, 52*, 390–398.

Ryan, B. (1971). *Blaming the victim*. New York: Pantheon.

Sacks, K. B. (1994). How did Jews become white folks? In S. Gregory & R. Sanjek (Eds.), *Race* (pp. 78–102). New Brunswick: Rutgers University Press.

Saenger, G., & Gilbert, C. (1950). Customer reactions to the integration of Negro sales personnel. *International Journal of Opinion and Attitude Research, 4*, 57–76.

Sagiv, L., & Schwartz, S. H. (1995). Value priorities and readiness for out-group social contact. *Journal of Personality and Social Psychology, 69*, 437–448.

Samelson, F. (1976, May). *From "race psychology" to "studies in prejudice": Some observations on the thematic reversal in social psychology*. Paper presented at the Eighth Annual Meeting of the International Society for the History of the Behavioral and Social Sciences, Washington, DC.

Sampson, E. E. (1976). *Social psychology and contemporary society*. New York: Wiley.

Sampson, E. E. (1977). Psychology and the American ideal. *Journal of Personality and Social Psychology, 35*, 767–782.

Sampson, E. E. (1988). The debate on individualism: Indigenous psychologies of the individual and their role in personal and societal functioning. *American Psychologist, 43*, 15–22.

Sampson, E. E. (1991). *Social worlds, personal lives: An introduction to social psychology*. San Diego: Harcourt Brace Jovanovich.

Schaller, M. (1992). In-group favoritism and statistical reasoning in social inference: Implications for formation and maintenance of group stereotypes. *Journal of Personality and Social Psychology, 63*, 61–74.

Schaller, M., Boyd, C., Yohannes, J., & O'Brien, M. (1995). The prejudiced personality revisited: Personal need for structure and formation of erroneous group stereotypes. *Journal of Personality and Social Psychology, 68*, 544–555.

Scheper-Hughes, N. (1992). *Death without weeping: The violence of everyday life in Brazil*. Berkeley: University of California Press.

Schwartz, S. H. (1992). Universals in the content and structure of values: Theoretical advances and empirical tests in 20 countries. In M. Zanna (Ed.), *Advances in experimental social psychology: Vol. 25* (pp. 1–65). Orlando: Academic Press.

Schwartz, S. H. (1994). Are there universal aspects in the structure and content of human values? *Journal of Social Issues, 50*, 19–45.

Schwartz, S. H., & Bilsky, W. (1987). Toward a psychological structure of human values. *Journal of Personality and Social Psychology, 53*, 550–562.

Schwartz, S. H., & Bilsky, W. (1990). Toward a theory of the universal content and structure of values: Extensions and cross-cultural replications. *Journal of Personality and Social Psychology, 58*, 878–891.

Scott, J. W. (1988). *Gender and the politics of history*. New York: Columbia University Press.

Sedgwick, E. K. (1990). *Epistemology of the closet*. Berkeley: University of California Press.

Segal, C. M., & Stineback, S. (1977). *Puritans, Indians and manifest destiny*. New York: Putnam.

Shanklin, E. (1994). *Anthropology and race*. Belmont, CA: Wadsworth.

Sherif, M., & Sherif, C. W. (1953). *Groups in harmony and tension*. New York: Harper.

Shields, S. A. (1975). Functionalism, Darwinism and the psychology of women: A study in social myth. *American Psychologist, 30*, 739–754.

Shils, E. A. (1954). Authoritarianism: Right and left. In R. Christie & M. Jahoda (Eds.), *Studies in the scope and method of "the authoritarian personality"* (pp. 24-49). Glencoe, IL: Free Press.

Sidanius, J. (1988). Political sophistication and political deviance: A structural equation examination of context theory. *Journal of Personality and Social Psychology, 55,* 37-51.

Sidanius, J., Pratto, F., & Bobo, L. (1994). Social dominance orientation and the political psychology of gender: A case of invariance? *Journal of Personality and Social Psychology, 67,* 998-1011.

Sidanius, J., Pratto, F., & Bobo, L. (1996). Racism, conservatism, affirmative action, and intellectual sophistication: A matter of principled conservatism or group dominance? *Journal of Personality and Social Psychology, 70,* 476-490.

Simon, B., & Hamilton, D. L. (1994). Self-stereotyping and social context: The effects of relative in-group size and in-group status. *Journal of Personality and Social Psychology, 66,* 699-711.

Skedsvold, P. R., & Mann, T. L. (Eds.). (1996). The affirmative action debate: What's fair in policy and programs? [Whole issue]. *Journal of Social Issues, 52.*

Slavin, R. E. (1985). Cooperative learning: Applying contact theory in desegregated schools. *Journal of Social Issues, 41,* 45-62.

Sniderman, P. M., & Tetlock, P. E. (1986). Reflections on American racism. *Journal of Social Issues, 42,* 173-187.

Snow, R. E. (1995). Pygmalion and intelligence? *Current Directions in Psychological Science, 4,* 169-171.

Snyder, M. L. (1982, July). Self-fulfilling stereotypes. *Psychology Today,* 60-68.

Snyder, M. L. (1984). When belief creates reality? In L. Berkowitz (Ed.), *Advances in experimental social psychology: Vol. 18* (pp. 247-305). San Diego: Academic Press.

Snyder, M., & Miene, P. (1994). On the functions of stereotypes and prejudice. In M. P. Zanna & J. M. Olson (Eds.), *The psychology of prejudice: The Ontario Symposium, Vol. 7* (pp. 33-54). Hillsdale, NJ: Erlbaum.

Snyder, M., Tanke, E. D., & Berscheid, E. (1977). Social perception and interpersonal behavior: On the self-fulfilling nature of social steroetypes. *Journal of Personality and Social Psychology, 35,* 656-666.

Spotlight on Research (1996). Is racism on the decline in America? *APS Observer, 9,* 12-13, 26.

Steele, C. M. (1997). A threat in the air: How stereotypes shape intellectual identity and performance. *American Psychologist, 52,* 613-629.

Steele, C. M., & Aronson, J. (1995). Stereotype threat and the intellectual test performance of African Americans. *Journal of Personality and Social Psychology, 69,* 797-811.

Steinberg, L., Dornbusch, S. M., & Brown, B. B. (1992). Ethnic differences in adolescent achievement: An ecological perspective. *American Psychologist, 47,* 723-729.

Stephan, W. G. (1985). Intergroup relations. In G. Lindzey & E. Aronson (Eds.), *Handbook of social psychology: Vol. 2* (pp. 599-658). New York: Random House.

Stephan, W. G., Ageyev, V., Coates-Shrider, L., Stephan, C. W., & Abalakina, M. (1993). On the relationship between stereotypes and prejudice: An international study. *Personality and Social Psychology Bulletin, 20,* 277-284.

Sternberg, R. J. (1995). For whom the bell curve tolls: A review of The Bell Curve. *Psychological Science, 6,* 257-261.

Stone, W. F. (1995, April). The rise, fall and resurgence of authoritarianism research. *SPSSI Newsletter, 14.*

Stouffer, S. A., Suchman, E. A., DeVinney, L. C., Star, S. A., & Williams, R. M., Jr. (1949). *Studies in social psychology in World War II* (Vols. 1 and 2). Princeton: Princeton University Press.

Strong, M. (1995, June). Inside the mind of a racist. *San Francisco Focus,* pp. 47-55, 88-89.

Swim, J. K. (1994). Perceived versus meta-analytic effect sizes: An assessment of the accuracy of gender stereotypes. *Journal of Personality and Social Psychology, 66,* 21-36.

Swim, J., Borgida, E., Maruyama, G., & Myers, D. G. (1989). Joan McKay versus John McKay: Do gender stereotypes bias evaluations? *Psychological Bulletin, 105,* 409-429.

Synnott, A. (1993). *The body social: Symbolism, self and society.* London: Routledge.

Tajfel, H. (1969). Cognitive aspects of prejudice. *Journal of Social Issues, 25,* 79–97.

Tajfel, H. (Ed.). (1978). *Differentiation between social groups.* London: Academic Press.

Tajfel, H. (1982). *Social identity and intergroup relations.* Cambridge: Cambridge University Press.

Tajfel, H., Flament, C., Billig, M., & Bundy, R. (1971). Social categorization and intergroup behavior. *European Journal of Social Psychology, 1,* 149–178.

Tajfel, H., & Turner, J. C. (1979). An integrative theory of intergroup conflict. In W. G. Austin & S. Worchel (Eds.), *The social psychology of intergroup relations* (pp. 33–47). Monterey, CA: Brooks/Cole.

Tavris, C. (1992). *The mismeasure of woman.* New York: Touchstone.

Taylor, C., & Gutmann, A. (1994). *Multiculturalism: Examining the politics of recognition.* Princeton: Princeton University Press.

Taylor, D. M., & Jaggi, V. (1974). Ethnocentrism and causal attribution in a South Indian context. *Journal of Cross-Cultural Psychology, 5,* 162–171.

Taylor, D. M., & Moghaddam, F. M. (1987). *Theories of intergroup relations: International social psychological perspectives.* New York: Praeger.

Taylor, D. M., Wright, S. C., & Porter, L. E. (1994). Dimensions of perceived discrimination: The personal/group discrimination discrepancy. In M. P. Zanna & J. M. Olson (Eds.), *The psychology of prejudice: The Ontario Symposium, Vol. 7* (pp. 233–255). Hillsdale, NJ: Erlbaum.

Thompson, B., & Tyagi, S. (Eds.). (1996). *Names we call home: Autobiography on racial identity.* New York: Routledge.

Tougas, F., Crosby, F., Joly, S., & Pelchat, D. (1995). Men's attitudes toward affirmative action: Justice and intergroup relations at the crosssroads. *Social Justice Research, 8,* 57–71.

Trachtenberg, J. (1943). *The devil and the Jews: The Medieval conception of the Jew and its relation to modern antisemitism.* Philadelphia: Jewish Publication Society of America.

Triandis, H. C. (1995). *Individualism and collectivism.* Boulder, CO: Westview.

Triandis, H. C. (1996). The psychological measurement of cultural syndromes. *American Psychologist, 51,* 407–415.

Turner, J. C., Hogg, M. A., Oakes, P. J., Reicher, S. D., & Wetherell, M. S. (1987). *Rediscovering the social group: A self-categorization theory.* Oxford: Basil Blackwell.

Tyler, T. R., & Lind, E. A. (1992). A relational model of authority in groups. In M. P. Zanna (Ed.), *Advances in experimental social psychology: Vol. 25* (pp. 115–191). New York: Academic Press.

Vanneman, R. D., & Pettigrew, T. F. (1972). Race and relative deprivation in the urban United States. *Race, 13,* 461–486.

Vernant, J. P. (Ed.). (1995). *The Greeks.* Chicago: University of Chicago Press.

Voyer, D., Voyer, S., & Bryden, M. P. (1995). Magnitude of sex differences in spatial abilities: A meta-analysis and consideration of critical variables. *Psychological Bulletin, 117,* 250–270.

Wallerstein, I. (1991). The construction of peoplehood: Racism, nationalism, ethnicity. In E. Balibar & I. Wallerstein (Eds.), *Race, nation, class: Ambiguous identities* (pp. 71–85). London: Verso.

Ward, S. H., & Braun, J. (1972). Self-esteem and racial preference in black children. *American Journal of Orthopsychiatry, 42,* 644–647.

Weber, M. (1930). *The Protestant ethic and the spirit of capitalism.* New York: Scribner's.

Webster, D. M., & Kruglanski, A. W. (1994). Individual differences in need for cognitive structure. *Journal of Personality and Social Psychology, 67,* 1049–1062.

Wegner, D. M. (1989). *White bears and other unwanted thoughts.* New York: Viking.

Wegner, D. M., & Erber, R. (1992). The hyperaccessibility of suppressed thoughts. *Journal of Personality and Social Psychology, 63,* 903–912.

Weigel, R. H., & Howes, P. W. (1985). Conceptions of racial prejudice: Symbolic racism reconsidered. *Journal of Social Issues, 41,* 117–138.

West, C. (1993). *Race matters.* New York: Vintage.

Westie, F. R. (1964). Race and ethnic relations. In R. E. L. Farris (Ed.), *Handbook of modern sociology* (pp. 576–618). Chicago: Rand McNally.

Whitbeck, C. (1976). Theories of sex difference. In C. C. Gould & M. W. Wartofsky (Eds.), *Women and philsophy: Toward a theory of liberation* (pp. 54-80). New York: Putnam.

Wilson, P. R. (1968). Perceptual distortion of height as a function of ascribed academic status. *Journal of Social Psychology, 74,* 97-102.

Winkler, J. J. (1990). *The construction of desire: The anthropology of sex and gender in ancient Greece.* New York: Routledge.

Wright, S. C., Taylor, D. M., & Moghaddam, F. M. (1990). Responding to membership in a disadvantaged group: From acceptance to collective protest. *Journal of Personality and Social Psychology, 58,* 994-1003.

Yee, A. H., Fairchild, H. H., Weizmann, F., & Wyatt, G. E. (1993). Addressing psychology's problems with race. *American Psychologist, 48,* 1132-1140.

Young-Bruehl, E. (1995). *The anatomy of prejudices.* Cambridge: Harvard University Press.

Zuckerman, M. (1990). Some dubious premises in research and theory on racial differences: Scientific, social and ethical issues. *American Psychologist, 45,* 1297-1303.

INDEX